For Paul — who also
likes a violet light!
Love,
Barbara

Wallace Stevens

The Intensest Rendezvous

Wallace Stevens:
The Intensest Rendezvous

BARBARA M. FISHER

University Press of Virginia
Charlottesville

THE UNIVERSITY PRESS OF VIRGINIA
Copyright © 1990 by the Rector and Visitors
of the University of Virginia

First published 1990

Library of Congress Cataloging-in-Publication Data
Fisher, Barbara (Barbara M.)
    Wallace Stevens : the intensest rendezvous / Barbara M. Fisher.
    p.   cm.
    Includes bibliographical references.
    ISBN 0-8139-1248-2
    1. Stevens, Wallace, 1879–1955—Criticism and interpretation.
    2. Love in literature.   I. Title.
PS3537.T4753Z637   1990
    811'.52—dc20   89-16608
                                                              CIP

Printed in the United States of America

TO HOLLY

Contents

Foreword by Angus Fletcher   ix
Preface   xxi
Introduction   xxiii

1. The Spirit's Own Seduction   1
2. Ambiguous Birds and Quizzical Messengers   21
3. Something for Nothing   35
   Contraries and the Necessary No   46
4. A Woman with the Hair of a Pythoness   54
5. The Archangel of Evening   64
   Star and Candle   66
   "From out the rinde of one apple"   74
6. Enough   85
   Miraculous Influence   94
7. Love of Place   107
   Place, Space, Topos   109
8. Native Passion   120
9. Six Significant Landscapes   128
   Holiday in Reality   129
   From *Credences of Summer*   132
   The Poem That Took the Place of a Mountain   135
   The Man on the Dump   139
   Celle Qui Fût Héaulmiette   143
   The River of Rivers in Connecticut   147

   Notes   159
   Index   179

Foreword

WALLACE STEVENS elicits wonder at his craft, which is one of exemplary recurrences and, as such, is almost theoretical in its gestures. He makes us aware that poetry, understood to mean poems, commonly repeats where prose departs anew. Prose may, of course, exhibit recurrences of narrative or discursive elements, but poetry is the definitive verbal art of intensified recurrence; literally, its verses turn and return. When rhymed couplets "tag" the open form of blank verse, as Dryden put it, the degree of repetition is merely increased and made more obvious. But blank verse also uses patterns of assonance for subliminal repetitions, which in complex stanza forms may assume architectonic shapes. Further, even as metrical techniques allow for recurrence of many subtly different kinds, the poet may invite the return of favored ideas and images, of thematic schemata. A personal rhythm always results: the poet's signature.

Characteristically the recent developments of criticism have sophisticated the formal problem—Hillis Miller's *Fiction and Repetition* sees two basic types of novelistic recurrence, of the identical and the different, and these two lead grandly to a widely broadened horizon of possibilities. With poetry there is perhaps a more strongly contained mode of repetition, as if the poem sought repetition as an end in itself, as if right repetition were a specific poetic goal. Even the proselike structures of free verse often lean toward anaphoric reduplication. For American poetry Whitman's example may be determining, not least in the case of Wallace Stevens. As Frank Kermode observed, Stevens repeats in the most egregious fashion. Poetry is at base cyclical; romantic poetry even mythologizes the cycle. Especially as his craft matured, Wallace Stevens became the late romantic master of the hypercylical.

In everyday life recurrence spells boredom, so the question arises: Why is a poet like Stevens not boring? or, why is so much of the late

Wordsworth so very dull? It would appear that Stevens discovered—perhaps even set out to discover—something that evaded the poet laureate, namely, a technique and a justification of formal repetition of elements.

The broad answer to our question appears to be this: if speaking the necessities of life, including the need for what is *not* necessary, is to be a poet, then Stevens has achieved the not-boring through the *forms* of his poems, in which he imitates or draws from the fact of natural redundancy, such as the rising and setting of the sun, the wanderings of the moon, the ever repeating or changing shapes of waves. The early Wordsworth had possessed such capacities for vital form, but over time seems to have lost them, at least for the forming of his later poems. When repetition is the iteration of a natural rhythm and the poet conveys such turning and re-turning, his work cannot be boring—in the strict sense that breathing, for example, is not boring.

There are various ways of discerning and addressing the craft of recurrence in Stevens: archetypally recurrent seasons, quasi-liturgical orders deriving from early religious experience, the obsessive nagging of certain metaphysical quandaries, phases of traditional philosophic rehearsal in ethics and aesthetics, recurrences within a lexicon of punning and wordplay, certain stamps of metrical order that return with the footfall of a steady march, the gait of a determined long-distance walker—there are indeed many sides to the Stevensian cycle, and these have received critical attention. Most recently Laury Magnus has defined the microstructures of Stevensian iterative syntax in her book *The Track of the Repetend*.

Barbara Fisher perforce takes a broader view of Stevens's poetics. Her notices of repetition in the poetry point to the largest aspirations, to a general philosophy of art that goes beyond the poet's self. As Blackmur once said, "This is a poetry of repetitions, within the poem and from poem to poem. Rebirth in the individual (poem or person) can only be a little repetition. It is the misery and the force not ourselves that is reborn; it is the music of these which is repeated everlastingly." Barbara Fisher's book shows us that the larger reason for repetition is love.

Twenty-six times within the eighteen lines of *Final Soliloquy of the Interior Paramour* Stevens repeats the morpheme *in-*. Commenting on the virtually numerological ease of the poem's organization, Fisher says that "the poem shimmers because its interiority has been turned inside-out, so to speak. Stevens reveals the inner presence, not only by means of the firm but invisible voice, but visibly, in the extraordinary number of times the word *in* gleams at us from various positionings." Stevens here is even craftier than usual. The theme of Eros and of the paramour and the poet's intense encounter with her throws the poetry into an ecstasy, a hypercyclical system of *ricorsi* in a Vichian sense. Such is the mode of the "intensest rendezvous." Love traced through so many forms by Fisher's choreographic touch, from poem to poem, from kind to kind, from logic to lumpen experience as the poetry gives these to us—this love, always operating upon the poet's choice of particular aims and objects, is shown to give an iterative formal disposition—or "positioning"—to every particular chosen topic of each poem and of the topoi within. In large and small ways the fearful powers of an ancient deity, Eros, determine a need for containment by cyclical "chantering" forms.

Harold Bloom has identified the onset of this art within the significant beginning of Stevens's achieved success. Thus Bloom describes *Domination of Black*, with its inturning variants of figure, such that one final metalepsis raises the poem's last lines to "an almost apocalyptic pitch of rhetoricity, of excessive word-consciousness (a text's equivalent of human self-consciousness)." Significantly, when the poem speaks of "the fallen leaves, / Repeating themselves," it marks what Bloom calls

> Stevens's true starting point as a poet. He was thirty-seven years old as he wrote, yet the short lines carry the resonances of a master, who knows fully what it may mean to say that the colors of the fallen leaves are *repeating* themselves. Thirty times and more in the next forty years Stevens's poetry would repeat, crucially, some form of the word "repeat," until Stevens could write of his Penelope meditating the repetitious but never culminating advent of her Ulysses:
>
>> She would talk a little to herself as she combed her hair,
>> Repeating his name with its patient syllables,
>> Never forgetting him that kept coming constantly so near.

And, as Bloom has shown here and elsewhere, the repeated may bespeak what is *not* repeated, through symbolic reversal. If this last may be the case, the reader may be allowed to wonder how eros and the vicissitudes of the erotic drive can properly be said to find a native expression. There may, however, exist a way of patterning repetition so that metaleptic reversals may be expressed thereby.

In dreams an imagery may reverse its common meaning by processes of *verneinung*, or "negation." The way to get poetic repetitions that would have such free play would be for a poet like Stevens to employ techniques most highly developed in another art, music. The governing rhetorical figure in Stevens is a figure equivalent to musical variations. As Frye says, "We cannot read far in Wallace Stevens's poetry without finding examples of a form that reminds us of the variation in music, in which a theme is presented in a sequence of analogous but different settings." The first example Frye gives is *Thirteen Ways of Looking at a Blackbird*, where "a series of thirteen little imagist poems are related by the common theme of the blackbird, and which, to pursue the musical analogy perhaps further than it will go, gives more the effect of a chaconne or passacaglia." When, in the later poetry, Stevens engages in far more richly interwoven thematic variations, the musical analogue points to the techniques of free variation-form as developed in the late Beethoven works. Limited though it is, the analogy Frye draws is a strong one.

Underlying the variational aspect of Stevens there is what might be called a principle of emotive coherence in the world of our perceptions. We see the moon rising over trees or snow, we see the high bed sheltered by curtains, we see the woman brushing her hair, we hear the wood dove, or the sound of waves on the shore, we smell the scent of a perfume—somehow these are percepts of an order to which we bring a desire for valuing, or to which we stand in a value-giving relation.

This mode of desiring is revealed in the way the verses turn and return to the subject, to caress its form again, to express its structure again, to set it forth again dressed in some new fashion of an ancient raiment. Always the relationship is one of passion, or affection, or obsession, and these are expressed through ritual or repeated returnings—possibly even so far sublimated that they render a Platonic anamnesis. For only eros and its force will account for this poetry of insistent variation. Such a cosmic force is encapsulated in its total effect in the single line: "Plato, the reddened flower, the erotic bird." Here love—for Eros becomes Amor in the romantic tradition—attains a Lucretian range of effect, touching all parts and corners of the Stevensian world or scene.

Such a force is imagined to motivate an entire universe of discourse, which in this case is a paramount effect, because without the energizing of an erotic drive, Stevens's poetry would lapse into a dried-out discourse of philosophic jargon. With it, the poetry is alive to all sorts of humorous undoings, or negations, of its arguments. Stevens the lawyer, on whose business life Barbara Fisher places a special emphasis, has the same mind, she reminds us, that makes up Stevens the poet. Both minds are at one in the way they "argue the case," for like other legally trained poets before him, Stevens knows how to let the facts of a poem thrust themselves upon the reader with the force of immediately persuasive evidence. Given the facts and the argument, the reader will sooner or later arrive at a proper construction.

There is room in this universe of lyrical argument for a defining use of the negative. This view is perhaps less dark and skeptical than that taken by Helen Vendler in her *Wallace Stevens: Words Chosen out of Desire*, because Fisher ascribes the mathematical role of negation to a very positively used zero-point. Or, more likely, these are two readings of Stevens, the one less optimistic than the other. In any case, between Vendler and Fisher (and possibly Lentricchia) there opens a debate as to the extent to which Stevens may be seen as affirming a set of values of some kind, or rather may be seen as presenting all values skeptically. (Certainly deconstructionists would opt for the latter.) The poet abides such debates because he retains in his poetry much of the reserve that gave a certain style to his private life.

Overall, Barbara Fisher's Stevens belongs firmly in the most powerful Western tradition of philosophy, the Platonic. Typically, in a late poem Stevens confronts the question of the nature of the Idea:

> The fiction of the leaves is the icon
>
> Of the poem, the figuration of blessedness,
> And the icon is the man. The pearled chaplet of spring,
> The magnum wreath of summer, time's autumn snood,
>
> Its copy of the sun, these cover the rock.
> These leaves are the poem, the icon and the man.
> These are a cure of the ground and of ourselves,
>
> In the predicate that there is nothing else.

The generalized Platonism of these lines lies not so much in a slavish adherence to the Theory of Ideas, as rather the exploration of the predicate in a more modern, Wittgensteinian fashion. Stevens asks and makes a poem of the Platonic questions: Are the leaves (in) or out of a poem the icons of (or in) the poem? Are such leaves the formal figurations of the good (the "blessedness")? What is the pharmacy, or cure, of the foundation of our thought, its ground? Such questions abound in Stevens, and Barbara Fisher wants us to see something of this abundance.

Most prominently Stevens's general Platonism appears in a celebrated admission: "Life is an affair of people not of places. But for me life is an affair of places and that is the trouble." Fisher introduces her seventh chapter, "Love of Place," with this citation. Place is a pun for the rhetorician's *topos*, but because the poet makes an "affair" of place, the whole is charged with a topological energy. Barbara Fisher does nothing less than establish the main lines of the topological order in which Eros plays and displays itself in the rhetoric of Stevens's world.

In this poetry every place is fully invested with the most intense feeling, while whatever is so invested with feeling is always placed by the poet within some larger order, even if it be placed in a specific nowhere. Even nowhere will be given a kind of mock specificity of location. Topos as poetic figure merges with topos as existential placement.

But the philosopher—or is it the visionary?—in Stevens tends to lessen the grip of the existentially mappable place and to allow it to flow outward, as by efflux, to its ideal domain or region or zone. The result is then that, as with our physical universe on the plane of highest energy, the plane of light, space itself becomes a sort of place, because space thickens and bends and follows an event-filled stream of the forces of the all-defining eros. To speak so might sound outrageously hermetic, as if one had caught the contagion of Sir Thomas Browne's "inexcusable Pythagorisme." But Wallace Stevens domesticates the hermetic. He controls its tendency to blank abstraction by constantly interrogating the poetic evidence. His habit of epistemological challenge is not there for the sake of philosophic display but to safeguard the activity of the image making and storytelling.

Like a clock thrown out into space to test the theory of relativity, the intimate domestic candle flame is cast out to become the Evening Star, which then returns as candle flame. Esoteric and exoteric keep changing places. The farthest notion of a divinity, the Sun, becomes the strong man, while the ethereal space of interacting ideas becomes an actual New Haven, or an actual Hartford, in an actual state (or is it "state"?), Connecticut.

Sun and Evening Star are only two among a large number of "persons" who, as personae among the parts of a world, divide up and structure various regions of imagined space. In each case, Fisher will demonstrate, the person of star or river or sea cloud or bird will hook the poem to some intensely felt location. Her Stevens is a kind of magic surveyor, who instead of drawing lines on a map or grid, draws the reality itself into being, as if he were making "real maps." (The parallel to Marianne Moore's "real toads" is what I have in mind.) Tracing these lines of force means tracing the vagaries of eros, in one zone, or region, or another. The tracery is topologically full of odd bends and twists and cuts. Here, even the town dump becomes a means of localizing the sublime meditation, for, as we follow Fisher's account of *The Man on the Dump*, we ask, What is the shape, and what meaning has the shape, of this dump? Repository of objects severed from desire, the dump is a model instance of a Stevensian region, and is so "described" by him, and by his critic.

The beauty of late Stevens evolves out of increasing powers in the poetic arguments. An early poem like *The Place of the Solitaires* in effect asserts without development that this solitary locus "is to be a place of perpetual undulation." By contrast, the much longer and more leisurely *Things of August* shows us how late in life Stevens could articulate a whole Lucretian field where desire forces the self to discover "the archaic space" where life is a state of impersonal, endless desiring:

> When was it that the particles became
> The whole man, that tempers and beliefs became
> Temper and belief and that differences lost
> Difference and were one? It had to be
> In the presence of a solitude of the self,
> An expanse and the abstraction of an expanse,
> A zone of time without the ticking of clocks,
> A color that moved us with forgetfulness.
> When was it that we heard the voice of union?

This poetry is wondrous because it makes palpable that merely relational language which earlier would have served only to scaffold some brilliant imagery or image play, while here, in its constructed or "argued" form, the relational language itself becomes the only image play worth the candle! Finally the mere links between the elements and forces are the true images. The play of relationships at last provides what this poem calls "a text that we shall be needing,"

> A text of intelligent men
> At the centre of the unintelligible,
> As in a hermitage, for us to think,
> Writing and reading the rigid inscription.

There is nothing picturesque about this highly abstracted language. Yet it gives pleasure, perhaps because the mature Stevens keeps thinking more and more actively. He shows us the arithmetic that makes the world go round; its terms, its pluses and minuses, are terms for the life-process, for the ordering of the whirling energies. Finally, for this Stevens the object of desire is some order of relation. Desire is known therefore only as a region of experience seeking its own order, its idea; therein the self knows itself to be alive. To acquire a self in this kind is to be a poet of the orders of one's own being, and one's being in the world as that world plainly, most plainly, is.

Romantic tradition is no stranger to this affair. Ever since Spenser gave a dual relation and location to the scene of his Mutabilitie Cantos, both in and not in Ireland, romantic poetry in English has known the magic localization of visions occurring *in illo tempore*. Stevens is no less driven than his romantic forebears to insist on the vision of the actual. *An Ordinary Evening in New Haven* states that

> We keep coming back and coming back
> To the real: to the hotel instead of the hymns
> That fall upon it out of the wind.

By refusing the devious allure of decorative tropes, the poet goes "straight to the word, / Straight to the transfixing object." What is most desirable is simply a clear view, but this is not a human limitation; it is a liberation. Clarity of return enforces a sharp definition of the aspect of place that counts, and thereby is poignant; the poet transforms the affair of place to an affair of people, finally, for it is only in human perception that the poignant aspect reveals itself. Stevens aims then at changing the outward properties of place to inward properties, and what is inward is what speaks of people. The paradoxically cool warmth of sentiment comes from a sharpened sense of topos, or "color," as Bloom observed. Speaking of his own lectures, in "The Irrational Element in Poetry," Stevens said: "I like to do these papers, because they clear my mind and make it necessary to take a good look at ideas that otherwise would drift about, vaguely, with no place to go."

Ideas with no place to go!—exactly where this poetry begins and then discovers its own course. Place and anecdote go together, furthermore. To Judge Arthur Powell and other southern friends Stevens owed a congenial enrichment of what the Florida lawyer Phillip May once called "your complete repertoire of recent stories." From Peter Brazeau's splendid interviews and commentary there emerges a poet-folklorist for whom Phillip May could always be locating "one or two places of interest to poets." This poet is less a metaphysician than a humorous skeptic questioning the significance of tall and not so tall tales passed on by a native informant. As a purveyor of tall tales himself, Stevens wants the humorous symbolic distance the teller requires to gain an ear. He needs to sense whether a local story is substantially revelatory of a specific region where the story is told. But Stevens is not a regional poet as such. He is, rather, a poet curious about region in general, about the very idea of the "region clouds" that catch his attention, since region is defined by a set of particulars known only through the eyes of some individual perceiver, some particular native informant. Hence for Stevens region is a universal category of what he calls "substance." Each region, or zone of human habitation, implies some ideal way of being alive to that zone or region. New England has its ways, Florida its way, Rome its way.

What most sharply localizes and catches the region is some inflection of language the poet links to it, for landscape and language trope into each other. Yet even here Stevens does not transcribe; he transforms.

Geoffrey Hill recalls Ransom's definition of trope, and it applies to Stevens's practice: "Figures of speech twist accidence away from the straight course," and this twist, Hill says, is a "precise description of the little swirl, or gyre, of stubborn reiterative outcry, disturbing but not halting the ceremonial procedure of . . . traditional verse forms." Or, as Judge Powell put it, "Sound effects are a part of his artistry, especially sound effects produced by making slight changes in a word."

This disturbing aim of art promises a kind of romanticism we do not always encounter, a witty romanticism. Stevens is almost Byronic. His version of romance is strengthened "to resist the bogus," while the poet becomes "like a man who can see what he wants to see and touch what he wants to touch." Speaking thus at Bard College in 1948, Stevens saw the poet as a knight of faith, a secular faith: "In all his poems with all their enchantments for the poet himself, there is the final enchantment that they are true. The significance of the poetic act then is that it is evidence. It is instance and illustration. It is an illumination of a surface, the movement of a self in the rock. Above all it is a new engagement with life. It is that miracle to which the true faith of the poet attaches itself." Truth here has the old sense of a betrothal, a "true faith," which implies a method of returning to first principles.

Precisely because this return is not a mere quixotic gesture, we need, as Barbara Fisher suggests, a clear notion of the liminal vision involved in Stevens's mythmaking and in his linguistic play. For the liminal is a general condition of betweenness, where, say, a word hovers between the two senses of its punning usage, where, say "troth" and "truth" oscillate as a single-double meaning. More broadly conceived, the liminal betweenness appears when any narrative shows a protagonist moving between two fixed states, caught for the moment in that halfway passage from one to the other. The most intensely wrought liminal utterance either describes or actually projects what is called prophecy, because there the betweenness is a suspension between time and the timeless, between pure idea and impure historic event. In the final chapters of her book Fisher has recourse to such notions to clarify the intensity of Stevens's developed poetic practice. Stevens himself in the late poem *To an Old Philosopher in Rome* brings to the fore a final essential of liminal vision, the role of the guide, here an idealized Santayana, who is imagined virtually living "on the threshold of heaven." From the philosopher to man meditating is but a short step; there is a close and necessary connection between liminal awarenesses of existence at a threshold and the disciplines of meditation. Roughly, the former provide the materials of life which the latter mind, in meditating, seeks to place in sharper perspective.

Like the Mallarmé described by a disciple, Paul Valéry, Stevens "sought and recognized the principle of desire that engenders the poetic act; he had defined and isolated its pure element—and he had made himself the virtuoso of that discipline of purity, the one who studies and plays faultlessly upon what is rarest in his nature." Stevens appeared at times to be, but never was, precious or obscurely elegant (as Blackmur early wanted readers to understand). He was not the virtuoso of an effete *poésie pure*, neither finicky nor grandiose. As he matured and as he grew older in his craft, he sought with increased austerity the pure forms of the impure. In this he was Byronic, a modern master of a chastened romantic irony. He was a tough-minded author, completely dedicated to the nobility of art, for as Frye says, "Stevens was one of the most courageous poets of our time, and his conception of the poem as 'the heroic effort to live expressed / As victory' was unyielding from the beginning." Frye aligns this courage with the Blakean virtue of persistence. In this light Stevens makes war not against mankind or the world but upon expendable and deceiving rhetoric—empty rhetoric.

The war against empty rhetoric implies a wider and deeper knowledge of the world as it is. Introducing her seventh chapter with an epigraph from Whitman—"The known universe has one complete lover, and that is the greatest poet"—Fisher juxtaposes a fragment of verse, from John Hollander's poem on Stevens, *Asylum Avenue*. In this fragment Hollander speaks to the poet: "it is as if it [the customary walk to work] were receptive to / the space you bring along with you." The American poet—Whitman, Stevens, Hollander—is a mental traveler. Archetypally, Whitman provides for successors the model of an imaginative travel that is required if the world-eros of Whitman's poem is to find expression as poetry, if the "one complete lover" is to become "the greatest poet." In Stevens's case the career develops slowly and not without breaks and disturbance; he shares with Dante what Osip Mandelstam once called "geological intelligence," a mind seeking harmony with the slow turnings of geological time. There are two geographies, the actual one of actual earth, and "the non-geography that exists there," the layout of our own thoughts, moods and feelings. Desire, erotic desire, then is the need-driven energy that twists or tropes the actual geography into the inwardly knowable shapes of the "non-geography." But always the poetry reaches to the scene of the actual in order to ground the liminal transit between actual and ideal.

The poet described in *The Intensest Rendezvous* is an author one can imagine living the life of a senior insurance company lawyer; one can imagine him conversing with, or trying to evade, Peter Brazeau's informants; one can imagine the enigma of his marriage; one can imagine his relation to his daughter. This poet lives somewhere. He goes somewhere. He sees some thing. He contemplates some bird, some tree (like the great larch tree he practically forced a visitor to go with him to stare at). He is, in short, an actual poet. Which means that at times he is the learned exegete of the riddle of uncertainty. At other times he is the quizzical messenger of the mixed and skewed accidents of native speech. He is always looking for an ideal folklore. To many readers this will appear an unfamiliar characterization of our greatest modern poet. To others the description will answer a felt need. Unlike other critics, Barbara Fisher discovers a very long vista of influence upon Stevens. Her poet looks back, not merely to classical precedent in poetry and philosophy, but to the great intermediary figures, Dante and Villon. This is an unexpected Stevens. This older Stevens meets the younger mind in his continuous love affair with French poetry in its late symboliste phase, and with the French language. All these inflowing powers find their point of union in the region of a native American humor.

This Stevens would seek a home in an ever darkening world of two great wars and many revolutionary changes. "Against the dark and time's consuming rage"—the line comes from the old poet of the first Elizabeth's reign, Samuel Daniel—Wallace Stevens proposes the figure of the poet as hero. The war of the imagination is with and against the cycles of nature, and to this purpose Stevens invents a wide range of variational forms, as we have seen. Like his immediate master, Walt Whitman, he would hope to be in touch with the rhythms of nature herself. The poetry, in the account that follows, will be shown to participate in life, obeying the triple behest of the poet's invented credo: abstraction, change, and pleasure—all three.

ANGUS FLETCHER

Preface

MANY FRIENDS, teachers, scholars, and colleagues have contributed to this book, more than I can name here, but a few must be singled out. I am deeply indebted to Laury Magnus for several close readings of the manuscript, her sustained encouragement, and the suggestions of an elegant critical mind. Allen Mandelbaum directed the study through its first stages; he made it possible for me to spend a summer in research, and later gave me the privilege of helping to proofread his verse translation of Dante's *Purgatorio*. I am beholden to Professor Karl Malkoff, who first opened up modern poetry for me, and to Lillian Feder for the benefit of her classical scholarship, range of erudition, and enthusiastic support. Professors Paul Oskar Kristeller and William Elton both provided a window to the thought of the Renaissance. To George Ridenour I owe my love of Blake; and to Patrick Cullen a strong appreciation of pastoral. From Felicia Bonaparte, Barbara Watson, and Betty Rizzo I learned that serious scholarship can combine palpable intelligence with a love of truth—and not a little wit. I want to express my appreciation in memoriam to Jason Saunders, who led me through the elements of Greek, taught me something of classical philosophy, and initiated me into the concepts of energy in Aristotle, of desire in Plato.

A colleague in clinical psychology, Dr. Jean Litz, alerted me to Stevens's poker-faced humor. My friend Susan Schrader helped to prepare the manuscript and suggested many excellent emendations. At different times, Maria Correa and Ellen Ervin spent untold hours transferring typescript to computer with a patience that defies description. My daughter, Alex, rescued the manuscript from a deranged floppy disk and miraculously delivered corrected copy complete with Greek script. Benji Fisher paused in his mathematical meditations long enough to supply the word that opens chapter 4—*If*. His observations on the notion of whiteness in *Moby-Dick* substantially contributed to the opening of chapter 5. My younger son, Sam, was moved at an early age to produce a poem entitled "Wallace Sneakers," and I am beholden to him since for keeping the light over my typewriter in working order.

The dear friend to whom this book is dedicated showed me, one bright day, where the Connecticut River broadens and enters into Long Island Sound; more than that, over the years she has shown me something of her father in herself. Finally, this book would not have taken its present shape nor contained its final chapters without the challenge and stimulation of a mind "as rare / As 'tis for object strange and high." To Angus Fletcher I am, simply, grateful.

Acknowledgments are due to the following publishers for generous permission to use copyrighted material: Alfred A. Knopf, Inc., *The Collected Poems of Wallace Stevens*, copyright 1923, 1931, 1935, 1936, 1937, 1942, 1943, 1944, 1945, 1946, 1947, 1948, 1949, 1950, 1951, 1952, 1954 by Wallace Stevens. *Opus Posthumous*, by Wallace Stevens, ed., with an introduction, by Samuel French Morse, copyright 1957 by Elsie Stevens and Holly Stevens. *The Palm at the End of the Mind: Selected Poems and a Play by Wallace Stevens*, ed. Holly Stevens, copyright 1967, 1969, 1971 by Holly Stevens, Vintage ed., 1972. *Letters of Wallace Stevens*, ed. Holly Stevens, copyright 1966. Wallace Stevens, *The Necessary Angel: Essays on Reality and the Imagination*, copyright 1942, 1944, 1947, 1948, 1949, 1951 by Wallace Stevens. Holly Stevens, *Souvenirs and Prophecies: The Young Wallace Stevens*, copyright 1966, 1976 by Holly Stevens.

A number of full-length poems and other short extracts are reprinted by permission of Faber and Faber Ltd., from *The Collected Poems of Wallace Stevens* and *The Necessary Angel: Essays on Reality and the Imagination*, by Wallace Stevens.

Lines from *The Divine Comedy of Dante Alighieri: Purgatorio*, translated by Allen Mandelbaum, English translation copyright © 1980 by Allen Mandelbaum, reprinted by permission of Bantam Books, a division of Bantam, Doubleday, Dell Publishing Group, Inc.

A version of chapter 2 appeared in *The Wallace Stevens Journal* 9 (Spring 1985) as "Ambiguous Birds and Quizzical Messengers: Parody as Stevens' Double Agent." A longer version of chapter 4 appeared in *Bucknell Review* 31, no. 2 (1988) as "Wallace Stevens' Pythoness."

Introduction

IT MAY AT FIRST seem surprising to think of Stevens's poems as diverse expressions of desire. But Stevens himself draws attention to the erotic dimension of his poetry in the final directive of *Notes toward a Supreme Fiction*. Here, at the center of the canon, ontology is explicitly connected to desire: *it must give pleasure*. And Stevens himself tells us axiomatically, in the *Adagia*, that for the poet, and possibly for the poem's ideal reader, love fastens upon the parts of poetry as though they were parts of a human body: "In poetry, you must love the words, the ideas and images and rhythms with all your capacity to love anything at all." [1]

In 1984 Helen Vendler remarked that something of vital importance has been missing in critical readings of Stevens. "Though the conceptual bases of Stevens' poems have been ably set out, and Stevens' intellectual and poetic sources are gradually being enumerated, the task of conveying the poems as something other than a collection of ideas still remains incomplete." [2] Vendler urged the need to tether Stevens's poems to human feeling, but so far the need has been only partially filled. While Vendler's is the first study to focus on desire in the poetry, it concentrates on negative emotion, the frustrations of desire, the bitter, "harsher" notes of song. The full range of emotion in Stevens's work and the positive transformations of desire that structure it have remained unaddressed. It has become clear, however, that to trace the motive forces within the Stevens canon is a delicate, complicated, chance-ridden task.

I believe with Vendler, and with Harold Bloom, that the poems of Wallace Stevens bespeak an intense emotional life. I believe, too, that intensity of feeling empowers not only the lyric moments but the epistemological strain in Stevens. Indeed, it is the basic premise of this study that desire does more than energize individual poems and passages. In the most general terms, I am proposing that erotic energy is the key to the dynamics of Stevens's work and, further, that it is precisely these dynamics—that is, the presence of eros and the transformations of eros—that determine the vital structures and the configuration of the entire canon.

This book, then, addresses these questions of desire, the turning objects of eros, the passional dimension in Stevens. Each chapter takes up a single aspect of desire, each suggested by a major preoccupation of the poetry, and explores the object or objects targeted by that desire through an examination of exemplary poems. It should not surprise readers of Stevens to find chapters devoted to the seductions of the unknown; to parody and playful jugglery; to violent forces of negation and ascetic deprivation; to the poet's interior paramour; to the search for significance (for "what will suffice") in aesthetic, spiritual, even moral spheres; and, finally, to landscapes both of the mind and the beloved physical earth.

That Stevens was a student of Plato is well known. His annotations to Freud's writings, however, and his references to Freud show the poet well aware of the force of the psychoanalyst's investigations into the life of the irrational. There is a certain felicity, therefore, in the use of both the classical and the contemporary theorists of eros to illuminate Stevens's poetry of desire. Freud's theory of sublimation best accounts for the self-transformational powers of eros, the multiple metamorphoses of sexual desire. (It is perhaps this aspect of eros—its protean changeability—that contributes a virtuoso quality to the Stevens canon.) But Platonic theory takes up where Freud (and Socrates) leave off: it carries sublimation all the way to the sublime. Plato's description of eros as the philosopher hungry for knowledge, as the restless daemon with the power to span the distance between physical and metaphysical realms, is crucial. It prepares us for Stevens's perception of romance as the mover capable of spanning the distance between "blood-world" and "pure idea." To put it another way, for this poet the romantic may serve a philosophical need, "To make the body covetous in desire / Of the still finer, more implacable chords."[3]

Stevens's interior paramour comes remarkably close to Auerbach's concept of *figura*: "the creative, formative principle, change amid the enduring essence, the shades of meaning between copy and archetype."[4] I have aligned Stevens's *figura* of the paramour with the "bride-chamber" imagery that inspired medieval monastics such as Bernard of Clairvaux and the Parisian Victorines. These twelfth-century theologians drew their iconic language from Neoplatonist philosophy, the allegorical genius of Origen, and the passion of the Hebrew canticles. Although Stevens warns us in *Les Plus Belles Pages* that "Theology after breakfast sticks to the eye," I have indulged in a species of literary archaeology as a result of these alignments, tracing the bearing on Stevens of the two medieval poets who appear to me to be most strongly present in his work. Taking into consid-

eration that Stevens had absorbed Ovid's *Amores* as a college student, I
believe that it was Dante and François Villon—the divine comedian and
the devilish parodist of *Le Testament*—who gave the modern poet his
paradigms of transcendent love and earthy sensuality. In this connection,
I have found M. M. Bakhtin's comprehensive work on parody particularly
useful in examining the erotic-theological uses of the mode in Stevens.

Dante travels through hell and purgatory in pursuit of a transcendent
love object. For medieval and Renaissance thinkers, the *via negativa* indicated a difficult ascetic path to spiritual emptiness and, they hoped,
spiritual ecstasy. Stevens parallels this ascetic mode in search of what he
calls "extraordinary experience"—that is, repeated attempts to achieve a
perceptual vacuum and hence an altered consciousness. I have suggested
that the important transition in Stevens's attitude toward negation, and his
essentially positive pursuit of the *negativa* is, philosophically speaking, a
transition from Nietzsche to Bergson, from decreation to the procreative
empty space of vitalism.

Finally, I have brought Angus Fletcher's critical theories of liminality
to bear on Stevens's poetry of the transitional states of being. Symbolically,
the moment of prophecy occurs at the threshold where *templum* and *labyrinth* meet. The ordering temple represents gratification of desire; the dis-
ordering labyrinth shows the iconography of terror. The vatic poets'
utterance is generated by the visionary conjunction of these two archetypal states of being.

This study assumes an erotic cause at the heart of the liminal, in
Stevens. The time-space-condition that Fletcher has called *threshold* becomes here a contained jurisdiction of libidinal energy. Alternations of
fear and desire resonate from this zone—elemental uncertainties, hesita-
tions, indeterminacies. One locates the contour of liminality in Stevens's
tangential "as ifs," in labyrinthine embeddings of syntax and simile, in the
veiled semiotics of obscurity, paradox, and riddle. But the liminal also
assumes a clear symbolic form in Stevens. Perhaps its most salient example is the last poem treated in this book—Stevens's last great poem of
passage—*The River of Rivers in Connecticut.*

It may be helpful to consider the orientation of the individual chapters with respect to the theme of desire, especially as the focus of a chapter
may be trained more on the transformation of erotic energy than on the
root experience. Briefly, then, chapter 1 takes up poems in which sensual
passion is redirected toward a sublime object and classes these poems
as "seduction parables." Chapter 2 discusses Stevens's use of parody as a
jongleur's method of attaining simultaneous relation to—and dialogic distance from—romantic forebears, theological dogmas, and erotic passion.

The final focus is on the ambiguous figure of Nanzia Nunzio, who combines these emotionally charged elements in a potent, comedic, blasphemously sexy striptease.

The third chapter considers the force of sexual desire as an agent of violence and destruction, and follows the reversal of desire into ascetic modes of expression. It also examines the several ways in which negation functions as a positive agent in Stevens; how notions of poverty, nakedness, and nothingness predicate the scene of an "immaculate beginning."

Chapter 4 is a portrait of Stevens's mysterious paramour. It isolates the oracular, erotic, spiritual, and cognitive dimensions of the figure and suggests that it conforms neither to Jungian archetype nor rhetorical muse. In recognizing the cognitive aspect, this chapter situates Stevens's paramour in a line of Wisdom figures beginning with Parmenides and continuing through Plato's Diotima, the Aphrodite Ouranos of Plotinus, and the *Noys* of Bernard Silvestris. It connects the paramour to Saint Bernard's construct of the soul as *sponsa*, or spouse, and aligns her dark, and most strongly erotic, aspect with the Shulamite of Solomon's love song.

Chapter 5 traces the evolution of fire imagery throughout the canon, particularly in the poems of love and war. This chapter shows Stevens applying classical metaphors of flame and fire for both sexual passion and spiritual intensity, and it underscores the ancient connection of the evening star with love. It shows the erotic impulse converted to the purposes of prophecy and notes the point in the very late poetry where fiery images of star and candle—cosmic and domestic flames—are conjoined. Chapter 6 concentrates on a close reading of *Final Soliloquy of the Interior Paramour*. This chapter develops the presence of Dante in Stevens's poetry and shows the dynamics that permit the interiorization of an external love object to have originated in the *Vita Nuova*.

The three last chapters take up Stevens's most open, most direct object of affection: his love of place. Chapter 7 presents a three-part exploration of the theory and poetics of place; chapter 8 plants Stevens firmly in native soil and considers him as a peculiarly American poet; and the final chapter, "Six Significant Landscapes," constitutes a gathering, a recapitulation of the major themes of the book. In the form of emblems, these landscapes—or mindscapes—show the complex topography of eros in the Stevens canon, the horizons of desire.

Wallace Stevens

The Intensest Rendezvous

Chapter 1

The Spirit's Own Seduction

Plato, the reddened flower, the erotic bird.   STEVENS

IN AN AGE as harsh as it is intelligent, phrases about the unknown are quickly dismissed." The year was 1937, the setting a New England college for women, and Wallace Stevens was shaping a defense of
the irrational element in poetry. The country had known eight years of
severe economic distress. Stevens was fifty-eight years old. He had weath-
ered the Great Depression and personal disillusionment; his first books of
poetry had gained recognition. In his detached, quiet, methodical way,
he spoke about the poet's need to make poems, the scholar's ardor to
search the unfamiliar, of the overwhelming attraction of the unknown: "it
has seductions more powerful and more profound than those of the
known" (OP, 228). Stevens was talking to this audience of young women
about ardor, seduction, need. He was talking about things he loved, prob-
ing the experience of desire. At the heart of this talk is the force that
empowers an exploratory poetics, the critical force that urges entrance
into the space of the irrational unknown. In an age as harsh as it is intelligent, Stevens is saying, the intelligence of a man whose soul is rooted in
the romantic must return, again and again, to the domain of the irrational. For in the irrational lie the sources of love and desire, all formulations of the romantic, and the springs of poetry.
    Nobody has accused Wallace Stevens of writing love poetry. But the
experience of desire is what Stevens's poems are about. Not since Whitman has an American produced a body of work so charged with erotic
energy, while among his contemporaries Stevens can be compared in this
area only to Yeats and to Dylan Thomas. In Stevens, desire is channeled
into unexpectedly varied kinds of expression. It surfaces in the poetry as
solitary yearning, as open sensuality and bride-chamber imagery, in forms
of play that include affectionate teasing and pointed irony, in the impulse

toward asceticism, and sometimes as complex meditations on the nature of seduction. The erotic element in Stevens's verse speaks as fluently in the vulgate as the sublime. The Stevensian eros may take to clowning, as in *Bantams in Pine-Woods* or emerge as a theological parody as in *The Dove in the Belly*. What is surprising is not the visionary aspect—"desire, set deep in the eye"—or the recurrent mode of troubled longing—"the soft / Touch and trouble of the touch of the actual hand"—nor the motifs of violence and savagery that attach to yearning throughout the canon. What is surprising when one considers the range of desire in Stevens's poetry, and special to it, is his persistent courtship of an interior love object and his double-edged notion of a "singular romance."

Certainly for Stevens the idea of romance attaches in a striking way to romantic poetry. As Holly Stevens has shown, Shelley is the doorway through which the young Stevens entered poetry—"words of the fragrant portals"—walked into the lyric garden, the elemental landscape of the romantics.[1] Their challenge to the poets who followed is contained in the well-known effusion that announces the closing chords of Shelley's *Ode to the West Wind*: "Be thou, Spirit fierce, / My spirit! Be thou me, impetuous one!" In the major work of the middle period, *Notes toward a Supreme Fiction* (2.6), Stevens echoes the call. This is no soaring Shelleyan skylark, but a domestic sparrow who inhabits a windy suburban garden: "Bethou, bethou, bethou me in my glade" (*CP*, 394).

How are we to understand this reverberation? Explaining the line, Stevens wrote: "*Bethou* is the spirit's own seduction."[2] This is still puzzling, although Stevens is clearly pointing to something that is both mystical and erotic. He does not elaborate, but in context "spirit" too is suggestive, echoic. Does it refer to Shelley's evocation of pneuma—"Spirit fierce"? Or to Milton's mightier Spirit, brooding on the Abyss? Is he, perhaps, indicating a potent triadic symbolism?—what Angus Fletcher, discussing ideas of harmony in Milton's *Comus*, calls the "general triad-making power the Attendant Spirit himself enjoys."[3] Or does Stevens simply mean to indicate the psyche? What is the source of the voice that calls *bethou me*, or more seductively yet, *be thou me?*

Bethou is both intimate and biblical, romantic and religious. Stevens's *bethou me*—his "tutoyez-moi"—derives from two traditions of discourse, one romantic and revolutionary, the other theological and medieval. R. P. Blackmur, one of the most illuminating of Stevens's early critics, once remarked that the poet was "in essence of a very old tradition, French and Platonic," and with characteristic insight dubbed him "a troubadour, a poet of the Court of Love."[4] While Stevens's relation to the romantic poets has been discussed in depth (most notably by Harold

Bloom),[5] his use of the language of Canticles and the imagery of speculative mysticism has not.[6] The poems that are the focus of this chapter should strongly demonstrate that the notion of spiritual intimacy in the modernist's verse owes something to Neoplatonic mystical theology and to the erotic religious poetry found in both French and English medieval canons.

Sensual images and language are in evidence in all three major phases of the poetry, but one discovers a concentration of erotic energy in a particular group of poems. These poems are not hedonist in nature but describe a paradoxically rich form of asceticism. Each of them is a meditation that illustrates the leap of desire from a physical origin to a metaphysical locus of attraction. Like *Final Soliloquy of the Interior Paramour* and *Re-statement of Romance*, these poems are forms of communication with an interiorized, transcendent love object. To define and sharpen the relationships in such mystical-erotic poems, Stevens invents parables of seduction. Two such parables are the cameo, *Cy Est Pourtraicte, Madame Ste Ursule, et Les Unze Mille Vierges*, and the near-hallucinatory *World as Meditation*. As the present chapter will show, they are significantly related to the very early and very late periods.

With respect to love and its objects, *love* and *desire* may be used interchangeably with *eros* and *erotic energy*. All such terms are global and abstract. Among them, however, *desire* is the controlling superordinate term. The range of meanings carried by *desire* runs from subtle to overpowering: inclination, disposition; appetite, wish, want; need, longing, yearning; and at the far end, lust, passion, craving—the vernacular "itch" and Saint Paul's "burn." In Stevens's poetry, these feelings become the tonal elements of "a savage and subtle and simple harmony" (CP, 468). Indifference, neutrality, coldness, dislike, and satiety indicate degrees of distance, remoteness, and are desire's natural opposites. On the other hand, Stevens's verse abounds in positive oppositions, as for example, "A responding to a diviner opposite" (CP, 468).

The expression of desire in Stevens's poetry is distinguished by its intensity, fluidity, and its mutability. Freud's libido allows to eros precisely this sense of a concentrated energy flow. In addition, while libido as the pleasure principle denotes the sexual urge, it generalizes to mean the driving force behind all human action. Even so, the theory of libido may not stretch far enough to encompass response to a diviner opposite, an idea that seems closer to Plato than to Freud. Stevens was familiar with Freud's writings and his theories of sexuality and, like Freud (who declared himself a "convinced Platonist"), Stevens acknowledged that he had been deeply influenced by the author of the *Symposium* and the *Phaedrus*.

Both Freud and Plato are concerned with the fact that desire is self-transformational. In Freudian language, the powerful sexual impulse that arises in response to a physical, visual, or verbal stimulus may undergo sublimation, the instantaneous redirection of sexual energy to a nonsensual object. In the Platonic vocabulary, Eros is the hungry daemon who—like the philosopher hungry for wisdom—can span the distance between the material plane and the metaphysical. An educated eros, in the *Symposium*, achieves an ascent. It moves from the begetting of children to the bringing to birth of poetry, laws, institutions; then to the contemplation of the beauty of the abstract sciences, to the beauty of ideal forms, to a final *ekstasis*—union with unchanging eternal good. One understands that for Plato, desire at each stage of the game is intent on some form of immortality.

In "The Irrational Element in Poetry" (referred to earlier), Stevens spoke of Freud as "one of the great figures in the world" who had "given the irrational a legitimacy that it never had before" (*OP*, 218–19). He moves easily in this essay from Freud's encounter with the irrational to the Platonic ascent of eros: "All mystics approach God through the irrational. Pure poetry is both mystical and irrational. . . . [and while] very few of us . . . write poetry in order to find God, it is probably the purpose of each of us to write poetry to find the good which, in the Platonic sense, is synonymous with God" (*OP*, 222). In this early piece, phrased with great care, Stevens has already brought together two critical ideas that will continue to develop through the life of the poetry: the seductive force of a strong metaphysical object; and the notion that poetry arises from a desire "to find the good," which he defines as philosophically synonymous with God.

Seen thus, desire is more than a motivating force; desire is an engine of conversion. What springs into life as an erotic impulse may be directed away from a primary sexual object toward a contemplative goal or mystical state, or sublimated to an aesthetic act or mental effort. Such an impulse may culminate in delight, vision, humor, invention, philosophic inquiry, poetry, or pure mathematics. It may carry one into the sphere of the sublime. Alternately, and certainly in Stevens's poetry, desire may culminate in violence, a consuming negation, or the urge to destroy. It will be aimed, in each case, at whatever best promises to satisfy the initial impulse. But because libidinal energy tends to course between two poles, some object must kindle the original impulse to *bethou*.

Stevens captures desire's cosmic leap when he muses on the singularity of the romantic: "it is a singular romance, / This warmth in the blood-world for the pure idea." (*CP*, 256). What does he mean by "romance"?

An adventure? A *romaunt?* A rendezvous? An illusion? On occasion he does use *romantic* to mean a sentimental fiction, as Margaret Peterson has shown in her valuable discussion of Stevens's various uses of the term.[7] But his technical or specialized use of the term indicates something very different. As a mode, the romantic seems to denote a process of constant renewal, a Heracleitan stream of invention. "It is curious," remarks Stevens in November 1944, "how subject the romantic is to change: tremendously alive one day and a curiosity the next" (*LWS*, 478). The late essay "Two or Three Ideas" (1951) outlines a theory of the romantic that transcends a period of literature or a particular set of poetics: "The romantic . . . has a way of renewing itself. . . . it can never effectively touch the same thing twice in the same way. . . . When, therefore, the romantic is in abeyance, when it is discredited, it remains true that there is always an unknown romantic and that the imagination will not be forever denied" (*OP*, 215).

A much earlier work, *Re-statement of Romance* provides a voice for the "unknown romantic." It can be read as an imaginative interchange between spirit and sense; and hence it provides one formal model for Stevens's ongoing meditation on the concept of *bethou*. As against an elemental Shelleyan struggle with the forces of nature, *Re-statement* comes across as a love poem, strangely cool and luminous. It addresses psychological space and a nameless inhabitant of the interior:

> Only we two may interchange
> Each in the other what each has to give.
> Only we two are one, not you and night,
>
> Nor night and I, but you and I, alone,
> So much alone, so deeply by ourselves,
> So far beyond the casual solitudes,
>
> That night is only the background of our selves,
> Supremely true each to its separate self,
> In the pale light that each upon the other throws.   (*CP*, 146)

As the pronominal fusion and subsequent separation of "ourselves" to "our selves" suggests, the poem differentiates mutuality and isolation, interdependence and independent identity. It probes, in a stripped-down conversational lyric, the problem of self-definition in the context of being together. The "pale light" that each casts upon the other is knowledge derived, not from a mirror but the lamp of another being. The problem for the reader is not so much in these questions of interchange, interesting as they are, but in the question of who is speaking, and to whom. What kind of romance is this?

Is the poet communing with a seductive but silent paramour during this rendezvous? Or is Reality interviewing Imagination? Perhaps we are voyeurs, overhearing the murmurs of a blood-world lover to his blood-world beloved. Or it might be a romance between a blood-world lover and a metaphysical mistress. Perhaps it is the conversation of a neoromantic with the high tradition he is in the act of renewing. Or conversely, the exchange of a postromantic with an "older woman," the tradition he is ever so gently repudiating. Possibly none of these are headed, so to speak, in the right direction. What we are hearing may be a ghostly inner voice addressing the outer person. The riddle of the speaker may not yield to a simple solution. But in pondering these things one has perhaps been entertaining angels unawares. For one is left with the sense of having been exposed to an uncanny intimacy.

In *Wallace Stevens: Words Chosen out of Desire*, Helen Vendler opened up the whole question of desire in Stevens's poetry. "To tether Stevens' poems to human feeling," she observed, "is at least to remove him from the 'world of ghosts' where he is often located, and to insist that he is a poet of more than epistemological questions alone."[8] Vendler has always been sensitive to the strength of feeling that courses through Stevens's curiously chaste words. Stevens himself, however, maintained that there is a deep bond between epistemological concerns and human feeling. *It is the unknown that excites the ardor of scholars. . . . it has seductions more powerful and more profound than those of the known.*

The early *Cy Est Pourtraicte*, portraying Saint Ursula, traffics in the seduction of the unknown, or at least the unseen. It illustrates "responding to a diviner opposite" by way of a saint's legend, a medieval *romaunt*. On the one hand, it suggests a Pre-Raphaelite painting, richly colored and experimental. From another point of view, it is a piece of mordant blasphemy. Either way, Stevens's portrait of the virgin martyr gives us an exemplary case of the relation of physical to spiritual experience. And it is precisely her martyrdom, the fact of her physical pain—the bloody and violent death coupled with knowledge of God—that dominates the piece and binds the bodily passion to the passion of the soul.

The erotic longing that directs its energies toward a sublime object is allegorized with delicate wit in *Cy Est Pourtraicte, Madame Ste Ursule, et Les Unze Mille Vierges*. Bearing a title that floats like a heraldic streamer over a scant thirty-one lines, *Ursule* unfolds a tale of desire, mystical seduction, and deadly counterseduction. Stevens places his virgin saint on her knees in an ordinary garden. Her prayer, like George Herbert's, is meant to serve as an engine against the Almighty:

> Ursula, in a garden, found
> A bed of radishes.
> She kneeled upon the ground
> And gathered them,
> With flowers around,
> Blue, gold, pink, and green.
>
> She dressed in red and gold brocade
> And in the grass an offering made
> Of radishes and flowers.
>
> She said, "My dear
> Upon your altars,
> I have placed
> The marguerite and coquelicot,
> And roses
> Frail as April snow;
> But here," she said,
> "Where none can see,
> I make an offering, in the grass,
> Of radishes and flowers."
> And then she wept
> For fear the Lord would not accept.   (*CP*, 21)

Ursula, in red and gold brocade, kneels in the grass "where none can see" to make a secret offering to the Lord. In place of the frail cultivated blossoms she has cut for display in the church, she offers up pungent red roots and hardy meadow flowers, addresses God intimately as "my dear," and weeps. In his own garden the Deity is apparently searching for just what Ursula so ardently wishes him to receive:

> The good Lord in His garden sought
> New leaf and shadowy tinct,
> And they were all His thought.
> He heard her low accord,
> Half prayer and half ditty,
> And He felt a subtle quiver,
> That was not heavenly love,
> Or pity.   (*CP*, 21–22)

Ursula's desire, uprooted like her radishes and wildflowers from the earth that nurtured them, wings its way upward to strike the good Lord who is both the source and object of her desiring. He, receptive to her "low accord / Half prayer and half ditty," feels a corresponding quiver. Perhaps, like the woman in *Sunday Morning,* he has been thinking:

> Is there no change of death in paradise?
> Does ripe fruit never fall? Or do the boughs
> Hang always heavy in that perfect sky.   (CP, 69)

Perhaps he has grown weary of interminable green thoughts and craves refreshment from the blood-world. In the later *Esthétique du Mal* the poetic consciousness also meditates on the possibility of infinite boredom:

> Perhaps,
> After death, the non-physical people, in paradise,
> Itself non-physical, may, by chance, observe
> The green corn gleaming and experience
> The minor of what we feel.   (CP, 325)

The double yearning that arises from the secular and spiritual halves of existence becomes unified in Ursula's low accord, for it is a chord composed of both sacred and profane notes, prayer and ditty. In a much later work Stevens will rearticulate the chord of desire in a simple parallel: "The physical pine, the metaphysical pine" (CP, 373). In the early poem, however, the good Lord's "subtle quiver" is the key to the ruling idea. It is an idea with pagan roots, the notion that active desire brings god and mortal together, effects an interchange, causes them to *bethou* and for a time become one another. In Stevens's poem, the Lord's quiver may be the first stirring or the final shudder of desire, but it is a "subtle" figure because it also suggests the divine quiver that holds, not the Augustinian beams of caritas but the fiery darts of eros.

The figure of the Lord's quiver and dart entered Christian theology in the third century by way of Origen's *Commentary on the Song of Songs,* the same work that introduced nuptial imagery into Christian mysticism. "The soul," says Origen in the prologue, "is moved by heavenly love and longing when, having clearly beheld the beauty and fairness of the Word of God, it falls deeply in love with His loveliness and receives from the Word Himself a certain dart and wound of love."[9] A passage from the *Commentary* helps to elucidate Stevens's ironic point in the portrait of Ursula. It gives us a rationale for the saint's romantic behavior and underscores the implications in the poem of repressed sexuality and immanent violence. Expounding Isaiah (49:2) on the figure of the dart and quiver, Origen says:

> If there is anyone anywhere who has at some time burned with this faithful love of the Word . . . who has received the sweet wound of Him who is the chosen dart . . . if anyone has been pierced with the loveworthy spear of His knowledge, so that he yearns and longs for him by day and by night, can speak naught but to Him, can think of nothing else, and is disposed to no desire nor longing . . . except for Him alone . . . that soul . . . has received her wound of Him of whom Isaias says: *And he hath made me a chosen dart, and in His quiver hath he hidden me.*[10]

Here is a concentration of erotic language: *burned, love, loveworthy, yearns, longs, disposed,* and *desire,* interspersed with images of penetration—*sweet wound, pierced, spear, dart, quiver.* Origen has set forth a clinical description of the malady known as lovesickness; Ovid himself can give no more graphic a definition. Stevens's young saint, weeping and kneeling in the grass, has simply fallen in love with God. But the exemplary status of Stevens's poem emerges only when one takes into account the legend that furnishes its backdrop.

Origen's ecstatic figure of the soul "pierced with the loveworthy spear of His knowledge" remained part of the rhetoric of Christian mysticism for over a millennium. It is peculiarly applicable, however, to Saint Ursula of Cologne, who is usually depicted as a crowned princess with an arrow—which is her attribute.[11] Ursula is said to have been born in Brittany in the fifth century, the daughter of a Christian king. Her beauty and intelligence drew many suitors but she refused them all. Finally, she agreed to marry Conan, the son of the English king, but stipulated that three well-nigh impossible conditions be met before the wedding could take place: she must have ten noble virgins for her companions, and she herself and each of her companions must have a thousand virgins in attendance; Prince Conan and the entire English court must convert to Christianity; she must have three years before the wedding in which to travel so that she might visit the shrines of saints.

The English ambassadors returned home ringing Ursula's praises and her conditions were agreed upon—perhaps to the maiden's dismay. Eleven thousand virgins were marshaled for her retinue and Conan arrived with them to accompany Ursula on the pilgrimage to Rome. When they reached the outskirts of Cologne on the return journey, their party was attacked by Huns who had laid siege to the city. Her "unze mille vierges" and her husband-to-be were slaughtered on the spot, but the leader of the Huns took a fancy to Ursula and offered to spare her life if she became his bride. When she refused, he raised his bow and drove three arrows into her body.

Stevens presents the virgin martyr as *Madame* Ste Ursule to indicate that a wedding has already taken place. In her own thoughts at least, Ursula has taken the vows of a nun. She is disposed, in Origen's phrase, to "no desire nor longing nor yet hope, except for Him alone." The saint's early death and her purity of spirit are memorialized by the white roses "frail as April snow" that she has placed upon the altars—enshrined tomb-like within the church. The crimson roots and wildflowers, together with Ursula's red-and-gold robe, signal that a more sensual passion, earth-sprung, is feeding the austere passion of the spirit.

Stevens's portrait of Ursula is structured by three arrows, three vectors of desire that mark the crucial moments of her life. These provide the poem's subtext, its foundation of meaning and its romance. We can infer that antecedent to the present moment of the poem, Ursula has been penetrated by the heavenly dart and that she continues to yearn and burn for the divine Archer. The poem's central moment shows the Deity moved in turn by the girl's intense longing:

> He heard her low accord,
> Half prayer and half ditty,
> And He felt a subtle quiver,
> That was not heavenly love,
> Or pity.

Struck by Ursula's passion, the good Lord's "quiver" becomes, with positive irony, the inevitable preliminary to the maiden's death.[12] Out of that quiver will come the final arrow that speeds their union. Thus, the savage hand that raises the Hun's bow and the hand of God converge. The future moment contained in the poem is that moment when Madame Ste Ursule, thrice-stricken, is poised between life and violent death, death and holy consummation. Martyrdom, with its overt brutality and innate knowledge, roots physical, bodily experience to metaphysical experience. It is a theme which Stevens allows to emerge by implication only in *Ursule* but which flows like an underground river just under the surface of the poetry.

Clearly the history of *Ursule* casts a long shadow behind what is essentially a slender poem. Its sprinkling of rhyme, the arch ending, its delicacy and poetic tact make it insouciant and graceful. But we learn that the garden in a Stevens poem is a locus of solitary desire, and further, that it may suggest violent change or death. At the end of *Peter Quince at the Clavier,* composed during the same period, we find parallels for the death that is foreshadowed in *Ursule:*

> So evenings die, in their green going,
> A wave interminably flowing.
> So gardens die, their meek breath scenting
> The cowl of winter, done repenting.
> So maidens die, to the auroral
> Celebration of a maiden's choral.   (*CP,* 92)

Ursule and *Peter Quince,* with its reorchestration of Susanna and the Elders, both engage directly with the force of arousal and the intersubjective mechanics of seduction. The violence that attends the saint's death is echoed in the elders' attempt to rape Susanna. The "melody" of the lovely woman, bathed as much in her own sensuousness as in the waters of the garden pool, is interrupted by the crash of cymbals and the "roaring horns" of lust. Assault and violation are a hidden presence in Stevens's *hortus conclusus,* merely biding their time. The self-seductive element, the contrapuntal aesthetic response that speaks to something both within and beyond the self, is set forth with extraordinary precision in the opening lines of *Peter Quince:*

> Just as my fingers on these keys
> Make music, so the selfsame sounds
> On my spirit make a music, too.   (*CP,* 89)

Meditations such as develop in these early pieces extend through the later poetry, always maintaining a sensual character and nearly always the tinge of violence. They structure the visions of *Sunday Morning,* the woman in her sunny chair with late morning coffee and oranges struggling to dissipate the "holy hush of ancient sacrifice." In the typical early poems Stevens elaborates on the romance between blood-world and pure idea, describing a dialogue of one, as Donne puts it in *The Extasie.* The poems contain a silent partner; one consciousness is paramount, a single voice speaks. Desire is trained on a metaphysical or sublime object. In each case, one is aware of the relentless attraction of the "diviner opposite." While the attractive force of the object pervades these poems, the focus falls sharply on the subject experiencing attraction, desiring.

These considerations govern the expression of one form of desire throughout the canon, but a change or broadening takes place during the middle period. The dramatic entrance of Nanzia Nunzio in *Notes,* in the passage that Stevens called "the poem about Ozymandias," is the moment in the poetry that contains his restatement of the romantic. Nanzia Nunzio, the messenger, proclaims poetic passion in the mystical language of sexual desire. The canto is full of erotic force, but the "diviner opposite" has been reduced to a figure of parody. The object of Nanzia's passion (this is surely one of Stevens's more complicated jokes) is a compelling but utterly unresponsive locus of attraction—a stony Ozymandias.

By the late poetry, there has been a striking change in the poet's ideas about desire and the object of desire. In the final period Stevens has increasingly come to think of desire as a good in itself—apart from its satisfaction. It has become the primal energy "which nothing can frustrate."

Stevens's notion of "the spirit's own seduction" is tied to his use of monastic nuptial imagery. All through the poetry, Stevens's language reflects an ancient tradition, the rhetoric of hierogamy, or sacred marriage. The contemplatives, as Stevens knew, drew their imagery from two very different streams of thought, compounding a Hebrew allegorical tradition—God as the Bridegroom of Israel—with a pagan philosophy of divine eros. The contemplative or "speculative" strain entered Christian theology by way of Neoplatonism. For early theologians like Origen, the Song of Songs yielded the paradigm of a spiritual union of God and Church. Gradually, however, the *sponsa Dei* and *Sponsus*, bride and Bridegroom, became particularized as the human soul and Christ. In this way, the bride-chamber imagery drawn from Solomon's erotic poem came to illustrate what was essentially a Platonic description of desire as *askesis*, an ascension.[13]

The erotic language of spiritual union flowered in the sermons of Bernard of Clairvaux and the Victorines (Richard and Hugh of St. Victor's in Paris) in the twelfth century. It prevails in religious poetry to the Virgin. It is evident in the writings of Aquinas, a century after Bernard, in the use of such terms as *extasis*, *zelus*, *liquefactio*, *fervor*, and *fruitio* to describe man's love for God. In the *Paradiso*, Dante puts the sexualized language of spiritual delight in Saint Bernard's tongue—he is (in Sinclair's translation) "all on fire with love" for the Queen of Heaven:

> E la regina del cielo, ond' io ardo
> tutto d' amor, ne fara ogni grazia,
> però ch' i' sono il suo fedel Bernardo.   (31. 100–102)

> (And the Queen of Heaven, for whom I am all on fire with love,
> will grant us every grace, since I am her faithful Bernard.)

As Stevens reminds us in *Madame Ste Ursule, amor* is "not heavenly love" but physical desire, not *caritas* but lust. One may ask where Stevens picked up this strand of theology. The answer may well lie in the young poet's college years. Stevens attended Harvard at a time when Charles Eliot Norton's translation of Dante was the subject of animated discussion. It seems likely that Stevens, who participated actively in the literary and intellectual life of the college, would be well aware of the discussions of the "Dantisti" and conversant with the theology of Bernard, a major presence in the *Commedia*. [14]

Poems in which solitary yearning must bridge the gap between material and imaginative realms may owe something to their romantic forebear, Shelley's *Alastor: or the Spirit of Solitude*. But when Stevens wants to suggest a more fertile, less frustrate context for desire, he will echo the marriage song of Solomon and the speculative tradition. *Study of Images II*, for example, posits a continuum in which theoretical constructs coexist with their opposites. Those who are familiar with the metaphors of betrothal, union, and birth used by the contemplatives will recognize the mystical-erotic strain in this poem. It is a peculiarly seductive vision for Stevens, an invasion of the metaphysical realm by a powerful erotic impulse—as if abstractions were organisms,

> as if the disparate halves
> Of things were waiting in a betrothal known
> To none, awaiting espousal to the sound
>
> Of right joining, a music of ideas, the burning
> And breeding and bearing birth of harmony,
> The final relation, the marriage of the rest.   (*CP*, 464–65)

There is unquestionably something in Stevens that sees a connection between theological mysticism and aesthetic experience. The fluid interchange among monastic, philosophic, and aesthetic pursuits is set forth in the first section of *Notes*:

> The monastic man is an artist. The philosopher
> Appoints man's place in music, say, today.
> But the priest desires. The philosopher desires.   (*CP*, 382)

In these lines, Stevens categorically rejects T. S. Eliot's celebrated theory of the divided sensibility. It is merely an attitude, Stevens seems to say, a rigid cast of thought, that blocks the interplay of mind and soul and human feeling. A "right joining" of the paths of perception may be no easy task, but when the three paths feed together it produces exuberant power, a virile force:

> the strong exhilaration
> Of what we feel from what we think, of thought
> Beating in the heart, as if blood newly came,
>
> An elixir, an excitation, a pure power.   (*CP*, 382)

Although this enjambment of blood-world and pure idea occurs all through the poetry, Stevens is understandably cautious when he refers to it in his prose discussions. He is first of all a man who profoundly values the existence of boundaries, of defining limits, the separation of one thing from another. Furthermore, he does not wish to be classed irresponsibly as a mystic. In the 1930s, as noted earlier, Stevens suggested with thoughtful diffidence that pure poetry "is both mystical and irrational," joining the whole Freudian exploration of sexuality and the subconscious to the meaning of the irrational. While Stevens was clearly aware of the ideas about mystical experience developed by William Jones in *The Varieties of Religious Experience*, he does not refer to James specifically in the early talk on the irrational in poetry.[15] Not until Stevens is in his seventies (in 1951) do we find him calmly stating in public that "the theory of poetry . . . often seems to become in time a mystical theology" (*NA*, 173). Stevens was enough impressed with H. D. Lewis's essay "On Poetic Truth" to enter it into his notebook (c. 1954). A passage from that essay draws the parallel modes of art and religion firmly together in Jamesian cadences: "And the wonder and mystery of art, as indeed of religion in the last resort, is the revelation of something 'wholly other' by which the inexpressible loneliness of thinking is broken and enriched" (*OP*, 237).

"The inexpressible loneliness of thinking" brings us to *The World as Meditation*, the poem about Penelope. Stevens's narratives about chaste and desirous virgins and matrons are not seduction poems in the traditional sense, but they are in that family. Perhaps they constitute an attempt to entice knowledge herself by the careful framing of a meditation. Each poem in this group concerns the flow of physical desire toward an object of thought; each one is an epistemological experiment in an erotic mode. In their very conception and structure they seek to repair, to "mend" Stevens might say, the Cartesian split. And in fact, the ligature of mind and body referred to above in *Notes*—"thought / Beating in the heart"—is repeated almost word for word in the poem about Penelope: "The thought kept beating in her like her heart." By the very late period

Stevens has succeeded in bringing together the objects of desire and thought. *Episteme* means "knowing," and *The World as Meditation* posits a knowing in both the contemplative and biblical senses—subject and object become one flesh.

This late poem in which Penelope contemplates the return of Ulysses is, in the simplest terms, about *composition*. Stevens, who is not generally given to epigraphs in his short pieces, introduces *The World as Meditation* with a quotation from Georges Enesco, concert violinist and composer. The rootless life of the musician on tour is opposed to the sustained and sustaining inner vision of the *compositeur*:

> J'ai passé trop de temps à travailler mon violon, à voyager. Mais l'exercice essentiel du compositeur—la méditation—rien ne l'a jamais suspendu en moi . . . je vis un rêve permanent, qui ne s'arrête ni nuit ni jour.

> (I have spent too much time practicing my violin, in traveling. But the essential exercise of the composer—meditation—has never been suspended . . . I live an ongoing dream that ceases neither night nor day.) [My translation]

The epigraph, just beyond the frame of the poem (or always verging on the poem), serves several purposes. It makes graphic the division between outside and inside. It formally counterposes French to the poem's English, prose to verse, a musician's thoughtful words to the poem's ordered music. It transfers the perspective of the traveler to the perspective of the one who waits at home. But it sets up consonances as well as oppositions: both epigraph and poem have to do with distance and isolation, circling motion and central stillness. Both conceive meditation as a visionary act—the composition of a continuous whole from the separated parts of a world.

Within the poem, Penelope is clearly *compositeur* of the world she contemplates, the dreamer of the "rêve permanent, qui ne s'arrête ni nuit ni jour." In *Sunday Morning*, the meditating woman conceives death as a final mothering:

> Death is the mother of beauty, mystical,
> Within whose burning bosom we devise
> Our earthly mothers waiting, sleeplessly.   (CP, 69)

In the later poem, "our earthly mothers waiting, sleeplessly" resolve into one Homeric woman. This poem enacts a scene of fascination and its Penelope-figure is something more complex than a model of domestic fidelity. She is a composite of welcoming wife and mother and bewitching seductress—Penelope, Circe, and Siren combing her hair. Joseph Riddel has characterized Stevens's Ulysses-principle as "that ever-changing thing itself for which the one longs from across the abyss of consciousness."[16] One might apply the same characterization to the Penelope-figure.

Stevens opens the poem with a question that returns, with a tense change, after the first five stanzas:

> Is it Ulysses that approaches from the east,
> The interminable adventurer? The trees are mended.
> That winter is washed away. Someone is moving
>
> On the horizon and lifting himself up above it.
> A form of fire approaches the cretonnes of Penelope,
> Whose mere savage presence awakens the world in which she
>   dwells.
>
> She has composed, so long, a self with which to welcome him,
> Companion to his self for her, which she imagined,
> Two in a deep-founded sheltering, friend and dear friend.
>
> The trees had been mended, as an essential exercise
> In an inhuman meditation, larger than her own.
> No winds like dogs watched over her at night.
>
> She wanted nothing he could not bring her by coming alone.
> She wanted no fetchings. His arms would be her necklace
> And her belt, the final fortune of their desire.
>
> But was it Ulysses? Or was it only the warmth of the sun
> On her pillow? The thought kept beating in her like her heart.
> The two kept beating together. It was only day.
>
> It was Ulysses and it was not. Yet they had met,
> Friend and dear friend and a planet's encouragement.
> The barbarous strength within her would never fail.
>
> She would talk a little to herself as she combed her hair,
> Repeating his name with its patient syllables,
> Never forgetting him that kept coming constantly so near.
>   (CP, 520–21)

The last and greatest of Stevens's seduction parables, *The World as Meditation* occupies a class of its own: as a meditation on meditation it is identical with its subject. A few points of form should be noted right away. The poem is dyadic in its warp-and-woof structures, triadic in overall design; its space is a rippling of expanding circles; its time dimension prophetic, dreamlike, and in its layered repetitions, suggestive of Bergsonian *durée*. Its thesis is a brilliantly simple, if unoriginal, proposition about desire.

The poem appears to be set for a double keyboard. Everything about it is designed to work on two levels. It sustains two meditations: Penelope's, which constantly prepares the scene of Ulysses' return, and the "inhuman meditation, larger than her own" which thinks the planetary scene into existence, imagining, inventing, composing its diurnal and seasonal cycles, its eternal returns. The poem itself then yields a third meditation, its stanzas cast in the familiar tercets of the late poetry—the triadic dimension. There is formal counterpoint of language and mode—French to English, prose to verse—but in the fourth stanza these elements are both united and reversed: the *exercice essentiel* of the epigraph literally turns around to become the poem's *essential exercise*. Of the lexical doublings, perhaps the most eye-catching is the strangeness of trees that are "mended." (Apart from its evident sense of revived spring leaf, can this be a reference to the "men dead" of Homeric epic?) Is Stevens punning, perhaps, on the Greek form (*men . . . de*) which classically introduces a pair of antithetical statements?[17] Finally, the poem frames a question about its major binaries: what is internal? what external? It seriously investigates the constantly changing boundaries between self and other and makes visual Bachelard's space of "intimate immensity."[18]

Among the more important binaries that come together are Penelope's thought and heart; her longing for Ulysses and his longing for home; the two hearts beating together in the imagined final embrace; and the two visions, domestic and planetary, which are joined at the moment sun and man become a unity (Riddel's "solar hero"). The binary modes of brutality and tenderness—the "savage presence" of the approaching male and the "barbarous strength" of the awaiting female—are drawn together in the sheltering tenderness of "friend and dear friend."

The world as meditation is a world of circles, spheres, and circlings. There are spheres of consciousness, spheres of influence, and a horizon, or circular boundary, from which desire approaches Penelope as regularly as the return of light. Beginning with natural cycles, the poem evolves cycles of return through the repetition of image and word, spiraling continually back to its beginnings. In contrast, its closing remains peculiarly open-ended. Like the blackbird of the early poem, the ending escapes entrapment in lethal circularity:

When the blackbird flew out of sight,
It marked the edge
Of one of many circles.   (CP, 94)

Encirclement for Stevens, even among enchanted circles, does not necessarily mean enclosure.

Time also describes a kind of circle. Temporality, expressed in the
repeated sunrise, is joined to the scene of approach—the "interminable"
advent of the desired one. The tenses of the poem move snakelike through
present, future, and past. We are absorbed into a zone of prophetic vision.
Like Homer's "best of diviners," the poem gifts us with all-encompassing
knowledge; we are able to see the things that were, that were to be, and
that had been before—all at once.

As in all the poems of the mystical-erotic group, the attraction of the
love object is intense. The poem about Penelope develops the proposition
set forth in *An Ordinary Evening in New Haven*: "The point of vision and
desire are the same" (CP, 466). And clearly, part of Stevens's "argument"
in *The World as Meditation* is concerned with the placement and re-
placement of eros; the meaning of *bethou me*; the interchange of identity
between lover and beloved. Penelope *seems* to be an unmoved mover in
the world she contemplates. Her call emanates like a radio signal from a
fixed point at the center. But she is herself a "point of vision and desire"
and may be understood as a projection of her husband's intense wish to
return home. In truth, desire streams from both the inner and outer
circles as the continually approaching "form of fire" kindles a parallel
warmth in the waiting woman: "awakens the world in which she dwells."
The world thus imagined follows the transformations of desire as it arcs
from blood-world sensuality to pure idea and back again; it examines the
internalization of the love object, and all its addictive fascination.

Stevens is not alone in his use of the circling-husband and waiting-
wife topos, but he is original, I believe, in situating the poetic consciousness in the one who waits. Donne's A *Valediction Forbidding Mourning*
prefigures *World as Meditation* in its circling and spheres of influence, its
positioning of the wife's "soule" as the "fixt foot" at the center of things.
Stevens will have known the poem about the twin compasses:

Such wilt thou be to mee, who must
    Like to th'other foot, obliquely runne;
Thy firmness draws my circle just,
    And makes me end, where I begun. [19]

For all its expanding bubbles of imagined bliss, Stevens's poem has a terrible starkness about it and a dark underside. *The World as Meditation* depends on its Homeric ancestor to provide more than the names of husband and wife and an echo of epic dimensions. It suggests a "final fortune"—Ulysses will eventually strike through to Penelope and home—and it provides a literary context for the experience of twenty years of married solitude. The "final fortune of their desire" may be read as the chief irony in Stevens's poem, for as Tennyson's *Ulysses* makes clear, the Homeric hero ("he of the multiple turnings," *polytropon*) will return twenty years older to a wife who is twenty years older. As fortune will have it, the final embrace is death. Stevens's Ulysses is being drawn home to a figure who represents chaste wife, seductive witch, and deadly siren—in that order. The closing stanza thus takes on a less than innocent meaning. Behind the loving Penelope, talking a little to herself as she combed her hair, is the mother of beauty, mystical, patiently waiting.

In the Penelope poem, Stevens illustrates the thesis spelled out in *An Ordinary Evening in New Haven:* desire is enough. In canto 3 Stevens tells us that all manifestations of love can be traced to an irreducible single origin—the desire for love. While love can be frustrated, he points out, desire cannot:

> And next to love is the desire for love,
> The desire for its celestial ease in the heart,
>
> Which nothing can frustrate, that most secure,
> Unlike love in possession of that which was
> To be possessed and is. But this cannot
>
> Possess. It is desire, set deep in the eye,
> Behind all actual seeing, in the actual scene.   (CP, 467)

Desire calls *bethou me* in the many poems that marry the abstract to the organic. Stevens's wish to physically grasp the "object / Of the perpetual meditation, point / Of the enduring, visionary love" (*CP*, 466) is surely the poet's desire to capture the music of ideas in black ink. The contemplative mode that chronicles the spirit's lust for the divine emerges hesitantly in the poetry, although it is clearly one of Stevens's major restatements of the romantic. And, whether the voice is Saint Ursula's or Penelope's, the reflecting consciousness of *Sunday Morning,* the unidentified speaker of *Re-statement of Romance,* or the clownish entrepreneur who with exquisite sensibility coaxes music from a clavier, it contributes to "the sound of right joining." On occasion, the contemplative tradition that feeds into Stevens's poetry will take him by the hand, as it were, and draw him to itself. At such a moment, Stevens's language becomes the language of Solomon; passionate, explicit, sexual, simple, composed:

> Her hand composed him like a hand appeared,
> Of an impersonal gesture, a stranger's hand.
> He was too conscious of too many things
>
> In the first canto of the final canticle.
> Her hand took his and drew him near to her.
> Her hair fell on him and the mi-bird flew
>
> To the ruddier bushes at the garden's end.
> Of her, of her alone, at last he knew
> And lay beside her underneath the tree.   (CP, 271)

Chapter 2

Ambiguous Birds and Quizzical Messengers

To compound the imagination's Latin with
The lingua franca et jocundissima. STEVENS

IN THE MONASTERY at Soissons there is a thirteenth-century manuscript finely illuminated in red, gold, and blue, whose text is a collection of miracle tales. One of these stories, translated from the Latin into Middle French, is set in the Bernardine monastery at Clairvaux. It tells of a minstrel, or jongleur, who, having entered the order with no other skill, performs his somersaults and juggling tricks in secret before the altar of the Blessed Virgin. This daily service takes place in a crypt seldom visited by the other monks; here the jongleur, clad only in a light undergarment, worships his Lady with skillful vaults. He pauses only to invoke the Queen of Heaven's blessing and to beseech her to accept his secular and unorthodox efforts as a token of loving reverence. The scene in the dimly lit chapel is described in rich detail:

> Then commenced he his merry play, leaping low and small, tall and high, over and under . . . he knelt upon his knees before the statue, and meekly bowed his head. "Ha!" said he, "most gracious Queen, of your pity and your charity scorn not this my service." Afterward he did the French vault, then the vault of Champagne, then the Roman vault . . . then, with his hands before his brow, he danced daintily before the altar. . . . Then he walked on his two hands with his feet in the air and his head near the ground. He twirled with his feet, and wept with his eyes. "Lady," said he, "I worship you with heart, with body, with feet and hands. . . . Now I am your very minstrel. Others may chant your praises in the church, but here in the crypt will I tumble for your delight."[1]

The tumbler's activities are discovered by a fellow monk who hastens to the abbot, imparts the startling information and is commanded, in turn, to hold his tongue until the abbot can see the spectacle for himself. Together they hide in the crypt, and the abbot does indeed observe the antics of the juggler who again tumbles and dances for his Lady's mirth and delight. When, streaming perspiration, he sinks to the ground in a near faint, the watchers are treated to a miraculous vision. They behold the Queen of Heaven descending from the vault of the crypt: "She was more beautiful than the daughters of men, and her vesture was heavy with gold and gleaming stones. In her train came the hosts of heaven, angel and archangel also. . . . Then the sweet and courteous Queen herself took a white napkin in her hand, and with it gently fanned her minstrel before the altar. Courteous and debonair, the Lady refreshed his neck, his body and his brow." [2] In another version, the watchers see the Queen of Heaven appear in the statue's place and are stricken with awe as she descends from the pedestal, approaches the tumbler and smiling, takes up the hem of her robe to wipe his brow.

The charm that lies in the tale of the tumbler and Our Lady is certainly to be found in the contrast between high *courtoisie* and the subdued fervor of monastic life, heightened by the libertine quality of the troubadour. These elements combine to give the miracle its poignance and point, and the tale thus accomplishes its teaching purpose; it is an exemplum of the glory of faith and the value of humility. But there is a further teaching to be gathered from the tale of the juggler, at least as profound as the literal directives concerning faith and humility. The underlying message of the tale is almost transparently clear: with love, one may court the sacred by means of the profane and be accepted—even touched—by the divine. [3]

Early in December of 1908, the month they became engaged, Stevens wrote to "My dearest Elsie" the story of the tumbler. [4] "Now, suppose," he queried, referring to his own "Book of Doubts and Fears" as much as to the juggler, "suppose that, instead of doing his best, he had grieved about his short-comings, and offered only his grief. Would the image have smiled?" A sudden whimsy turns this homily into a little dance, and he adds: "And a jig—and a jiggety-jiggety-jig. There is *my* juggling, my dear—and my somersault." [5] Stevens had revealed something of his character to his bride-to-be, and to future readers an aspect of his poetic identity—playful, awkward, irreverent, yet oddly touched by grace. There are moments in the poetry when, immersed in irreverence, Stevens appears to be signaling—like the tumbler to his Lady: "Others may chant your praises in the church, but here in the crypt will I tumble for your delight."

Wallace Stevens's poetry is full of harping angels, ambiguous birds, and quizzical messengers. These creatures can provide rattling good entertainment. Hosts of angels tumble about the stratosphere; inching bantam roosters magically, priapically, transform into "ten-foot poets"; a papal courier launches, amazingly, into a slow striptease. Such figures, taken all together, constitute a parodic layer in the poetry that relies to a considerable extent on Scripture for its subtext.

It seems as though Stevens periodically yielded to the attraction of this material. Through much of the poetry one finds him vaulting and somersaulting and skillfully juggling with concepts such as the doctrine of Virgin Birth, the Personhood of the Paraclete, and the Annunciation. At the opening of *Le Monocle de Mon Oncle*, he flings down a liturgical invocation like a gauntlet. Within this frame of reference, titles like *The Dove in the Belly* or *The Owl in the Sarcophagus* assume a satirical edge, while *The Bird with the Coppery, Keen Claws* takes on a quietly blasphemous significance.[6] It becomes evident that Stevens frequently chooses theological material as an object of parody and, as often as not, a point of doctrine with sexual overtones.

What is Stevens up to? Here is a modern poet with a trained legal mind who in 1942 writes to a friend, "I loathe anything mystical." On the other hand, here is a thoughtful man who includes among his aphorisms: "God is in me or else is not at all [does not exist]." Finally, there is the Stevens who has celebrated a seventy-third birthday, in October 1952, writing with disarming ambivalence: "At my age it would be nice to be able to read more and think more and be myself more and to make up my mind about God, say, before it is too late, or at least before he makes up his mind about me."[7] With these observations in mind, one may suggest that in poems anchored to a theological undertext, Stevens is using parody, satire, even burlesque, to accomplish a double purpose.

All parodic invention uses a low mimetic, or imitative, method that establishes identity and disavowal at the same time. A *Dunciad* relies upon an *Iliad* to sharpen its satirical point, while its Goddess of Dulness—a purely allegorical figure—underscores by its very impiety the vanished religious significance of an antique pantheon. In a less gentle but equally familiar use, parody attacks its antecedent. By means of ridicule and caustic mimicry it seeks to expose, disarm, and debase its model. As M. M. Bakhtin has shown, parody pokes fun at, questions, "dialogizes," enlivens, assaults, and sometimes engulfs the antecedent work, but takes delight in assuming its aspect.[8] Parody, as it were, loves to stalk about in its father's bathrobe and slippers. It pretends to be its parent while commenting *on* the parent, which leads to Stevens's dual use of the mode.

Parody offers a playful way to talk about things that are felt to be meaningful but are no longer taken seriously. It constitutes one sort of permissible discourse with institutions of the past. Stevens uses parody to establish a link with traditional sources—the "romantic tenements" of aesthetic form and poetic utterance, the confluence of poetry and religion in a sacred text. But Stevens is also using parody to separate himself, to maintain distance from these same sources. Perhaps the use of parody to gain such diametrically opposed ends is a relatively recent development, occurring at a time that is preoccupied, not so much by problems of a possible theology, or an alternative to theology, but by great and subtle adjustments to its absence. Two selections from *Harmonium—The Bird with the Coppery, Keen Claws* and the opening stanza of *Le Monocle de Mon Oncle*—show how Stevens uses parody to attack, on the one hand, and to evoke the past, on the other. Perhaps the strangely poignant burlesque in *Notes toward a Supreme Fiction*, centered about a quizzical messenger of indeterminate gender, most fully illustrates Stevens's double use of the parodic mode, a use both sacral and sacrilegious.

The word *parody* derives from the Greek παρῳδία, *parodia* (*para-*, beside, and *oidia*, singing), literally "at the side of the singing" or, roughly, "countersong." Bakhtin's theory of parody is developed from this notion of countersong. The Russian formalist contends that since antiquity, every "high" genre (epic, lyric, tragedy) has generated a countervailing mode, a comical parodic counterpart.[9] It is precisely this parodic countersong that fulfills the condition of mirroring reality, says Bakhtin, for it provides "the corrective of laughter and criticism to all existing straightforward genres, languages, styles, voices: *to force men to experience beneath these categories a different and contradictory reality* that is otherwise not captured in them."[10]

Gilbert Highet classes parody as a venial form of satire, not the poisoned dart but the distorting mirror. His definition of the mode stresses intention: "Parody is imitation which, through distortion and exaggeration, evokes amusement, derision, and sometimes scorn."[11] Highet usefully refers to the evidence of self-parody in poetry, noting a Wordsworth sonnet that features a stuffed owl, and Swinburne's mercilessly mellifluous *Nephelidia*. Both of these poems exaggerate the styles of their respective authors, and both pass judgment on their own artistic personae by slyly implying that they are prey to self-indulgence. (Students of Stevens will recognize similar prodigies of self-parody in *Bantams in Pine-Woods*, for example, where the poet attempts to dissociate himself from his own *avoirdupois*: "Fat! Fat! Fat! Fat! I am the personal. / Your world is you. I am my world." There is the almost contrapuntal self-parody in section 25 of *The Man with the Blue Guitar*. This is the irregularly rhymed section that begins "He held the world upon his nose" and ends seven couplets later with "A fat thumb beats out ai-yi-yi"—unmistakably the thumb print of the poet in his character of plump and mocking jongleur.)[12]

In contrast to Bakhtin's agonic theory of parody with its echoing social resonances, Highet's argument presents parodic imitation as a neutralizing agent. It dilutes and disarms whether it masquerades as epic or heroic verse, or whether it blandly imitates the form while mocking the content of the prior work, as does Byron's murderous parody of Southey's *Vision of Judgment*.[13] One of Stevens's early pieces conforms to both these sets of criteria, for it both attacks and seeks to neutralize the power of the object it attacks. Essentially satiric, its mimicry and mockery are directed against ideological content. On one level, this poem attempts to neutralize the theological construct of the Paraclete—that least graspable person of the Trinity whose emblem is the Dove. On quite another level, the poem locks in combat with its object and "dialogizes," or argues against it. We shall see, however, that yet a third element enters the ideological debate that smolders at the core of the piece.

Over the jungle of the parakeets presides the Bird with the Coppery, Keen Claws. He is the controlling influence of this cosmic jungle, a "parakeet of parakeets" in whose image, presumably, the prevailing life-form is echoed. He would be Mozartian, doubtless, if he sang, for he is a classically "perfect cock." But except for a "pip" he does not sing—the pip, among other things, denotes a disease of poultry that may result in blindness—and as it turns out, this regal bird is as blind as Milton. His "church" is a sun-bleached rock and he is an unmoved mover who "exerts his will" upon the jungle universe, holding it in an impersonal death grip with his brazen claws.

In its formal structure, the poem mirrors the parakeet's relation to the jungle below. It is no accident that the opening line of each stanza stands aloof from the rhymed couplets beneath:

> Above the forest of the parakeets,
> A parakeet of parakeets prevails,
> A pip of life amid a mort of tails.

> (The rudiments of tropics are around,
> Aloe of ivory, pear of rusty rind.)
> His lids are white because his eyes are blind.

> He is not paradise of parakeets,
> Of his golden ether, golden alguazil,
> Except because he broods there and is still.
>
> Panache upon panache, his tails deploy,
> Upward and outward, in green-vented forms,
> His tip a drop of water full of storms.
>
> But though the turbulent tinges undulate
> As his pure intellect applies its laws,
> He moves not on his coppery, keen claws.
>
> He munches a dry shell while he exerts
> His will, yet never ceases, perfect cock,
> To flare, in the sun-pallor of his rock.   (CP, 82)

Discussing what he calls the "sacred irreverence" of this poem, Daniel Fuchs observes: "For all his magnificence, the king of the parakeets remains a caricature of a god of reason."[14] And like the blind deity of *Negation* (CP, 98), he adds, "God becomes a parody of omniscience and omnipotence."[15] In truth, Stevens might easily have designed his brooding bird in satiric antithesis to the divine being that hovers over the opening passage of *Paradise Lost*, that Spirit who,

> from the first
> Wast present, and with mighty wings outspread
> Dove-like satest brooding on the vast Abyss
> And madst it pregnant.

Unlike Milton's mighty Spirit, whose brooding brings forth the universe, the "parakeet of parakeets" broods and "is still." Against the maternal character of "mighty wings outspread / Dove-like," Stevens opposes a peacock-like parakeet who, in a pluming and phallic display, deploys his tails "upward and outward." Conversely, the parakeet's image is further debased by a detumescent "mort of tails."

Stevens's travesty of the Paraclete touches on a number of doctrinal nerve centers, including the will of God, the Aristotelian notion of an unmoved mover, a determined or predestined universe, the problem of evil, man made in God's image, the sun-Son identity, the church as rock, and ("alguazil") questions of law and judgment. The absolute and remote aboveness of Stevens's bird is a satiric echo of the doctrine that God's love for God is the essence of perfection. In sum, *The Bird with the Coppery, Keen Claws* can be read as a devastating critique of formal religion.

Stevens's departures from reverence and the covert nature of his attack place this sharp-clawed poem into that class of tendentious humor that Freud called "cynical." According to Freud, the target of cynical wit "may well be institutions, dogmas of morality and religion . . . which enjoy so much respect that objections to them can only be made under the mask of a joke and indeed a joke concealed by its facade."[16] From this point of view, the coppery, keen claws in this poem are the poet's own. But there is another, more personal angle to the ideological debate in the piece, and it deserves attention if one is exploring Stevens's special uses of parody.

Louis H. Leiter, in an extremely sensitive reading, has shown that Stevens chose clusters of words for this poem that convey antithetical meanings. He reduces the opposed forces in the poem to evocations of life and death: energy and flux on one side of the coin and morbid paralysis on the other. At the poem's "thematic center," Leiter discerns "stasis, a state of suspended animation." He concludes: "The 'perfect' cock is perfect because it is neither alive nor dead."[17] The "perfect," one should add, is also a tense, and one by which Stevens relegates this bird to the past. The "perfect cock" is the denizen of that time "when bishops' books / Resolved the world. We cannot go back to that" (*CP*, 215).

Leiter's reading has as much to tell us about the poet as the poem. Stevens's relation to the idea of deity is, of course, the animating concept of *The Bird with the Coppery, Keen Claws*. The very ambivalence of the key concept suggests that the poem is a position paper on the subject of faith. Belief is neither fully alive nor yet entirely dead, but caught in a state of suspended animation. Stevens does not approach, at this point, the positiveness of a Coleridgean suspension of disbelief. Although he generally responds to the motion with irony or avoidance, the mere *prospect* of belief lurking in the corner is a powerful agent. The possibility of faith is strong enough to generate the poem and its satiric imagery, but also strong enough to effect the paralysis, the stasis at its center. *Desire* for belief is infiltrating the Stevensian parodic discourse as a silent but extremely effective agent.

Precisely these questions of faith and irony—the remnants of belief and the overlay of cynicism—bring us to the poem that Harold Bloom singled out as the most important of the early period: *Le Monocle de Mon Oncle*. In the first stanza of *Monocle*, we find Stevens using parody to look forward and backward at the same time—overtly adapting to the time that is, and covertly searching for and questioning the spiritual values of a time that was.

Le Monocle de Mon Oncle was first published in 1918, at the close of

World War I, when Stevens had just turned thirty-nine.[18] The poem consists of twelve eleven-line stanzas that approximate the ballade stanza. The title, which can be loosely rendered as "seeing things from my uncle's point of view," substitutes a one-eyed vision of things as they are for the blindness of the parakeet's world. The tone modulates from bitterness to nostalgia to the more tranquil mood of the final stanzas, which seem to reflect a genuine stoic assent.

The first stanza of *Monocle* demands attention. It begins explosively, with an invocation that doubles as invective, and it begins unusually, for Stevens, with four lines of quotation:

> "Mother of heaven, regina of the clouds,
> O sceptre of the sun, crown of the moon,
> There is not nothing, no, no, never nothing,
> Like the clashed edges of two words that kill."
> And so I mocked her in magnificent measure.
> Or was it that I mocked myself alone?
> I wish that I might be a thinking stone.   (*CP*, 13)

Most readings of *Monocle* tend to pass quickly over the fact of the quotation. With one exception, it has not been remarked that, of the four lines contained within quotation marks, two are clearly liturgical in nature while the verses following are secular and conversational, perhaps a replication of the poet's own words.[19] Why should two such divergent forms of discourse be so convened? It has generally been assumed that Stevens is echoing sacred litany in the most casual sense, and with blasphemous intent. There has been no comment, therefore, on the curious insertion of litany and the vocative into a secular work. But something more intricate than blasphemy, more mysterious than a casual echo, is at work here.

Bloom calls it a bravura first stanza, "one of the most ferocious ironies in our poetry, where the imagery of presence and absence refers less to the muse . . . or the beloved . . . than to the language of passion."[20] Helen Vendler offers an interpersonal reading. Against Bloom's notion that the passage has to do with the loss of a language (that is, a negation of expression in its broadest sense), Vendler observes a deterioration of the marriage relation. The last "energies of love and faith," she notes, are "now exhausted in a depleted marriage" and "a sardonic pity and antagonism separate the conscious poet from his self-deceiving wife."[21] Vendler's reading is perhaps more biographical than it need be, although both interpretations contribute to an understanding of the stanza. But the absence of a passionate language and the depletion of "energies of love and faith" become far more meaningful when these ideas are carried beyond the immediate context of marital life. What is revealed in the opening passage of *Monocle* is as much historical as the liturgical vocative suggests, as figural as the sacred image invoked, as paradigmatic as it is biographical—or ironic. These are large assertions, but they are rooted in a text that may well be the source of Stevens's opening quotation.

One medieval French work stands forth as a candidate for the source of the opening lines. This is the fifteenth-century *Ballade; pour prier Nostre Dame* from *Le Testament* of François Villon. A true ballade (three ten-line stanzas with a refrain and a seven-line envoi), it introduces a liturgical note into a larger secular work, the larger work in itself a rollicking sardonic parody of a legal will and testament.

The *Ballade* is a supplicatory hymn "bequeathed" by Villon to his mother, "ma pauvre mère." It is conceived as a legacy from the impoverished poet (and thief, pimp, jailbird, and general scoff-law) to his similarly impoverished mother. He gives her a prayer to offer up to the Blessed Virgin. It is written in the mother's voice, from the point of view of a humble, hardworking, unlettered widow—everything her son is not—so that the entire ballade, including the envoi, is a quotation. What first singles out Villon's *Ballade* as Stevens's "prior text" is the startling similarity of the opening lines. Stevens, who held that "French and English constitute a single language,"[22] begins to express "his uncle's point of view" with the invocation to Our Lady: "Mother of heaven, regina of the clouds, / O sceptre of the sun, crown of the moon." One hears the identical cadence in Villon's opening lines:

> Dame du ciel, regente terrienne,
> Emperiere des infernaulx paluz.[23]
>
> (Lady of heaven, regent of earth,
> Empress of the infernal marshes.) [My translation]

Here, then, is parody with a profound double purpose, for a quotation admitted into a text comes surrounded by its original text—and context. Villon's poem supplicates the Son through the Mother by way of his own mother, and we recognize that in making his own humble mother the agent of intercession to the divine Intercessor, Villon is himself pleading for grace in a graceful way. His great refrain refers to son and mother both: "En ceste foy je vueil vivre et mourir" (In this faith I will to live and to die). If the doubleness of the supplication weren't perfectly clear at the outset, it is thrust at the reader in the envoi, where Villon signs his name to the piece in an acrostic.

Stevens's quotation of Villon underscores the double purpose of parody because it employs mockery in both of its senses: as "imitation"—or attempting a likeness—and as "ridicule"—holding up to derision. The opening verses of *Le Monocle de Mon Oncle* may very well express anger and bitterness by means of mocking exaggeration, but they also reproduce sacred litany. They import a theological vocative into an atheological context. Bakhtin, who treats parody with some seriousness, refers to this doubleness when he characterizes Hellenistic and medieval parodies as "the complex and contradictory process of accepting and then resisting the other's word, the process of reverently heeding it while at the same time ridiculing it."[24] By virtue of the opening invocation, Stevens makes Villon his poetic uncle, aligns his poem with the earlier text, and identifies it with the embedded sacred character of the source he has quoted. But by means of what Bloom called ferocious irony, he distances his work from the earlier text and rejects the substance of the thing he mocks. Stevens is thus engaged in discourse and disavowal at the same time.

The two verses that immediately follow the opening quotation state the central theological problem posed in *Monocle*. After the hard rain of negatives, which in one sense act positively to cancel each other out "(not nothing . . . never nothing"), there follows a more tranquil reflection: "And so I mocked her in magnificent measure. / Or was it that I mocked myself alone?" Notice the sequential repetition of "mocked," which first seizes the attention and directs it to the past and then—like the quotation of a quotation—sets up a meditative echo chamber entirely appropriate to a poet who has just introduced into the world of his poem a reverberating series of intercessions. As Vendler suggests, the poem does concern "energies of faith and love," their depletion and replenishment. Without precluding any reference to personal relations, however, these verses clearly extend beyond the single sense of a poet taking his wife to task.

The remembering mind in these verses, about to wish it were a "thinking stone," is dealing with a cosmic sense of loss. Under cover of the rhetoric of cynicism, these two lines about mockery—the one a statement, end-stopped, and the other a questioning of that statement—set forth various aspects of the question of faith: trust in others; belief in oneself; faith in a divine Other. Stevens is dealing here with contemporary problems of alienation and identity, and nowhere more than here does he capture so forcefully the bitterness of human disillusion.

The "she" who is invoked, and mocked, and denied "in magnificent measure," is an imperfect woman seen in the shadow of the perfect divine woman. As medievalists know, the Queen of Heaven is also the Empress of Hell, "Emperiere des infernaulx paluz." In *Le Monocle de Mon Oncle*

the imagery of the infernal marshes exists, not as an epithet in the invocation, but as the psychological terrain of the entire poem. It takes the
angel of parody to work this quagmire without sinking, to keep a foothold
in both the celestial and infernal regions at once, and to arrange the secret
rendezvous with the past.

The presence of Villon is not confined to the first stanza. The character of the poem, in which a man approaching his fortieth year takes
stock of his life—and leave of his youth—reflects Villon's satiric *Testament*, which begins: "In the thirtieth year of my age / Having drunk my
fill of shame (my translation)," after which the poem laments his lost
youth ("Je plains le temps de ma jeunesse") and declares himself on the
verge of old age ("Jusques a l'entree de viellesse"). In stanzas excluded
from *Monocle*, Stevens refers to "Poets of pimpernel, unlucky pimps / Of
pomp, in love and good ensample" (*OP*, 19), which is as close as you can
come to Villon without naming him. In the second stanza of *Monocle*,
the legal theme of the will and testament is picked up in "I am a man of
fortune, greeting heirs." Finally, in the eighth stanza, Stevens makes a
parodic reference to Villon's famous *Ballade of the Hanged*, sometimes
known as *Villon's Epitaph*. The hanged men of the medieval ballade who
(in Swinburne's translation)[25] are "more pecked of birds than fruits on
garden wall," become in Stevens's poem the middle-aged couple who
"hang like warty squashes":

> Distorted by hale fatness, turned grotesque.
> We hang like warty squashes, streaked and rayed,
> The laughing sky will see the two of us
> Washed into rinds by rotting winter rains.   (*CP*, 16)

In *Monocle* the parodic play ranges from major chords of "magnificent measure" to a fugal inversion of Villon's hanging theme, grotesquerie
in a minor key. It is not until the Ozymandias canto in *Notes toward a
Supreme Fiction* (2.8), composed nearly a quarter-century later, that we
discover Stevens using parody deliberately as a medium in which divergent impulses can safely meet. This canto is hedged with irony and deeply
erotic, but it is particularly illuminating because it documents Stevens's
reopening of discourse with something romantic, mystical, and long dis-
avowed. It presents an aesthetic question in theological terms by compar-
ing the mystery of poetic invention to the mystery of the Annunciation.
In the Ozymandias canto, Stevens's parodic genius struts out in a bold
divertissement, with all the theatrical panoply, the jewels and the feathers—and the sublime deadpan delivery—of the classic American
burlesque number. This is an entirely new vault of the tumbler, the

sleight-of-hand man, who is still engaged, however cryptically, in paying court to a sacred image.

The canto that Stevens called "the poem about Ozymandias" develops, like Shelley's original poem, as a narrative account of an exchange between a traveler and a broken monument—in this case the monument of romantic poetry. And like the angel of the Annunciation, Stevens's Nanzia Nunzio arrives on the scene with the express purpose of initiating an intimate sort of discourse. Although the interchange takes the form of a conversation, the burden of discourse is invested, not in Ozymandias, but in the would-be spouse who comes to confront him. In the figure of Nanzia Nunzio, however, there is more than immediately meets the eye. For one thing, the Annunciation implied in the name turns out to be a paradoxical sort of revelation: although the announcement is accompanied by a slow strip in the finest burlesque tradition, the substance of the message is that there is no such thing as nakedness. And although Stevens introduces Nanzia Nunzio as a woman, the inflections of the bisexual name and the symbolism implicit in the messenger's characteristics suggest that the "contemplated spouse" is something more than a woman. Certainly, the twenty-one verses that constitute the canto introduce one of the most baffling, ambiguous, superbly sensuous creatures in Stevens's poetry:

> On her trip around the world, Nanzia Nunzio
> Confronted Ozymandias. She went
> Alone and like a vestal long prepared.
>
> I am the spouse. She took her necklace off
> And laid it on the sand. As I am, I am
> The spouse. She opened her stone-studded belt.
>
> I am the spouse, divested of bright gold,
> The spouse beyond emerald or amethyst,
> Beyond the burning body that I bear.
>
> I am the woman stripped more nakedly
> Than nakedness, standing here before an inflexible
> Order, saying I am the contemplated spouse.
>
> Speak to me that, which spoken, will array me
> In its own only precious ornament.
> Set on me the spirit's diamond coronal.

Clothe me entire in the final filament,
So that I tremble with such love so known
And myself am precious for your perfecting.

Then Ozymandias said the spouse, the bride
Is never naked. A fictive covering
Weaves always glistening from the heart and mind.   (*CP*, 395)

In her circling "trip around the world," and in her virginal quality the figure corresponds to the moon. Her light is reflected light, suggested by the sparkle of jewels and the shine of gold; her "nakedness" is complete when she is "divested of bright gold." On the other hand, her "burning body" is clearly a solar symbolism and its erotic force stands in counterpoise to the sense of constraint that attends the "vestal long prepared." By the end of the third tercet, then, we find that the characteristics of the two heavenly bodies that exert the most influence on the earth have been made to coincide in the person of the "contemplated spouse."

Her name, divided neatly into two distinct halves, also represents two distinct but interpenetrating sets of characteristics. *Nanzia* bears a feminine inflection but suggests a "Nancy," an effeminate or homosexual male. *Nunzio* has a masculine ending, and literally means a papal emissary. But the name begins with "Nun," which conveys the idea of the chaste bride and the notion of "taking the veil." Thus Ozymandias—a standing parody of Shelley's monumental irony—is confronted by a figure whose name is replete with theological implications, whose gender is curiously dual, and who seems intent upon stripping herself "more nakedly / Than nakedness" itself. And this creature seductively refers to itself as the "contemplated spouse."

This last is the most heavily loaded term of all, for it points directly to the lyric eroticism of the Song of Songs, and to the holy union of *Sponsus* and *sponsa* in the tradition of Christian mysticism.[26] The ambivalence that Stevens imparts to the gender of his emissary is a reminder, too, that the Bridegroom of speculative theology is the object of contemplation for both monk and nun. In the monastery and the convent, the language of love becomes the language of prayer, and the desire of the soul may be expressed as the desire for physical love, "So that I tremble with such love so known / And myself am precious for your perfecting."

In the most general interpretation, the scene in the desert represents a confrontation of the "canonical body" of accepted works by a living creative impulse. In a more specific sense, the passage describes a serious flirtation with romanticism. Nanzia's flaming body indicates an *inventio* of great power, an aesthetic of great worth. It is the emblematic rendering of what Stevens called, in *Esthétique du Mal*, the "genius of the body," although in this canto it requires "the spirit's diamond coronal" for completion.

In the most private, and most limited, reading, the poet himself is the dynamic messenger who confronts the poetry of the not too distant past—the petrified canon—and who asserts a Coleridgean "I AM" again and again in the canto, six times in all (seven, if we count the "myself am" of the sixth stanza). In this reading, Nanzia Nunzio announces Stevens's open confrontation of the romantic tradition and, through intentional parody, his assumption of the romantic temper. Stevens's earlier figure of the Youth as Virile Poet (see NA, 39–67) is here transformed with some amusement into the figure of the nubile stripper. And the "dual person" inherent in the imaginative, creative act is embodied in the double identity of the messenger, and in the mocking echo of her double "I am": "As I am, I am / The spouse."

The intermingling of aesthetic, erotic, and theological elements dominates the tone of the Ozymandias canto in *Notes*. But the parodic reference to Shelley's sneering monarch governs its intention and underscores Stevens's quizzical relation to the romantics. If romantic poetry and idealist thought stand canonized as an inflexible order, the androgynous Nanzia Nunzio is eminently flexible, exquisitely plastic, and it is her burning body that dominates the desert scene. The power of this canto derives, not from its emblems, its elegance, or its allegorical significance, but from its infusion of erotic energy. It is the parodic recall of the Scriptural Annunciation, however, that provides the dimension of depth. Like the mocking "Angelus" of François Villon's *Petit Testament*, Stevens's Nanzia Nunzio is a perverse reminder of "Le Salut que l'Ange predit."[27] With a jongleur's finesse, Stevens has summoned up a red-robed archangel kneeling reverently before the chosen woman, holding a lily in place of the ancient herald's wand, and conveying news of the divine salutation with utmost gravity and grace.

Chapter 3

Something for Nothing

The mortal no
Has its emptiness and tragic expirations.
The tragedy, however, may have begun,
Again, in the imagination's new beginning,
In the yes of the realist spoken because he must
Say yes, spoken because under every no
Lay a passion for yes that had never been broken.   STEVENS

THE FREQUENCY OF TERMS of negation in Stevens's poetry is striking. Along with the salient *nothings*—the "nothing that is not there and the nothing that is" (CP, 10)—Stevens's categories of bleakness include images of emptiness, whiteness, invisibility; northern cold, ice, and snow; pure transparent crystal and dark water without reflections, "like dirty glass" (CP, 503). Negation is implied in the general landscape of winter: "bare limbs, bare trees and a wind as sharp as salt" (CP, 419). But it is also the "barrenness of the fertile thing that can attain no more" (CP, 373), the "essential barrenness" of summer. Stevens expresses negation in terms of poverty ("impoverished," "pauvred," "poor") and nakedness. In the most organic representation it becomes blindness—"his lids were white because his eyes were blind" (CP, 82)—and the silence of "sacked speech" (CP, 530), the mute incapacity of *The Man Whose Pharynx Was Bad* (CP, 96).

Negation can attain cosmic dimensions. As Frank Doggett has shown,[1] Stevens's early poem *The Reader* presents an unrelieved vision of entropy:

> It was autumn and falling stars
> Covered the shrivelled forms
> Crouched in the moonlight.

> No lamp was burning as I read,
> A voice was mumbling, "Everything
> Falls back to coldness." (*CP,* 147)

In the late *Auroras of Autumn,* negation appears as the principle of the serpent—"form gulping after formlessness"—a principle not far from the deconstructionist's *éffacement,* disappearance into a labyrinth of undifferentiation. But negation can be intensely personal, as in *Esthétique du Mal:*

> How cold the vacancy
> When the phantoms are gone and the shaken realist
> First sees reality. (*CP,* 320)

Sometimes negation takes the form of social distancing, not pleasant solitude but isolation, not healing privacy but loneliness. Such is the Baudelairean nature of the poet in *Esthétique:*

> He disposes the world in categories, thus:
> The people and the unpeopled. In both, he is
> Alone. (*CP,* 323)

Or it may be the detached view of life seen from inside the cemetery grounds:

> It is curious that the density of life
> On a given plane is ascertainable
> By dividing the number of legs one sees by two. (*CP,* 157)

This mathematical detachment forks and leads to extreme remoteness or to its contrary—a paradoxical "desire to be at the end of distance" (*CP,* 527).

Finally, negation can be a discipline, the way to a positively altered awareness. Stevens's experiments, in the poetry, to achieve the "feel" of a perceptual vacuum have their parallels in mystical theology. Like the ascetics who traveled the *via negativa* in their search for God, Stevens moves toward a metaphysical "centre" by draining preconceptions, will, mythologies of various sorts, memory itself from what John of the Cross called the caverns of the soul. In *Credences of Summer* Stevens sets about the emptying of the world in terms of a visionary geometry:

> Trace the gold sun about the whitened sky
> Without evasion by a single metaphor.

Look at it in its essential barrenness
And say this, this is the centre that I seek.   (CP, 373)

The All, a golden sphere, is overlaid on Nothing, a disk of flat whiteness. The circling of the sphere imposes both edge and center on the formless. It gives to empty space an inside and an outside and to the poetic consciousness an intuition of "the centre that I seek." It is Stevens's peculiar genius to set forth this vision in unelaborated terms of sun and sky.

Almost every major study of Stevens has addressed some aspect of negation in the poetry.[2] It is clear that a number of exceptional critical minds have dwelt on the austere turn of Stevens's thought, the ascetic, acerbic, or "harsher" aspects of the poetry. What has been missing, very simply, is a recognition of the *positive* value of negation in Stevens's work.

The *negativa* in Stevens's poetry has nothing to do with negativity as a retreat from reality. The ascetic's desire for an altered perception, or revealed knowledge, or for an ecstatic mystical experience is accompanied by deliberate self-deprivation—a removal from material *and* spiritual comforts and from familiar intellectual anchorings. The *via negativa* is not clinical "negativism," what Freud spoke of as the "passion for universal negation . . . displayed by many psychotics."[3] But apart from noting Stevens's turn for the ascetic, how does one gauge the positive dimensions of negation in the poetry?

Stevens posits negation, to begin with, by the repeated use of paradox. One effect of paradox is comparable to the effect of a Zen koan: it catapults the mind out of the universe of systematic logic. Stevens uses paradox to negate mere verifiability, to bypass the constraints of linear thinking, and to open the mind to the irrational. There is also the positive motif of nakedness occurring all through the poetry, and the image of stripping down. There are echoes of Henri Bergson's vitalist proposition— itself an echo of Plato—that all human action begins in the desire to fill an emptiness, to "embroider 'something' on the canvas of 'nothing.'" There is the correlation of nothingness to transparence and purity. Finally, there is the positive function of negation as the ground of all distinctions. The most fundamental use of the negative provides Stevens with far more than a voyage to a spiritual center, or the starting point of a journey to affirmation. Stevens is deeply aware that the negative confers the power of disjunction—not only the ability to deny but the capacity to separate one thing from another, to isolate the particular, to set limits, establish boundaries, to *define*.

Stevens's ascetic tendency appears in a number of poems as a compelling urge to burn away, empty out, strip off. It is a passion to penetrate to the very soul of things. In the grip of this mood Stevens abandons verbal gesture, ornament, the flirts of fancy, and seriously courts the void. The temptations of the florid and the baroque vanish when this side of his temperament takes hold; the language becomes noticeably stripped down and spare. Sensuous objects are relinquished for a glimpse of the *res* itself. Stevens wants at these moments to work his way back, somehow, to first perception. There is a signal intensity to this project:

> Let's see the very thing and nothing else.
> Let's see it with the hottest fire of sight.
> Burn everything not part of it to ash.   (CP, 373)[4]

One thinks of Donne's impatient prayer to "breake, blowe, burn and make me new." Doggett has accurately characterized this austere mode in Stevens, although he limits his observations to the later poetry. He finds a "chastening and a reduction . . . the imagery is more spare, the mere assertion more frequent, the flamboyant lyricism is subdued . . . the composition more economical."[5] This is indeed a different mode from Stevens's lyrical "floraisons," choirs and chorales, but surely it is not confined to the late poetry. This is the same reduced mode of early pieces such as *The Snow Man* and *Valley Candle*.

At the conclusion of *Extracts from Addresses to the Academy of Fine Ideas*, one finds Stevens navigating toward a "subtle centre." Here is a version of the *via negativa* that is neither religious nor secular, but a neutral ascetic exercise aimed at refining and altering perception:

> if one breathed
> The cold evening, without any scent or the shade
> Of any woman, watched the thinnest light
> And the most distant, single color, about to change,
> In the exactest poverty, if then
> One breathed the cold evening, the deepest inhalation
> Would come from that return to the subtle centre.   (CP, 258)

In *The Snow Man* the listener accomplishes precisely such a return. By an act of contemplation he has become identical with the "mind of winter." Through successive stages of distancing, a human consciousness has achieved an alien perception. Each reader of this poem becomes involved in a magical transfer of consciousness, from the mind of the observer to the "mind" of the man of snow. One has arrived at "the exactest poverty," the ultimate uncluttered vision. For Stevens, this chilling being-seeing of nothingness is an end in itself. At the same time "to be at the end of distance" constitutes what he has called an "immaculate beginning." On several counts, then, the poem unfolds a paradoxical vision. The mind's apprehension of pure nothingness is an apprehension of the impossible. And the final verse turns upon a formal paradox that is both logical and ontological—as well as rhetorical:

> For the listener, who listens in the snow,
> And, nothing himself, beholds
> Nothing that is not there and the nothing that is.　　(*CP*, 10)

This famous final verse generates a resounding series of contradictions. What does this do to the reader? In her study of the Renaissance tradition of paradox, Rosalie Colie remarked of one classical example (the "Cretan Liar" paradox) that "its negative and positive meanings are so balanced that one meaning can never outweigh the other, though weighed to eternity."[6] One might say exactly the same about the last verse of *The Snow Man:* "Seeming to open out, the paradox turns in, acknowledging the wide world of alternatives and denying autonomy to most of them. The very 'infiniteness' of paradox . . . is balanced by its tautology, for all paradoxes are self-enclosed statements with no external reference point. . . . Self-limiting, they deny limitation."[7] The formal paradox produces a sort of mental vertigo, or disorientation, and teaches among other things that knowledge can elude rational structures.

In "The Language of Paradox" (published, in 1942, in a collection that included Stevens's "Noble Rider and the Sound of Words"), Cleanth Brooks argued that paradoxical structures could be found at the heart of poetry. We tend to think of the mode as "clever rather than profound, rational rather than divinely irrational," he said, "yet there is a sense in which paradox is the language appropriate and inevitable to poetry. It is the scientist," he concluded, "whose truth requires a language purged of every trace of paradox."[8] And in truth, while a poet may indulge in dizzying contradictions, the logician must take a genuine paradox very seriously.

Antinomy is the class of paradox that brings about "crises of thought" in the domain of logic, says W. V. Quine. A paradox is an antinomy, according to Quine, "if we find that it is, if and only if it is not."[9] Just as Stevens conceives poetry at times as an agent of demolition, so does the logician and philosopher see antinomy as a "destructive force," a destroying angel. "It can be accommodated by nothing less," Quine declares, "than a repudiation of part of our conceptual heritage." A true antinomy posits an ominous negation of known logical structures. It leaves the logician intellectually naked, so to speak, while the poet may use it to amuse or intrigue, or more seriously to suggest an ambivalent reality.

For Stevens, a naked figure represents the most positive kind of negation. Nakedness suggests clean lines, a washed transparency, elegance of structure and grace of movement. Stevens can make the state of nakedness seem enterprising, Edenic, natural, and romantic, all at once: "the rainy rose belongs / To naked men, to women naked as rain" (*CP*, 252). Nakedness is precious to Stevens both for what it reveals and what it removes. The systematic uncovering of Nanzia Nunzio in *Notes toward a Supreme Fiction* (2.8) is, among other things, a pantomime of stripping down to the "first idea." Stevens explained what he meant by the term in a letter to Henry Church. "If you take the varnish and dirt of generations off a picture," he wrote, "you see it in its first idea. If you think about the world without its varnish and dirt, you are a thinker of the first idea" (*LWS*, 426–27). *If you think about the world without its varnish and dirt* . . . Here again one sees Stevens intrigued with the possibility of an unblemished vision, a perception "naked of any illusion."

As often as not, it must be admitted, the thing revealed remains as mysterious as before. Again and again one finds Stevens unveiling an obscurity, an enigma, a riddle. Consider the gnomic quality of the passage in *Things of August* (1.3) that ponders "the spirit's sex." Is Stevens playing, perhaps, with psychology's notion of psyche? Odd questions arise about a new "aspect, bright in discovery":

> a new aspect, say the spirit's sex,
> Its attitudes, its answers to attitudes
> And the sex of its voices, as the voice of one
> Meets nakedly another's naked voice.   (*CP*, 489)

Nanzia Nunzio declares herself to be "stripped more nakedly / Than nakedness," but removing the ornaments from Nanzia's blazing body does not leave her entirely bare:

>   the bride
> Is never naked. A fictive covering
> Weaves always glistening from the heart and mind.   (*CP*, 396)

Nanzia's truth remains veiled and in some profound way she herself remains inaccessible. She is the impassioned sibyl of the senses, incomplete without the "spirit's diamond coronal." It is not until the very late poetry, and *The Sail of Ulysses*, that we encounter the truly naked sibyl who,

waiting at the terminus of a difficult *via negativa*, possesses the dark jewel
that Nanzia Nunzio craves. This is Stevens's "sibyl of the self,"

> whose diamond,
> Whose chiefest embracing of all wealth
> Is poverty, whose jewel found
> At the exactest central of the earth
> Is need. (*OP*, 104)

Like Yeats, Stevens wants to cast off the coat covered with embroid-
eries—"For there's more enterprise / In walking naked."[10] One of the most
poignant moments in the early poetry shows the vulnerability of man
stripped of illusion, stripped of his gods. In this post-Darwinian, post-
Nietzschean world, man is nakedly alone under the sun, yearning for
something beyond the "bare spaces of our skies":

> The body walks forth naked in the sun
> And, out of tenderness or grief, the sun
> Gives comfort, so that other bodies come,
> Twinning our phantasy and our device,
> And apt in versatile motion, touch and sound
> To make the body covetous in desire
> Of the still finer, more implacable chords. (*CP*, 108)

Stevens spoke of the death of the gods, modern man's heritage of
spiritual solitude, in a passage noted both by J. Hillis Miller and Helen
Vendler.[11] "It was their annihilation, not ours, and yet it left us feeling
that . . . we too had been annihilated. It left us feeling dispossessed and
alone in a solitude, like children without parents, in a home that seemed
deserted. . . . They left no mementoes behind, no thrones, no mystic
rings, no texts either of the soil or the soul. It was as if they had never
inhabited the earth" (*OP*, 206–7). This survey of desolation, in "Two or
Three Ideas," becomes the threshold upon which, characteristically, Stevens will introduce a startlingly positive idea—the "peculiar majesty of
mankind's sense of worth." Such a progression is built into the structure
of the poetry. In Stevens's poetic universe, *that which is not* almost invar-
iably brings about *that which is*. In terms of philosophies, we are seeing
Stevens moving from the Nietzschean tragic vision to a Bergsonian vitalism.

In *Creative Evolution* Bergson defines human action as a response to
absence: "Every human action has its starting point in dissatisfaction, and
thereby in a feeling of absence. We should not act if we did not set before
ourselves an end, and we seek a thing only because we feel the lack of it.

Our action thus proceeds from 'nothing' to 'something' and its very essence is to embroider 'something' on the canvas of 'nothing.'"[12] Stevens, as we know, held Bergson in some esteem. For him, too, the *negativa* is a starting point rather than a static condition. One of the most positive values that Stevens derives from negation is expressed in the thesis that threads in and out of the poetry: each thing contains the seed of its opposite; each thing implies its antithesis. Out of nothing, something comes.

Sometimes the poem itself is the "something" that is embroidered on the empty canvas. But apart from its intrinsic application to the act of poetry, negation as the prior condition to creation or development is formulated in various other terms—existential, ethical, mystical, erotic. Consider the much-quoted lines that open *The Well Dressed Man with a Beard*: "After the final no there comes a yes / And on that yes the future world depends" (*CP*, 247). There is the paradoxical proposition that resembles a Blakean proverb of hell: "The good is evil's last invention" (*CP*, 253). There is the meditation in *Prologues to What Is Possible*, a near-mystical apprehension of first creation: "The way the earliest single light in the evening sky, in spring, / Creates a fresh universe out of nothingness by adding itself" (*CP*, 517). There is the observation in *Notes* that compresses Bergson's theory of action into two lines of verse: "And not to have is the beginning of desire. / To have what is not is its ancient cycle" (*CP*, 382). There is the extraordinary evocation of poiesis, in *An Ordinary Evening in New Haven*: "things seen and unseen, created from nothingness, / The heavens, the hells, the worlds, the longed-for lands" (*CP*, 486). Finally, there is the "harping" angel-poet of *Notes*—another Blakean manifestation?—who, filled with "inexpressible bliss," chants the paradoxical poetics of the *via negativa*:

> there is a time
> In which majesty is a mirror of the self:
> I have not but I am and as I am, I am.   (*CP*, 405)

Bloom observes that "I have not but I am" is a "confession not of loss but of the influx of power."[13]

Although Stevens embarks on the way of negation through the gateway of Bergsonian vitalism, the path is an old one that stretches back past Christian monasticism to classical times and Orphic ascetic ritual. Plotinus, in the third century, described the painful process by which one aspires to leave behind all measures of quantity, quality, extension, all familiar shape and form: "The mind reaching toward the formless finds itself incompetent to grasp where nothing bounds it . . . in sheer dread of holding on to nothingness, it slips away. The state is painful; often it seeks relief by retreating from all this vagueness to the regions of sense, there to rest on solid ground."[14] In the sixteenth century, John of the Cross (Stevens's "Dark Juan" of *The Old Lutheran Bells at Home*) wrote of the search for God in the interior "caverns of the soul": "These caverns are the faculties of the soul: memory, understanding, and will . . . they can be filled with nothing less than the infinite. By focusing upon what they would suffer when void, we can comprehend, to some degree, the profundity of their joy . . . when they are filled with their God, for one contrary can cast light upon another."[15] In the twentieth century, C. G. Jung described the mode of negation as spiritual poverty: "Just as the vow of worldly poverty turns the mind away from the riches of this earth, so spiritual poverty seeks to renounce the false riches of the spirit . . . to dwell with itself alone, where, in the cold light of consciousness, the blank barrenness of the world reaches to the very stars."[16] Stevens memorializes the struggle "to renounce the false riches of the spirit" in one of the most devastating passages in the poetry:

> The poem lashes more fiercely than the wind,
> As the mind, to find what will suffice, destroys
> Romantic tenements of rose and ice.　　　　　(*CP*, 239)

The Sail of Ulysses describes a passage through four ways of obtaining knowledge: by reason, by intuition, by revelation, and by negation. Ulysses embarks upon his nocturnal journey "under the middle stars" from a Cartesian point of crossing where knowing and being converge: "'As I know, I am and have / The right to be'" (*OP*, 99). In the third canto, the excursions of analytic reason are interrupted by another cadence. Here, the aesthetic imagination forcibly wrenches design out of the formless by intuitive means:

> Thinking gold thoughts in a golden mind,
> Loftily jingled, radiant,
> The joy of meaning in design
> Wrenched out of chaos.　　　　　(*OP*, 100)

By the fifth canto, the rational voice has been brought to another full stop with the proposition "We come / To knowledge when we come to life." Another more mysterious voice now rises in counterpoint:

> Yet always there is another life,
> A life beyond this present knowing,
> A life lighter than this present splendor,

> Brighter, perfected and distant away,
> Not to be reached but to be known,
> Not an attainment of the will
> But something illogically received,
> A divination, a letting down
> From loftiness, misgivings dazzlingly
> Resolved in dazzling discovery.   (*OP*, 101–2)

The third voice in this fugal exercise speaks of mystically revealed knowledge. A sense of brilliant illumination, the passivity of the will, the experience of something "illogically received" in "dazzling discovery" is the experience recorded by the great mystics. This is the knowledge given in oracles and prophecies, and the passage cited above does indeed herald an apocalyptic vision—a time when "We shall have gone behind the symbols / To that which they symbolized . . . Like glitter ascended into fire" (*OP*, 102).

By the end of the fifth canto we have encountered three modes of knowing, passing from analytic reason to creative intuition to mystic insight. But the journey into the night, like Marlow's journey to the Heart of Darkness, like "Dark Juan" traveling into *la noche oscura*, suggests the fourth mode of knowledge in itself. The *via negativa*, the passage into darkness, carries the seeker away from the "crystal atmospheres of the mind" and toward the shadowy origins of knowing and being—toward the figure of the sibyl.

The eighth and final canto develops the way of negation systematically as a series of inward-directed stages or steps—a descent into the self. It opens with a question—"What is the shape of the sibyl?"—and begins by defining what it is not. It is not art or illusion. Art is the "englistered woman," the "gorgeous symbol seated / On the seat of halidom, rainbowed."[17] Her wealth and majesty are aesthetic riches, her realm a plane of sensuous images "piercing the spirit by appearance" and "delving show." Thus, the journey to the interior begins with a rejection of external beauty. In this passage to knowledge, a thing of beauty is not only not "a joy forever" but itself must pass into nothingness. The "shape of the sibyl" becomes dimly manifest the moment one sees that her worth lies in what is not attached to her. This realization is the movement toward the *sibyl of the self*,

> The self as sibyl, whose diamond,
> Whose chiefest embracing of all wealth
> Is poverty.   (*OP*, 104)

At the midpoint of the canto, the approach to the region of the formless takes on the quality of painful confusion remarked by Plotinus. The next stage is accomplished as the "blind thing fumbling for its form" recedes into sheer nothingness:

> the sibyl's shape
> Is a blind thing fumbling for its form,
> A form that is lame, a hand, a back,
> A dream too poor, too destitute
> To be remembered, the old shape
> Worn and leaning to nothingness.

The central line stares out at us—"A dream too poor, too destitute"—its center a cluster of o's and double o's suggesting blind eyes, the zero state, centrality and nothingness all at once. Dissolution of the old shape of things, however, is precisely the point of upturn. In the emptied cavern a faint purpose emerges, like the appearance of Hope in Pandora's emptied casket, and a series of upward steps evolves:

> Need names on its breath
> Categories of bleak necessity,
> Which, just to name, is to create
> A help, a right to help, a right
> To know what helps and to attain,
> By right of knowing another plane.

The ascent from the sibyl's dark domain to knowledge and another plane is a Bergsonian "embroidery": *something* has been traced on the canvas of emptiness. But the rapid ascent from nothingness and need and "bleak necessity" also involves a dramatic alteration of perception. Art has become something other than mere "delving show":

> The englistered woman is now seen
> In an isolation, separate
> From the human in humanity,
> A part of the inhuman more,
> The still inhuman more.   (OP, 104–5)

Distinct in its isolation from "the human in humanity," art is recognized as a spiritual intermediary, a link with the "inhuman more." *The Sail of Ulysses* concludes with the notion of something huge and "wholly other"—its presence enlarged by repetition, a shadowy doubling—engaging the human consciousness on one level while, on another, it pursues its own mysterious course:

> The great sail of Ulysses seemed,
> In the breathings of this soliloquy,
> Alive with an enigma's flittering . . .
> As if another sail went on
> Straight forwardly through another night
> And clumped stars dangled all the way.   (OP, 105)

Contraries and the Necessary No

The journey along the *via negativa* in *The Sail of Ulysses* shows the Stevens of the very late poetry still entertaining the notion that something is mysteriously born ex nihilo, and still intrigued by the dance of linked contraries. Stevens's interest in the workings of opposition and contrast began early, and all through his life the phenomenon of bound contraries seems to have been associated with thoughts of pleasurable variety. "When I was a boy," he wrote to Hi Simons, "I used to think that things progressed by contrasts. But this was building the world out of blocks. Afterwards I came to think more of the energizing that comes from mere interplay, interaction. Thus the various faculties of the mind co-exist and interact, and there is as much delight in this mere co-existence as a man and a woman find in each other's company" (*LWS*, 368). Stevens goes on to list the kinds of interaction that bring energy to the "faculties of the mind." What is revealed is an aesthetics of measure; a stately mental choreography is in progress: "Cross-reflections, modifications, counterbalances, complements, giving and taking are illimitable. . . . While it may be the cause of other things, I am thinking of it as a source of pleasure, and therefore I repeat that there is an exquisite pleasure and harmony in these inter-relations, circuits."

Two propositions continue to shape the poetry: the idea that each thing is contained within its opposite; and the idea that each thing tends to become its opposite.

> Logos and logic, crystal hypothesis
> Incipit and a form to speak the word
> And every latent double in the word.   (CP, 387)

The latent doubleness of things, the embedding of antithetical pairs one within the other, and the "exquisite pleasure and harmony" of their inter-relations is set forth in one of the most beautiful passages in the poetry:

> Two things of opposite nature seem to depend
> On one another, as a man depends
> On a woman, day on night, the imagined

On the real. This is the origin of change.
Winter and spring, cold copulars, embrace
And forth the particulars of rapture come.

Music falls on the silence like a sense,
A passion that we feel, not understand.
Morning and afternoon are clasped together

And North and South are an intrinsic couple
And sun and rain a plural like two lovers
That walk away in the greenest body.   (CP, 392)

As much as any in Stevens's poetry, these stanzas from the second section
of *Notes* ("It Must Change") have to do with attraction and conversion—
the physics of "moving toward" and the dynamics of a thing "turning into"
something else.Consider, however, that this most epithalamic of passages
celebrates the *particulars* of rapture. In it, no member of a matched pair
loses its singular identity in fusion or synthesis. Each retains discreteness,
definition, particularity. The imagined is spatially separated from the real;
music remains distinct from silence; feeling is not understanding. Sun
and rain do not swallow and displace one another but create an atmosphere of rainbow as they coexist in (*plui, pleur*) plural interaction.

   Stevens's era was invaded by startling ideas about "inter-relations, circuits," the erotic life, uses of wit, God as an illusion without a future,
problems of desire, of obsession, of repression—all introduced by Freud.
The poet responded to Freud with his customary thoughtful ambivalence,
so far as one can judge. Stevens referred to Freud's "The Future of an
Illusion" in a talk on "Imagination as Value." "If we escape destruction at
the hands of the logical positivists, and if we cleanse the imagination of
the taint of the romantic, we still face Freud," Stevens observed.[18] In
1947, roughly ten years after Stevens credited Freud with giving the irrational "a legitimacy that it never had before," he quipped in verse that
"Freud's eye was the microscope of potency." The final stanza of *Mountains Covered with Cats* opens with a wink—a Freudian pun on eye-I-
ego—and closes (or more accurately, remains open-ended) with an unnerving paradox:

Freud's eye was the microscope of potency.
By fortune, his gray ghost may meditate
The spirits of all the impotent dead, seen clear,
And quickly understand, without their flesh,
How truly they had not been what they were.   (CP, 368)

It is an odd portrait. Stevens gives us Freud as a type of scientific Tiresias, the blind prophet who could see clearly "The spirits of all the impotent dead." Tiresias is the classical model of sexual ambivalence, just as the formal paradox is the model of logical ambivalence. This five-line stanza, riddled with double entendres, meditates on potency and the impotent, on what can been seen and what can nearly be seen, on the quick, the dead, and the ghostly—in sum, on various kinds of threshold, the zone of ambivalence.[19] Freud's explorations of antithesis, ambivalence, and negation will cast some light on Stevens's deployment of contraries and his poetics of negation.

Freud himself appeared fascinated with the concept of antithetical primal words.[20] As defined by Karl Abel (whose 1884 philological study supplied Freud with the term), these are "words with two meanings, one of which is the exact opposite of the other." (In modern English for example, *certain* can mean both "vague" and "sure"; *cleave* denotes both "splitting apart" and "adhering to.") Freud shared Abel's concern with the problem of innate contradiction built into language. Quoting Abel, he agreed that it was strange that a single word could "bind together in a kind of indissoluble union things that were in the strongest opposition to each other."[21]

Three aspects of these antithetical root terms stimulated Freud's interest. First of all, they appeared to have some bearing on his studies of ambivalence. Second, he believed there was a correlation between "primitive" syntactic structures and the "archaic," or regressive, nature of dreams.[22] Finally, the play of contradictory elements in the dreamworld was facilitated by a striking absence of negation. "'No' seems not to exist so far as dreams are concerned," he observed in a paper published in 1910: "Dreams feel themselves at liberty to represent any element by its wishful contrary; so that there is no way of deciding at first glance whether any element that admits of a contrary is presented in the dream-thoughts as a positive or a negative."[23]

Freud's focus on the absence of "No" in the dream language provides an entry into Stevens's use of negation as a positive structuring principle. The dream state, according to Freud, is a reversion to a stage of consciousness that precedes the development of the critical or evaluative faculties. It is therefore preaesthetic, premoral, and prelogical. "No" is the precondition of aesthetic judgment because it introduces contrast and delineation. It is the precondition of moral consciousness, which begins with an observance of Thou Shalt Not. Most simply, both art and ethics originate in a single act: the defining of limits. Blake talks about negation as a stimulus of moral energy—"Damn braces; bless relaxes." In ontological terms, the realization of not-being must precede the study of being. Thus, if all conditions are interchangeable and all options affirmative, as Freud noted of the dream state, differentiation cannot exist, nor the information that derives from contrastive analysis. Modern psychologists are still attempting to sort these things out and doubt has been cast on Freud's mythology. Given the climate in which Stevens was writing, however, and if we accept Freud's archaeology of the mind, the dreamworld would seem to reflect a primitive state of awareness. The dream, with its absence of definition and chameleon interchange of contraries, returns the dreamer to that stage in the history of consciousness that precedes the development of moral categories, aesthetic discrimination, and philosophic distinctions.

Stevens's poetic terrain includes this dream-limbo of the undifferentiated. Often it is an initiating stage or condition, a "chaos" or "disorder," a dim profusion of things struggling to attain a shape. In *Connoisseur of Chaos* the poet imagines a great design emerging from disorder: "But suppose the disorder of truths should ever come / To an order, most Plantagenet, most fixed" (*CP*, 216). In *The Sail of Ulysses* the moment of discernment is one of terrible joy; the act of creation is simultaneously destructive: "The joy of meaning in design / Wrenched out of chaos" (*OP*, 100). Negation civilizes. It makes possible the system of internal restraints and deferrals, the editing that allows us to exist in a social milieu and to live with ourselves. It changes an aboriginal and chaotic fluidity, a nameless nature of things, into a cosmos of clearly defined ideas, clearly articulated oppositions. The institution of the negative brings order to the disorder of truths. Antithesis brings clarification to image, thought, and speech: "Tell X that speech is not dirty silence / Clarified" (*CP*, 311). As Freud noted in the essay on negation, the "achievement of the function of judgement only becomes feasible . . . after the creation of the symbol of negation has endowed thought with a first degree of independence from the results of repression and at the same time from the sway of the pleasure principle."[24]

While negation permits such positive structurings and enrichment in Stevens's work, it is the mystical *negativa* that lends austerity and rigor to the "poem of the mind." One finds, however, that there is a modulation in the range of the negative mode. Particularly in the later work, the notion of austerity is withdrawn from the heights of a solitary sublime and dropped to a level that more closely approximates plainsong.

During the period that followed the publication of *Notes*, Stevens cultivated an asceticism that could include the dirt—if not the varnish—on things. He now wished to inspect the unromantic rubbish at the dump:

> the wrapper on the can of pears,
> The cat in the paper-bag, the corset, the box
> From Esthonia: the tiger chest, for tea.   (*CP*, 201)

Moving out from the mystique of nothingness, from the purity, sterility, and what Fletcher would call the "daemonic" energy inherent in the purged allegory of a "mind of winter,"[25] a mature Stevens was reaching for the apparent realism of a "plain sense of things." The ascetic side of the poet was now demanding the plain instead of the pure, the ordinary instead of the outré. Stevens had become intent on the pragmatic aspect of negation—which posited a mystique of its own.

In the spring of 1949 Stevens wrote to Bernard Heringman while at work on *An Ordinary Evening in New Haven*, Vendler's "resolutely impoverished poem." Stevens outlined his new object: "My interest is to try to get as close to the ordinary, the commonplace and the ugly as it is possible for a poet to get. It is not a question of grim reality but of plain reality. The object is of course to purge oneself of anything false."[26] There is a relative ease in sailing toward a mystical *negativa*, or in bringing a playful exercise in negation to a paradoxical conclusion. The labor is in confronting the banal, unornamented, unswept scene. However, it is not in the visionary fireworks of *An Ordinary Evening in New Haven* that Stevens takes up the challenge of a depressive reality but in a much shorter poem of the same period. *The Plain Sense of Things*, cast as a reflective narrative in the manner of Frost, comes as close to an "existential ordinary" as a Stevens poem will get. It attempts to close off the last route of escape from the commonplace, to exclude the troping paradox, the shimmer of possibility—not as perfectly perhaps as it might.

Like Shakespeare's "bare ruin'd choirs, where late the sweet birds sang," Stevens's meditation on the plain sense of things evokes a state of mind, a season of life, a time of year "after the leaves have fallen." It mirrors the psychological reality of a vision—not so much despairing as resigned—in which all other moods appear to have been falsely optimistic, all other visions illusory. The coloration tends to sepias and grays rather than black and white; the region is limbo rather than hell.[27] This is Dickinson's pervasive Hour of Lead, a mode of perception that disallows hope, that feels eternal, that masquerades as truth and darkens both past and future. It is not the great chord of tragedy but an unresolved diminished seventh. One feels a corrosive impotence and passively notes the blank evenness of things, the disappearance of choice:

> After the leaves have fallen, we return
> To a plain sense of things. It is as if

We had come to an end of the imagination,
Inanimate in an inert savoir.

It is difficult even to choose the adjective
For this blank cold, this sadness without cause.
The great structure has become a minor house. (*CP*, 502)

The verses are cast as short, flat statements of fact, and end-stopped with unusual frequency. Lexically, the poem trudges through a mire of disaffirmation: "fallen," "end," "inanimate," "inert," "difficult," "blank," "without cause," "lessened," "old," "badly," "failed," "silence," "waste." The tongue has trouble with the repetitive haltings of "In-an-i-mate in an in-ert" while the mind is troubled by the vague image of the unmoving, the lifeless, embedded in the inactive. The numbness extends to memory; it is difficult to choose even an adjective. Mortality is reduced, in stanza three, to a "repetitiousness of men and flies." Stevens the poet has surely succeeded in getting as close to the commonplace and the ugly as it is possible for a poet to get:

The greenhouse never so badly needed paint.
The chimney is fifty years old and slants to one side.
A fantastic effort has failed, a repetition
In a repetitiousness of men and flies.

To borrow a phrase from an earlier poem, "Bad is final in this light" (*CP*, 293). But symbolisms crouch in the ordinary scene and cannot be blanked out. The house is the world, the body, the housing of the mind, the skull—and the cosmos, once conceived as the House of God. The greenhouse is a glass coffin, an enclosed garden. And who or what has engaged in this "fantastic effort"? The neutral tones and "the great pond" of this poem are reminiscent of Thomas Hardy's alienated vision, although in Hardy's landscape a measure of pathos survives. One has the sense of gazing at a faded, slightly cracked old snapshot:

We stood by a pond that winter day,
And the sun was white as though chidden of God,
And a few leaves lay on the starving sod;
       —They had fallen from an ash, and were gray.[28]

Stevens's "plain sense of things" avoids sentiment and maintains its distance, both from the human "we" and the inhuman "God." But it turns upon the irresistible paradox: "Yet the absence of imagination had / Itself to be imagined." With the reappearance of the word *imagination* in the final stanzas of *Plain Sense*, the world is dismantled to the point where the Word and the Name are both "Mud." A debased perception creeps out of this originating element, this pre-Adamic slime—not a spoken imperative but the silent shiftiness "of a rat come out to see." And what the rat sees, what we see, are the ravages of Solomonic beauty, the aftermath of creation. It can be seen as such—and this is the point—only through the lens of imagination:

> The great pond,
> The plain sense of it, without reflections, leaves,
> Mud, water like dirty glass, expressing silence
>
> Of a sort, silence of a rat come out to see,
> The great pond and its waste of the lilies, all this
> Had to be imagined as an inevitable knowledge,
> Required, as a necessity requires.   (*CP*, 503)

The scene/seen through this lens recalls the degenerated cosmos of Sonnet 94, where "Lilies that fester smell far worse than weeds." Stevens's final stanzas reflect on the nonreflective surfaces of mundane existence, the "ordinary" scene before him. He is rendering a textured landscape as it might be composed in the mind's eye of a painter; a semi-ironic study of decomposition. But a great disorder in Stevens's world is always an order—as the poet tells us in *Connoisseur of Chaos*—a *command*. Perhaps a sublime imperative. *Plain Sense* moves from the ordinal to the ordained. It suggests an ordinal or primary perception that leads to a sense of something foreordained: "inert savoir" leads to "inevitable knowledge." Stevens's irrepressible delight in wordplay leaps out in the last line which at first reading appears to conclude things with a kind of pedantic gravity. But we see that "necessity" is flanked by two requirings, and we suspect that "all this" must return to motion, life, and bloom as the inventing mind restrings, reharmonizes, rechoirs the world as divine necessity rechoirs.

Stevens's achievement is essentially antisynthetic. His treatment of opposed or contradictory elements, all through the poetry, is an effort to keep them from disappearing into each other. It is important to Stevens, much as it was for Blake, that all things retain particularity and each its intrinsic worth. In his need to keep things defined, Stevens must combat the general tendency of living organisms and living ideas toward merger, synthesis, symbiotic entrenchment.

The closest parallel to this aspect of Stevens's poetics lies, not in philosophy or the arts, but in biochemistry. "There is a tendency for living creatures to join up, establish linkages, live inside of each other," observes Lewis Thomas. The tendency toward fusion, he adds, violates the "most fundamental myth of the last century, for it denies the importance of specificity, integrity, and separateness in living things.[29] The immediate parallel with Stevens's struggle to keep things apart and identifiable is, in terms of molecular biology, the immune system—the organism's defense against invasion by hostile agents. While the tendency toward merger is powerful, there is an equally powerful mechanism for differentiation, as Thomas points out: "Inflammation and immunology must indeed be powerfully designed to keep us apart; without such mechanisms . . . we might have developed as a kind of flowing syncytium over the earth, without the morphogenesis of even a flower."[30]

Negation keeps things apart, unmixed, distinct, and thus available. As Freud observed, with "the help of the symbol of negation, the thinking-process frees itself from the limitations of repression and enriches itself with the subject-matter without which it could not work efficiently."[31] Clearly, Stevens does not wish to be deprived of any part of experience. For him, the "mind of winter" is as necessary a morphogenesis as the heavy-laden roses "now in midsummer come." So we find the various oppositions set forth in the poetry: nothing and something, poverty and abundance, transparency and color, silence and sound, gaiety and *malheur*, mud and snow, Chocorua and Key West. So too are the contrarieties of Stevens's temperament given voice in the poetry; the ascetic and the sensual, the pragmatic and the mystical, the baroque and the sublime, the comic vision and the metaphysical, the gestured and the plain, while Stevens—true jongleur—keeps them all spinning.

Stevens outlines his own "complicate" poetics in *Notes* in the culminating vision, the near-Miltonic flight of the aspiring Canon. It is a poetics of *positive* negation; a poetics of choice:

> Forth then with huge pathetic force
> Straight to the utmost crown of night he flew.
> The nothingness was a nakedness, a point
>
> Beyond which thought could not progress as thought.
> He had to choose. But it was not a choice
> Between excluding things. It was not a choice
>
> Between, but of. He chose to include the things
> That in each other are included, the whole,
> The complicate, the amassing harmony. (CP, 403)

Chapter 4

A Woman with the Hair of a Pythoness

His anima liked its animal
And liked it unsubjugated.   STEVENS

IF STEVENS'S "INTERIOR PARAMOUR" is a Jungian anima figure or a moth-eaten muse, as a number of readers have supposed, why doesn't she conform to the models? Why does she display characteristics that are sharply at variance both with the psychological construct and the classical figure? *Can* Stevens's intensely personal "paramour" be construed as a "collective projection of the masculine unconscious," as Michel Benamou believed? Can one comply with Benamou's easy assurance that "Jungian psychology accounts rather well for this voice in the poetry?"[1]

To carry this line of inquiry a step further: can Stevens's complex response to the feminine be reduced to "an image of the great earth mother which will apear in various forms throughout the work"? Edward Kessler rightly identifies Stevens's vision of the feminine with recurring images of "summer" and "south," but he believes that the same visionary element is to be understood as mere "physical sensation." According to Kessler, Stevens's woman is "not an ideal but the earth itself," or "the part of the world that can be enjoyed without explanation or meaning."[2]

The approach shared by Benamou and Kessler with other Jungian critics relies upon a simple convention: a set of human traits is assignable by gender. Thus Kessler finds Stevens's image of woman "ambiguous or contradictory" where the poet evokes a composite figure.[3] He refers to the "disturbing" invocation that opens *To the One of Fictive Music*—("Sister and mother and diviner love")—and to the "troublesome opening" of *Le Monocle de Mon Oncle*: "Mother of Heaven, regina of the clouds, / O sceptre of the sun, crown of the moon." In truth, it *is* a troublesome opening that has drawn a good deal of critical attention. But it is particularly troublesome if one is compelled to interpret "heaven," "clouds," "sun," and "moon" as "the great earth mother" or mindless physical sensation. When one thinks of the range of Stevens's meditation on the feminine principle, the limitations of such a critical stance are striking. A Jungian reading simply cannot account for the striding poet-singer, the haunting genius of the shore in *The Idea of Order at Key West*. Jung's system of archetypes, far from opening a window on Stevens's poetry, forces the reader to transpose all that is inventive, all that is intellectually active—poiesis itself—beyond the reach of the feminine.

Homer's invocation to the "Goddess" and Hesiod's to the "divine muses" continue, in English poetry, as the address to Urania, the "heavenly muse." A. Walton Litz refers to this tradition when he calls the One of Fictive Music a "muse-goddess." Stevens's invocation, says Litz, is an address to "naked imagination, pure and simple, a figure of Muse and Virgin and earthly woman who is mistress of the music celebrated in the second stanza."[4] What we get is a kind of Ur-version of the Supremes: a combination of Polyhymnia, Saint Cecelia, and perhaps Stevens's young wife (a music teacher), who was precisely a "mistress of music" and whose long golden hair is memorialized here and elsewhere in the poetry.[5] What seems clear is that this early lyric has both ironic and erotic overtones. It contains a half-amused nod to the Heliconian sisterhood which serves as the introit to a more serious reflection on poetic musing—classically a category of "divine madness."

Harold Bloom firmly escorts the muse into Freudian territory. The One of Fictive Music is a "familial muse" says Bloom, and amplifies: "Stevens takes the Oedipal risk, as Keats and Whitman did, and invokes the muse as his actual mother and as the other women of his family."[6] In his discussion of *Final Soliloquy of the Interior Paramour*, the finely wrought chamber piece of the very late poetry, Bloom uses *muse* interchangeably with *paramour*. He claims, however, that Madame La Fleurie—"a bearded queen, wicked in her dead light," the land as receiver of the corpse—is the "last version of the American muse-as-mother," and so a "more authentic version of the interior paramour."

But Stevens's paramour is neither dread mother nor classical muse, nor for that matter, "imagination, pure and simple." The literary muse, conventionally summoned from above and beyond, represents inspiration that strikes from without; she is external to the poet. In contrast, the paramour is an inner presence. She dwells in the "hermitage at the centre," always within range of the poet's consciousness. She is conceived as an interior love object, not an externalized force. Finally, where the classical muse speaks to or through the poet, Stevens speaks *with* the paramour. "Fool," cries Sidney's famous muse: "look in thy heart and write." In contrast, the discourse between the modern poet and his paramour develops as an interchange: "those exchanges of speech in which your words are mine, mine yours" (NA, 67).

Stevens significantly defines the inner presence as a "separate self." In *Re-statement of Romance* the mysterious voice observes, "Only we two may interchange / Each in the other what each has to give," and concludes with a murmured assurance

> That night is only the background of our selves,
> Supremely true each to its separate self,
> In the pale light that each upon the other throws.   (CP, 146)

As one considers the manifestations of this separate self in the poetry, it becomes evident that Stevens's paramour has—like Theodore Roethke's flexible inamorata—"more sides than a seal." She is portrayed with various shades of green, purple, blue, argent, rose, and gold and surrounded by degrees of radiance ranging from "pale light" to flaming brilliance. As Kessler points out, she is related to summer—"the unbroken circle of summer" (CP, 438)—and to the south, the most fertile of Stevens's directional emblems.

But *paramour* is a term that contains both "love" (-*amour*) and "darkness" (-*moor*) and Stevens's paramour reveals a shadowy night side as well as a bright:

> Donna, donna, dark,
> Stooping in indigo gown
> And cloudy constellations,
> Conceal yourself or disclose
> Fewest things to the lover—   (CP, 48)

In the early "Florida" poems, the poet is the "scholar of darkness" and the paramour becomes "Night, the female, / Obscure, / Fragrant and supple" (CP, 73). Bloom, I think, comes as close as one can to describing the emotional tension that courses between poet and paramour. But does she reach her final flowering in the all-swallowing Madame La Fleurie? Or is this appearance in the late poetry merely a grim Gothic flourish? Generally one finds that the dark aspect of Stevens's paramour recalls—not the lethal earth queen—but her antithesis: the "black but comely" Shulamite of Solomon's love song.

Although Stevens does not give the figure a name, and indeed, occasionally refers to it as "nameless," he invests the paramour with a range of epithets and descriptive terms that indicate a compound nature. It is not easy to convey, in brief, the subtlety, the diversity, the strength of Stevens's delineation of the feminine—from tigress and she-wolf to regal abstraction. From Susanna and Saint Ursula to Bonnie and Josie dancing in Oklahoma, to the contemplative woman of *Sunday Morning*, to the "green queen" with the Marvellian "green mind" of *Description without Place*, to the "United Dames of America" to the "burning body" of Nanzia Nunzio, to the bearded circus freak Madame La Fleurie.

   Stevens's paramour is Eve, who "made air the mirror of herself" (*CP*, 383), and the "naked, nameless dame" whose hand "wove round her glittering hair" (*CP*, 271). She is the terrestrial globe, the "Fat girl" of *Notes toward a Supreme Fiction* and the seductive south, whose "mind had bound me round" in *Farewell to Florida* (*CP*, 117). In *The Owl in the Sarcophagus* she is memory,

> the mother of us all,

> The earthly mother and the mother of
> The dead.   (*CP*, 432)

In *The Candle a Saint* she "walks among astronomers," again "green kindled and green apparelled," reflecting a Platonic ideal form, an abstract icon of intelligence:

> The noble figure, the essential shadow,

> Moving and being, the image at its source,
> The abstract, the archaic queen.   (*CP*, 223)

Stevens invokes her with immense longing and bitter irony as "Mother of Heaven, regina of the clouds" (*CP*, 13) but, in the very late poetry, as the serene being "that was mistress of the world" (*CP*, 460). Like Shelley's Epipsyche, she is *A Golden Woman in a Silver Mirror* (*CP*, 460); like Plato's Diotima, she is the "sibyl of the self" (*OP*, 104); like Saint Bernard's *sponsa Dei*, she is "the spouse, the bride" (*CP*, 396), "the desired . . . sleek in a natural nakedness" who dwells in the hermitage at the center (*CP*, 505). But, like Blake's Divine Human Imagination, she is also the "maker of the song she sang" (*CP*, 129). She is the tripartite One of Fictive Music (*CP*, 87), the separate self "that speaks, denouncing separate selves" (*CP*, 441), the ambiguous "lover that lies within us" (*CP*, 394). Finally, she is the "inexplicable sister of the minotaur" (NA, 52) the "woman with the hair of a pythoness" (NA, 29).

"The Noble Rider and the Sound of Words" opens with the winged horses and the charioteer of the *Phaedrus*. Toward the conclusion of the essay, Stevens almost casually introduces the image of the pythoness, perhaps his version of Plato's mantic priestess. "All poets address themselves to someone," he writes, "and it is of the essence of that instinct . . . that it should be to an elite, not to a drab but to a woman with the hair of a pythoness." This is not the image of a Medusa, as one may first imagine, with hair composed of wildly twining snakes. Once summoned up, however, the Medusa image does not dissipate entirely; it remains long enough to ensure the barbarity of the "python" image, to intensify its uncanny quality, and to sharpen its archaic outline. The Pythoness is a sibyl, of course, who speaks in riddles but speaks the truth. The figure represents, for Stevens, an interior reader and an oracular voice that is archaic, erotic, prophetic, priestly, and unfamiliar. Stevens's half-savage, half-divine Ariadne-figure provides an essential clue to the nature of his paramour and underscores the riddling presence of the pythoness. The poet himself defines his "muse" as an expression of "the intelligence that endures" (NA, 52), and invokes her with a peculiar intensity in almost Yeatsian terms: "Inexplicable sister of the Minotaur, enigma and mask, although I am part of what is real, hear me and recognize me as part of the unreal. I am the truth but the truth of that imagination of life in which with unfamiliar motion and manner you guide me in those exchanges of speech in which your words are mine, mine yours" (NA, 67).

If one looks across the poetry as a whole, it becomes apparent that in common with his contemporaries—Yeats, Eliot, Pound, Williams— Stevens's feminine principle possesses a mythic dimension. Unlike his contemporaries, Stevens's idea of Woman reflects a noetic as well as a mystical ancestry. Although Stevens's paramour derives in part from the *sponsa Dei* of the speculative theologians (i.e., the anima as the mystical bride of Christ), she descends too from the oracular sibyls of the classical period. Her noetic, or intellective, quality aligns her with her great predecessor in the *Symposium*: Diotima, Socrates' instructor in the philosophy of love. Stevens's paramour thus stands in the long line of female representations of Wisdom. As the "intelligence that endures," she is the direct heiress of Wisdom in Proverbs, of the postclassical Sophia, and of Nous, the Neoplatonic figure of thinking.[7] In short, Stevens's paramour stands at a far remove from a Jungian concept of the anima.

Let me be clear. According to Jung, the anima is the image of the feminine that exists in the male psyche. It is a projection of the "mother imago" that extends to the image of "the daughter, the sister, the beloved, the heavenly goddess" and an entity called the "earth spirit Baubo."[8] Jung stresses the universality of the projection, which he discusses rather curiously in terms of contagion and disease: "Every mother and every beloved is forced to become the carrier and embodiment of this omnipresent and ageless image which corresponds to the deepest reality in a man. It is his own, this perilous image of woman." The equivalent "imago" in the psyche of a woman is the animus or image of the father, which Jung invests with qualities of "reason or spirit." Woman is "compensated by this masculine element," as Jung believes, and his discussion of anima and animus serves to reduce what is masculine and what is feminine into two antithetical "projections": male rationality and female sensuality: "The animus corresponds to the paternal Logos just as the anima corresponds to the maternal Eros."[9]

One cannot fail to be impressed by the beautiful symmetry of this scheme. But in a later writing Jung contradicts his original explanation of the anima. No longer is it a projection of the masculine psyche, nor the "deepest reality in a man." It is not even "his own, this perilous image of woman." Rather suddenly, it has developed into the "true nature" of woman. In "Marriage as a Psychological Relationship," Jung now says, "In men, Eros . . . is usually less developed than Logos. In woman, on the other hand, Eros is an expression of their true nature, while their logos is often only a regrettable accident."[10] It is not my intention, in noting this contradiction, to deny Jung's contribution to the study of symbolic expression. The point I would like to carry home has to do with the use of Jungian theory to read Stevens's poetry. For the rigid division of attributes which Jungian psychology accepts as "archetypal," and which Jung puts forth as a universal and unalterable truth, can hardly be said to "account rather well" for Wallace Stevens's paramour—a creature rich and sometimes strange, but impressively manifold.

The anima, as such, acquires a more Freudian coloration in *Esthétique du Mal*, where Stevens is clearly taking "the Oedipal risk" in this homage to Baudelaire. This is a wonderfully orchestrated passage that modulates in its portrait of desire and the artist from rhythmic sensuality to savage syncopation. One notes, however, that the anima figuration remains vivid, energetic, various:

> He sought the most grossly maternal, the creature
> Who most fecundly assuaged him, the softest

> Woman with a vague moustache and not the mauve
> *Maman.* His anima liked its animal
> And liked it unsubjugated.   (*CP*, 321)

The passage goes on, joining the anima playfully with "its animal":

> It is true there were other mothers, singular
> In form, lovers of heaven and earth, she-wolves
> And forest tigresses and women mixed
> With the sea. These were fantastic.

It is not really helpful, I think, to define this complex figuration in terms of disease or to discuss Stevens's paramour as an aberration, a "schizoid self," as Mary Arensberg does in her study of the figure.[11] Nor does it add to an understanding of Stevens's poetics to think of his paramour as a mere "syntactic event" (Arensberg here refers to Michael Beehler's critical approach) or to consider the paramour, as Beehler does, "an illusion, constructed within a linguistic hall of mirrors."[12] Nor can we think of the paramour as "an invented fiction . . . generated from within the poet's own psyche," if she is a "separate self," and the "intelligence that endures" as well as an integral part of the poet. Possibly the figure expresses the very psyche that is said to be generating an "invented fiction" of itself.

While the oracular and noetic components of Stevens's paramour are evidenced in images of the pythoness, the Ariadne figure, and the "abstract, the archaic queen," the passional element derives its force from the Song of Songs. If one bypasses the theological mystique that attaches to the bride and bridegroom of Canticles and returns to Solomon's love song, one is brought back to the headiness of purely physical pleasure: "Let him kiss me with the kisses of his mouth," the Shulamite sings, "for your love is better than wine." The Shulamite who provides the model for the soul in love calls her virile bridegroom the "dove that art in the clefts of the rock," a "young hart upon the mountains," and "an apple tree among trees of the wood." She, in turn, is "a garden inclosed . . . my sister, my spouse"; she is "fair as the moon, clear as the sun," and "black but comely." Thus, the Shulamite is a particularly rich source for Stevens's "beloved," for both her shining aspects and her dark face are mirrored in the paramour.

The shining and dark aspects of the paramour are both related to summer and the south, but the dark face is most often associated with the southern night. Black is neither absence of color nor lack of light, for Stevens, but an erotic and enveloping ambiance rich with anticipation and the suggestion of limitless possibilities. It is the "essential dark," the originating *materium* out of which all creation flows. In *Two Figures in Dense Violet Light* a nameless paramour urges the lover of darkness to

> Be the voice of night and Florida in my ear.
> Use dusky words and dusky images.
> Darken your speech.   (CP, 86)

Stevens succeeds both in revealing and concealing the presence of the dark-faced paramour (paramoor) in *Six Significant Landscapes*:

> The night is of the color
> Of a woman's arm;
> Night, the female,
> Obscure,
> Fragrant and supple,
> Conceals herself.
> A pool shines,
> Like a bracelet
> Shaken in a dance.   (CP, 73–4)

The inamorata is "lascivious as the wind" in the early *O Florida, Venereal Soil*, and the poet a "scholar of darkness." Here, the "Venus-like" body of the beloved place and climate is absorbed into the figure of the paramour. As in so many of the "Florida" poems, the exterior place is projected into a psychological interior, the space within, and shaped into a woman's image. The terrain itself pictures forth the emotional life. Thus in *Farewell to Florida* one has the sense of a profound leave-taking, something more than the simple fact of a journey north.

The Shulamite cries to the elements, in her yearning: "Awake, O north wind; and come, thou south; blow upon my garden, that the spices thereof may flow out" (4:16). In *Farewell to Florida* (CP, 117–18), the poet turns away from such a call as this with a sublime pathos. The poem stands at the opening to *Ideas of Order* (1936), and some have interpreted the passage from south to north as a passage to a new poetics. Surely it is a crossing poem that marks the closing of a era. But the freedom it heralds seems to have been dearly bought:

> Go on, high ship, since now, upon the shore,
> The snake has left its skin upon the floor.
> Key West sank downward under massive clouds
> And silvers and greens spread over the sea. The moon
> Is at the mast-head and the past is dead.

> Her mind will never speak to me again.
> I am free.

Bloom finds the second stanza an extraordinarily sensuous evocation, not of a state of the union, but of "a state of mind."[13] It is "so erotic a stanza," says Bloom, "that the reader needs to keep reminding himself that this Florida . . . is a trope of pathos, a synecdoche for desire and not desire itself." Yet in this stanza desire twists into dearth and death; the north and south winds called up by the Shulamite to fan and enflame desire become "my North of cold whistled in a sepulchral South." In this stanza erotic language remains attached to a configuration of place and to a woman's mind, while south and north become directional emblems of remembrance and Lethean forgetfulness:

> Her mind had bound me round. The palms were hot
> As if I lived in ashen ground, as if
> The leaves in which the wind kept up its sound
> From my North of cold whistled in a sepulchral South,
> Her South of pine and coral and coraline sea,
> Her home, not mine, in the ever-freshened Keys,
> Her days, her oceanic nights, calling
> For music, for whisperings from the reefs.
> How content I shall be in the North to which I sail
> And to feel sure and to forget the bleaching sand . . .

One feels the wrench of these lines. This is departure from a beloved who is still loved, and the agon between south and north, here, is one between passion and reason. The *mania* of love and poetry is rejected for the "contentment" of ordinary existence. It is a difficult moment, a hard passage toward north and "sanity," for as we learn in the final stanza, "My North is leafless and lies in a wintry slime / Both of men and clouds, a slime of men in crowds."

One can sail determinedly north and away from Florida, but can one leave an "interior paramour" behind? In this context, a connection emerges between the passion and finality of *Farewell to Florida* and the appearance shortly thereafter of the singer of the shore in *The Idea of Order at Key West*. In the *Farewell* we learn that "the snake has left its skin upon the floor." In *The Idea of Order* there is the sudden striking materialization of the paramour as an externalized presence—the one time in the poetry that the "sibyl of the self" jumps out of her skin, so to speak, like the snake. In the *Farewell* Stevens plays on the idea of *leaving*, connecting it with the loss of prophetic power, the barbarous scattering of sibylline leaves: "leaves in which the wind kept up its sound." The poet journeys toward a "leafless" north, the absence of passion and its power. As John Hollander has shown, Stevens displays "a great command of the dynamic range of echo, from the almost blatantly allusive to the most muted and problematic of phantoms."[14] Clearly, the fugal play on *leaves* and *leave-taking*, in this poem in particular, echoes Shelley's West Wind ode. More pointedly, it calls up Dante's epic simile of the dead souls at the gate of hopelessness.

The singer of Key West is the genius of presence, the composer of the here and now. But she is also the genius loci and an unusual one in that respect too. For the locus is not so much a place as a triple threshold—she strides along the margins of sea and shore and sky. Her song not only "makes" the world—that is, composes the natural world into an intelligible and harmonious order—but opens up the entrance from the known world to whatever lies beyond the "fragrant portals, dimly starred." In *The Idea of Order at Key West*, Stevens unmasks the "enigma and mask": "The sea was not a mask. No more was she" (CP, 128). But unmasked, she is like Echo: pure presence reduced to voice. We can hear her continuo over the pounding surf, but only the poet sees the moving rhythmic figure and only he knows who the nameless "she" really is.

In *Farewell to Florida* the poet means to detach from the paramour. He intends to sever all ties except the continuity of memory:

> To stand here on the deck in the dark and say
> Farewell and to know that that land is forever gone
> And that she will not follow in any word
> Or look, nor ever again in thought, except
> That I loved her once.   (CP, 118)

The relinquishment in Stevens's "to know that that land is forever gone" has the same quality of bitter knowledge that controls the close of Thomas's *Fern Hill*. Stevens does sail north to a wintry "slime of men in crowds," and in the splendid *Idea of Order* manages to thrust the paramour outside the self. The singer, the maker, the sibylline presence, the lover that lies within, is situated on an exterior plane, moving along the edges of a marginal world, haunting the dimly starred threshold of the possible. Fortunately, she does not remain in exile. Toward the end of the poetry, when Stevens is in his seventies, we are given *Final Soliloquy of the Interior Paramour*, and we understand that she has been with him all along.

Chapter 5

The Archangel of Evening

At their flaming head he westward trooped it like that chosen star
which every evening leads on the hosts of light.
MELVILLE, *Moby-Dick*

I am the archangel of evening and praise
This one star's blaze.
Suppose it was a drop of blood . . .   STEVENS

IN CHAPTER FORTY-TWO OF *Moby-Dick* (the famous chapter on "The Whiteness of the Whale"), Ishmael says: "It was the whiteness of the whale that above all things appalled me." The sublimity of Ishmael's pun—the whiteness *appalled* me—grows as the idea of whiteness grows. The complexion of the monster becomes the complexion of the man, for, as we are warned, "there lurks something in the innermost idea of this hue which strikes more of panic to the soul than that redness which affrights the blood." And indeed, as the remarkable catalogue unfolds, whiteness twists from bridal garments, milk-white beasts, altar flame— images of purity, innocence, redemption—into an emblem of terror. White is also the shark, the polar bear, the albatross. No longer a color or brightness, or mere albino lack of color, white trails "clouds of wonderment and pale dread." Like Freud's taboo, whiteness in *Moby-Dick* bespeaks the sacred and the unclean, inspires holy dread and unholy horror. With a genius-leap of ambivalence, Melville has converted whiteness into the cosmic blaze of moral energy, on the one hand, and made it the texture of evil, on the other.

In Stevens's poems, whiteness carries a variety of meanings—as does blackness—but white and black are significantly devoid of moral content. If there is a poetics of good and evil in Stevens, and I believe there is, it is not to be found in whalish whiteness. Yet Melville's disquisition on the sources of wonder and dread points in the right direction, and one passage in particular leads into the heartland of Stevens's moral terrain. Melville's White Steed of the Prairies, his "magnificent milk-white charger," possesses a divinity that commands worship but also enforces "a certain nameless dread." While the fabulous horse is described quite literally in stellar terms, the passage taken as a whole suggests that the figure is an apotheosis of the American west:

> He was the elected Xerxes of vast herds of wild horses, whose pastures . . . were only fenced by the Rocky Mountains and the Alleghanies. At their flaming head he westward trooped it like that chosen star which every evening leads on the hosts of light. The flashing cascade of his mane, the curving comet of his tail, invested him with housings more resplendent than gold and silver-beaters could have furnished him. A most imperial and archangelical apparition of that unfallen, western world, which to the eyes of the old trappers and hunters revived the glories of those primeval days when Adam walked majestic as a god. [1]

Stevens might have called Melville's celestial stallion one of the original inhabitants of the west. Certainly, a number of things in the passage correspond with Stevens's somewhat quieter notions of good: the evening star as a marvelous portent—"that chosen star"; the "archangelical apparition" that in Stevens's late poem becomes the "archangel of evening"; the allusions to a biblical text and an "unfallen, western world."

In Stevens's universe, nightfall and the west do not connote death, decline, all-swallowing darkness. On the contrary, they establish the temporal-spatial coordinates for the appearance of first light, the recurring symbol of first creation. Like Melville's unfallen world, Stevens's west is the scene of renewal, regeneration, and supernatural energy. Like Melville's sublime horse, the evening star in Stevens's poetry acts both as a wondrous sign and a guide to direction. It is, therefore, in Stevens's evocations of star-blaze and candle flame that one finds ideas of spiritual energy, generative force, guidance, and direction clustered together. The evening star has always been considered the star of love, and Stevens will evoke it as such. But he will also refer to it as a mechanism of divination, as an oracular being. These considerations strongly suggest that an examination of the star and candle poems will reveal not only the poet's moral concerns—his poetics of good and evil—but show the evolution of the linkage in Stevens's poetry between moral concerns, sexuality, and prophecy.

Star and Candle

The evening star rises as a potent symbol very early in the Stevens canon and the evening candle is lighted at about the same time. As both candle and star appear and reappear in the poetry, it becomes evident that Stevens is drawing a parallel between human and cosmic lamps. By the time of the last poems, it is clear that star and candle represent more than illumination in the dark; both are fire emblems of creation and consciousness. In the early *Le Monocle de Mon Oncle*, the evening star burns with generative fury:

> In the high west there burns a furious star.
> It is for fiery boys that star was set
> And for sweet-smelling virgins close to them.   (*CP*, 14)

Similarly, in the very late *A Quiet Normal Life* we learn "There was no fury in transcendent forms. / But his actual candle blazed with artifice" (*CP*, 523). The star can symbolize promise, a covenant. In *Prologues to What Is Possible* the "smallest lamp" of self "which added its puissant flick" is a single human intelligence. Consciousness *as such* appears, "The way the earliest light in the evening sky in spring, / Creates a fresh universe out of nothingness by adding itself" (*CP*, 517).

While Stevens establishes a correspondence early on between the planet that appears first in the evening sky and the candle or lamp lighted by human hands at dusk, a significant change occurs as one moves from the early to the very late poems. The fragile light of *Valley Candle*—the unprotected flame that represents conscious life, spirit, invention—that "burns alone" in the dark, only to be snuffed by the wind, slowly grows into the sustained radiance that illuminates *Final Soliloquy of the Interior Paramour*. In poems of the middle period, the candle comes more and more to light up familiar, homelike objects, and to suggest Stevens's genetic as well as his aesthetic heritage. In the final period, candle flame and star fire share a common substance, and both possess a warmth and a glow that contrasts sharply with the "crystal-pointed" fires of the earlier poetry.

A glance at *The Reader, Nuances of a Theme by Williams*, and *Valley Candle* quickly illustrates some of the qualities shared by the early poems of this cluster: remoteness, alienation, cold, inevitability, apocalyptic loss, existential despair. *The Reader*, as noted in chapter 3, describes an entropic universe. The stars are falling, no lamp burns, a disembodied voice "mumbles" and the text is fading out:

> It was autumn and falling stars
> Covered the shrivelled forms
> Crouched in the moonlight.
>
> No lamp was burning as I read,
> A voice was mumbling, "Everything
> Falls back to coldness.   (*CP*, 147)

The very shape of things seems atrophied in this relatively early piece. But while *The Reader* contemplates ultimate loneliness, it is not alone of its kind. The quoted voice in Stevens's poem that predicts cold nothingness echoes similar exercises in negation such as Byron's *Darkness* or Coleridge's *Coeli Enarrant* ("The Exposition of the Heavens").[2] This particular ancestor of Stevens's poem is itself a quotation of sorts. "I wrote these lines," Coleridge noted, "in imitation of Du Bartas as translated by our Sylvester." While Coleridge's late poem may or may not be what is mumbling in the entrails of Stevens's little piece, it possesses a sparkling black wit of its own well worth looking at in this context:

> The stars that wont to start, as on a chace,
> Mid twinkling insult on Heaven's darkened face,
> Like a conven'd conspiracy of spies
> Wink at each other with confiding eyes!
> Turn from the portent—all is black on high,
> No constellations alphabet the sky:
> The Heavens one large Black Letter only shew,
> And as a child beneath its master's blow
> Shrills out at once its task and its affright—
> The groaning world now learns to read aright,
> And with its Voice of Voices cries out, O!

In the early *Nuances of a Theme by Williams*, Stevens invoked the star—in its morning aspect this time—carefully avoiding mythic overtones. The poem was a tribute to William Carlos Williams but even more to an experimental poetics freed of classical baggage, the clinging shreds of allusion. Stevens celebrated Williams's "ancient star" on an impersonal plane, underscoring its otherness, its isolate character, its phenomenal detachment from all but the fact of its own manifestation:

> *It's a strange courage*
> *you give me, ancient star:*
>
> *Shine alone in the sunrise*
> *toward which you lend no part!*

Shine alone, shine nakedly, shine like bronze,
that reflects neither my face nor any inner part
of my being, shine like fire, that mirrors nothing.   (CP, 18)

Ronald Sukenick described this poem as the examination of "an alien reality, utterly nonhuman." It concerns an existential being, he pointed out, about which the poet "cannot generalize, which is impervious to abstract thought, and onto which he cannot impose meaning nor project his own identity."[3] Harold Bloom has ascribed this aspect of remoteness in Stevens, rightly I believe, to an Epicurean-Lucretian cast of thought.[4] It is the Lucretian impulse that counsels stoic detachment, objective distance from joy as well as suffering. It is a Lucretian philosophy that admits of supernatural beings but conceives them as utterly unconcerned with human welfare, like the star that "mirrors nothing" human. But it is also the Lucretian impulse to break with superstition, the accretions of myth and magic that attach to natural phenomena.

This stoic discipline of detachment is given meaningful expression in the star poems, which permit Stevens to develop ideas of distance and insularity. But it is not confined to them. Like the star in *Nuances*, the flame in *Valley Candle* shines alone. The poem sets forth an existential vision of isolation and mortality in six stark lines:

My candle burned alone in an immense valley.
Beams of the huge night converged upon it,
Until the wind blew.
Then beams of the huge night
Converged upon its image,
Until the wind blew.   (CP, 51)

Is the setting a grim reference to the psalmist's valley of the shadow of death, or to the youngest prophet's valley of decision, where the "sun and moon shall be darkened, and the stars shall withdraw their shining" (Joel, 3:14, 15)? Does it perhaps call up the Great Valley of Stevens's Pennsylvania childhood? Surely, the wind in *Valley Candle* is a figure of Ananke close to the "wind of history" in Eliot's *Gerontion* or the wind that cries eternal desolation in Yeats's (also early) *He Hears the Cry of the Sedge*. In Stevens's poem, the inevitable wind acts twice in a process of decreation. First it snuffs out life; then it dissipates the image, or memory, of the individual and his works.[5] It is a stunning, if brief, paean to negation.

By the time of *The Man with the Blue Guitar* (1936), the lurking threat of the "huge night" has been replaced by a positive concept of "essential dark." Primal darkness, night, the color black have begun to represent, for Stevens, the symbolic matrix of all conceptualization and creation. As the dark resolves into a positive context, or ground, the star and candle images can be seen to develop from an erotic center, the "amorist Adjective aflame." What is "aflame" in *Blue Guitar* appears first in the heavens like a show of fireworks, a wonderfully controlled explosion of light: "First one beam, then another, then / A thousand are radiant in the sky" (*CP*, 172). But the canto spans heaven and earth. The thousand starry lights telescope into a "chandelier," and we see that the distance between celestial designs and "things as they are"—between the marvelous and the familiar—is also abridged:

> One says a German chandelier—
> A candle is enough to light the world.
>
> It makes it clear. Even at noon
> It glistens in essential dark.
>
> At night, it lights the fruit and wine,
> The book and bread, things as they are.

It is not a long way from "A candle is enough to light the world" to the fusion of light sources that characterizes only the very late poems. By the final period of *The Rock*, the distance between candle flame and star fire has diminished almost to the point of disappearance. Stevens's elegy for Santayana, *To an Old Philosopher in Rome*, orchestrates the magical imagery of bell, book, and candle in an evocation of Rome as a spiritual threshold and a double city. Stevens theoretically locates the old philosopher in the poem's Stoic and Platonic architectures—the "pillared porch," the upward vault of the life-spirit. The earthly "Holy City" becomes the threshold of transit between mundane existence and visionary reality, and Stevens here uses a theological figure of consubstantiation to express the living psyche. Santayana's intellectual and spiritual energies are rendered in terms of flame and light:

> A light on a candle tearing against the wick
> To join a hovering excellence, to escape
> From fire and be part only of that of which
>
> Fire is the symbol: the celestial possible.   (*CP*, 509)

By the time of *Final Soliloquy of the Interior Paramour*, star fire and candle flame are conjoined in a single lamp. The opening line—"Light the first light of evening"—initiates a simple domestic act and invokes the cosmic principle that "lights" the evening star. In *Valley Candle* the doubling of darkness serves to erase all hope of return. In *Final Soliloquy* the doubling of light in the first verse—*Light* the first *light*—is a repetition that promises continuance and renewal. If *Valley Candle* can be read as a younger man's questioning of existential purpose, then *Final Soliloquy* stands as the elder poet's response: "We say God and the imagination are one . . . / How high that highest candle lights the dark" (*CP,* 524).

I do not know whether Stevens read George Santayana's essay "Cross-Lights" in the collection of soliloquies composed for the most part in England during World War I, and published in 1922—just one year before the publication of *Harmonium.* But Santayana's influence on the young poet during his Harvard years was an abiding one, to judge from Stevens's letters (and his literary biographers),[6] and "Cross-Lights" develops an image of fiery intelligences close to the images that inform Stevens's star poems. Santayana writes, "They say the sun is a very small star," and he goes on to connect this fact with human life: "Each living being is a sort of sun to itself; this spark within me, by whose light I see at all, is a great sun to me; and considering how wide a berth other spiritual luminaries give me, I must warm myself chiefly by my own combustion, and remain singularly important to myself."[7] This concern with the singularity of the individual and the sense of remoteness it fosters—"I must warm myself chiefly by my own combustion"—changes, says Santayana, when one directs the attention outward: "This importance . . . vanishes in so far as my little light actually burns clear, and my intent flies with it to whatever objects its rays can reach, no matter how distant or alien. Yet this very intelligence and scope in me are functions of my inward fire: seeing, too, is burning."

Seeing, too, is burning. Stevens will echo Santayana's thought many years later in *Credences of Summer:*

> Let's see the very thing and nothing else.
> Let's see it with the hottest fire of sight.
> Burn everything not part of it to ash.   (*CP,* 373)

The idea of intelligence as a phenomenon of combustion and Santayana's polarities of detachment and connection are carried forward by Stevens in the star poems. The need to maintain objective distance is an essential component of these pieces—indeed, of the poetry as a whole. But the impulse toward insularity runs counter to an equally strong concern with subjective relation; the web of connection between self and other, people and things. In the early *Stars at Tallapoosa,* terms of connection and distance structure the dialectic: "The lines are straight and swift between the stars." A correspondence between star and man is drawn in bold "lines" of verse. Stevens is primarily interested here, not in slow natural growth or transient manifestation, but in kinetic energy, velocity, the principle of momentum:

> These lines are swift and fall without diverging.
>
> The melon-flower nor dew nor web of either
> Is like to these. But in yourself is like:
> A sheaf of brilliant arrows flying straight,
> Flying and falling straightway for their pleasure,
>
> Their pleasure that is all bright-edged and cold.   (*CP*, 72)

This calculated play on "lines" suggests thought-waves made visible, connections seen, whether on a cosmic scale or in lines of verse flying, falling one after the other onto the page. But the pleasures of "flying and falling" take on a sexual meaning in the final stanza. The cold motion of star fire converts without warning to sudden heat and becomes the vehement pleasure of young bodies. The principle of momentum is transferred to the motion of organic life,

>   the nimblest motions,
>   Making recoveries of young nakedness
>   And the lost vehemence the midnights hold.   (*CP*, 72)

Stars at Talapoosa is a crossover poem. In it we can observe a movement away from the remoteness of *Nuances* and the overwhelming powerlessness of human life that pervades *Valley Candle*. Stevens is at pains in this poem to forge a delicate connection between the physical universe that can be seen and the universe of human feeling. Both one's relation to other bodies and one's distance from other bodies, he seems to say, are reflected in the very composition of the cosmos. The poem expresses this "cross-lighting" in elemental images of heat and cold, momentum and light-waves, rhythmic energies. With remarkable economy Stevens has made the verse line into connective tissue. In such a medium, the crystalline fires of stars and of distanced objective thought can be linked with the hot "vehemence the midnights hold."

A somewhat earlier piece, *Homunculus et La Belle Etoile*, shows Stevens sharply dividing the fleshly passion from the intellective. In *Homunculus* Stevens pays ironic tribute to Aphrodite Pandemos, the fleshly passion, and then his respects to Aphrodite Ouranos, the philosopher's passion—and to the divine Plato who differentiates them. Stevens introduces the "sea-born" goddess in a coolly devilish mood:

> In the sea, Biscayne, there prinks
> The young emerald, evening star,
> Good light for drunkards, poets, widows,
> And ladies soon to be married.   (CP, 25)

Stevens illustrates the classical division of love into higher and lower aspects by picturing the heavenly planet reflected in the sea, alluding perhaps to the medieval epithet for Mary—*Stella maris*, or "Star of the sea." This shining light appearing in the heavens sparks desire in the various creatures:

> This light conducts
> The thoughts of drunkards, the feelings
> Of widows and trembling ladies,
> The movements of fishes.   (CP, 26)

We learn that "this emerald"—this watery "green queen"—is a reflection of the light that "charms philosophers" and a meditation follows in which the "vulgar" Aphrodite gives place to her loftier twin. The mood grows less detached, although it remains ironical, as Stevens begins to play with charming optatives. To those enchanted, the heavenly aspect of the goddess is revealed as "no gaunt fugitive phantom":

> She might, after all, be a wanton,
> Abundantly beautiful, eager,
>
> Fecund.

La Belle Etoile concludes rather more seriously than its opening would lead one to expect. The contrast between the sufferings of love and philosophic calm is underscored, while the notion of heavenly love diminishes to an effective tranquilizer:

> It is a good light, then, for those
> That know the ultimate Plato,
> Tranquillizing with this jewel
> The torments of confusion.   (CP, 27)

The luminary that appears in the high west is, of course, the planet Venus, the subject of hymns and odes from Sumerian times to the English romantics.[8] Stevens recognizes this relation of the planet to antiquity when, in a late poem, he refers to it, ceremonially, as "The most ancient light in the most ancient sky" (*CP*, 481). When Stevens summons up the evening star, he cannot help recalling "nuances" of a history that stretches back in poetry and myth to the most ancient of the known religions and to equally ancient astronomical tables. The evening star's erotic significance has remained constant, however. Whether the planet shines forth as Inanna, Ishtar, Ashtaroth, Aphrodite, or Venus—or as Blake's fair-hair'd angel of the evening—it has continued to presage the act of love.

But the star shines in Stevens's poetry, as elsewhere, with a double nature of a far darker sort than that imparted by the classical division of earthly and heavenly love. The evening star, Hesper, is also the morning star, or Phosphor the light-bringer. In Scripture, the "light-bringer" is the Archangel Lucifer, who becomes the Prince of Darkness. Stevens, familiar with Scripture from childhood, will have known the passage from Isaiah (14:12–15): "How thou art fallen from Heaven, O Lucifer, son of the morning! . . . for thou hast said in thy heart . . . I will exalt my throne above the stars of God. . . . Yet thou shalt be brought down to hell, to the sides of the pit." Thus the star that rises in the evening as the amorous beacon of love becomes the fallen archangel at night's end, headed for the blackest pit of hell.

The appearance of the evening star brings with it long-standing notions of safety within and danger without. In a letter to Harriet Monroe, written December 23, 1926, Stevens refers to the Sapphic fragment that invokes the genius of evening: "Evening star that bringest back all that lightsome Dawn hath scattered afar, thou bringest the sheep, thou bringest the goat, thou bringest the child home to the mother." Christmas, writes Stevens, "is like Sappho's evening: it brings us all home to the fold" (*LWS* 248).

The quality that is both lyrically pastoral and profoundly domestic is reflected strongly in Blake's *To the Evening Star*, although the appearance of the star in Blake's poem signals the pleasant beginning of activity rather than the end of the day's labor:

> Thou fair-hair'd angel of the evening,
> Now, while the sun rests on the mountains, light
> Thy bright torch of love; thy radiant crown
> Put on, and smile upon our evening bed!

Blake's ode, that begins with childlike wonder and anticipation, goes on to turn Sappho's pastoral image inside out. Instead of domestic animals returning to the fold, Blake introduces beasts of prey roaming the night:

Soon, full soon
Dost thou withdraw; then the wolf ranges wide,
And the lion glares thro' the dun forest:
The fleeces of thy flocks are covered with
Thy sacred dew: protect them with thine influence. [9]

Blake, too, likes his animal "unsubjugated." With the advent of the un-tamable creatures, Blake suggests the savage component of erotic passion. Apart from the palimpsest of sexual arousal which easily reveals itself as the subtext of the poem, one is confronted by the sharpness of the contrast Blake has drawn between warmth and safety within the home circle, bes-tiality and incipient violence stalking without. While this contrast goes back to classical evocations of the evening star, the romantic poem paral-lels with remarkable fidelity the thematic changes established in the Ho-meric hymn *To Aphrodite*. Like Blake's fair-haired angel, the love goddess in the hymn is invoked as she "who loves to smile," an ancient cult epi-thet. As she moves over mountainside, field and fold, predators follow in her track: "After her came grey wolves, fawning on her, and grim-eyed lions, and bears, and fleet leopards, ravenous for deer." [10] But the influ-ence of the goddess, the classical hymn continues, "put desire in their breasts, so that they all mated, two together, about the shadowy coombes." [11]

In Stevens's poetry too, one may find danger, violence, bloodshed, following silently in the track of the evening star, particularly in the star poems that deal with war. The two poems we are about to examine are not concerned with the heroic aspect of martial conflict. On the contrary, they show Stevens's concern with a Satanic repetition of the unheroic in the history of war—the experience of fear, fatigue, loneliness, and defeat. This is the *esthétique du mal* one finds "Only in misery, the afflatus of ruin, / Profound poetry of the poor and of the dead" (CP, 509). Charac-teristically, these poems also hint at a reverse face to the coin.

"From out the rinde of one apple"

The "vehemence" or violence that accompanies sensual pas-sion is represented in mythology by the alliance of Venus and Mars, the mutual attraction between love and war. *Martial Cadenza* carries this mythic coding of aggression in its title along with the physics of the cad-enza: "flying and falling." This poem, published in 1942 during World War II, and *One of the Inhabitants of the West*, composed ten years later during the period of postwar prosperity, are natural companion pieces. In both, references to martial conflict and violent death occur in a deliberately "tranquillized" medium. The language in both poems is austere, and the feeling restrained—particularly in the later piece—almost to the point that Helen Vendler called "tonelessness." [12] But in each poem, the point of view takes on the clarity, the detachment, the distance, and the intensity of the star that serves as its focal center.

Both poems are structured by a metaphysic that Swinburne expressed as A *Vision of Spring in Winter.* They describe the pushing into being of each cardinal principle from out of the heart of its retreating identical opposite. While *Martial Cadenza* develops an ecstatic vision of peace in a war-torn world, *One of the Inhabitants of the West* introduces the inevitable drop of blood into a peaceful text.

The theology that concerns the interpenetration of good and evil comes to Stevens, by way of Blake and Swinburne, from Milton. In the *Areopagitica* Milton expounds a rationale for the experience of evil: "It was from out the rinde of one apple tasted, that the knowledge of good and evill as two twins cleaving together leapt forth into the World. And perhaps this is that doom which *Adam* fell into . . . of knowing good by evill."

Martial Cadenza, a meditation on time shaped by the fact of war—wartime—similarly explores the good by contrast with a known evil. The poem opens on a note of promise:

> Only this evening I saw again low in the sky
> The evening star, at the beginning of winter, the star
> That in spring will crown every western horizon,
> Again . . . as if it came back, as if life came back.   (CP, 237)

The star appears "like sudden time in a world without time," and pinpoints the beginning of Stevens's reflection on what time really means in time of war. A world without time, as Bakhtin would point out, is a *chronotope*, a world apart from ordinary chronometric time. [13] Time as such is suspended in wartime, its passage calculated not in days, hours, minutes, or seasonal holidays, but in terms of battles fought and the progress of victory or defeat. A battle zone after the battle becomes "A zone of time without the ticking of clocks," as Stevens puts it in *Things of August* (CP, 494). Into this zone of epic defeat creep ghost armies, legions of men who stand silently, their weapons and (severed?) arms strewn about the battlefield. These are the dead of wars past and present:

> armies without
> Either trumpets or drums, the commanders mute, the arms
> On the ground, fixed fast in a profound defeat.   (CP, 238)

In the third stanza, the armies of the defeated dissolve into the blacked-out skies over Europe. The star, like the meditating mind in the poem, seems remote:

> What had this star to do with the world it lit,
> With the blank skies over England, over France
> And above the German camps? It looked apart.

It is, of course, precisely the distant perspective of the star that places the warring nations below in a common family. They stand near each other on the planetary map, while the star looks apart. At the close of the stanza, Stevens achieves a remarkable parallel between the life of the star and human action in a theater of war; they are both the center of "constant fire." The star, whose existence depends on continuous combustion, is mirrored in the deadly fire of munitions, cannon, exploding bullets, and bombs. But the star stands apart from the zone of war and from the temporality of past and future. In *Martial Cadenza* the star generates an ever-recurring present: "Itself / Is time," and one must consider what an extraordinary declaration this is:

> Itself
> Is time, apart from any past, apart
> From any future, the ever-living and being,
> The ever-breathing and moving, the constant fire.

Marital Cadenza concludes with one of the truly ecstatic visionary moments in Stevens. The star is seen as a mystical constant, "the vivid thing in the air that never changes, though the air change." At its end the poem circles back in a brilliant flourish to its beginning, a mimesis of the star's eternal return. The miracle of renewal is embodied in the chordlike repetition of "again" in the poem's cadenza:

> Only this evening I saw it again,
> At the beginning of winter, and I walked and talked
> Again, and lived and was again, and breathed again
> And moved again and flashed again, time flashed again.

The evening star in this poem of war appears in the winter sky like a shining portent. It promises a renewal of the simplest peacetime pleasures: walking, talking, breathing, moving, living. Its periodic recurrence in the night sky institutes the measure by which one receives and understands the covenant of return, the passage of time: "Itself / Is time."

While *Martial Cadenza* expounds "War's miracle begetting that of peace," as Stevens elsewhere has it, *One of the Inhabitants of the West* suggests a reverse side to the coin. This poem, with its intricate structure of a text within a text, its spare but telling language, its hovering sense of miraculous nativity and of final judgment, its controlling reference to war, and its Blakean coda, illustrates the center of a "pastoral text" with a single drop of blood. *Inhabitants* comes across as different *in kind* among Stevens's poems, although it is not apparent immediately what the nature of the difference might be. Most readers have dealt briefly or not at all with this very late piece. Surely it is one of the most puzzling texts in a canon full of riddles; and just as surely one feels that something of moment is being announced. It can do no harm to keep a few questions in mind as we look at it. Who, for instance, is speaking? What is meant by the "reader of the text"? What information is locked into the title? Finally, what is the substance of the message? The poem follows in its entirety:

> Our divinations,
> Mechanisms of angelic thought,
> The means of prophecy,
>
> Alert us most
> At evening's one star
> And its pastoral text,
>
> When the establishments
> Of wind and light and cloud
> Await an arrival,
>
> A reader of the text,
> A reader without a body,
> Who reads quietly:
>
> "Horrid figures of Medusa,
> These accents explicate
> The sparkling fall of night
> On Europe, to the last Alp,
> And the sheeted Atlantic.
>
> These are not banlieus
> Lacking men of stone,
> In a well-rosed two-light
> Of their own.
> I am the archangel of evening and praise
> This one star's blaze.

> Suppose it was a drop of blood . . .
> So much guilt lies buried
> Beneath the innocence
> Of autumn days."
>   (*CP*, 503–4)

The first thing we may notice is the poem's formal division into three parts: the title; a prelude composed of four sets of tercets; and the body of the work, two stanzas of unequal length enclosed in quotations. The formal structure of *Inhabitants* inevitably recalls Stevens's early fascination with the prophetic element in Blake.[14] Stevens's poem takes precisely the same form as Blake's shorter prophetic works, *America: A Prophecy* and *Europe: A Prophecy*. Both of these works begin with what Blake calls a "Preludium" of four stanzas, followed by "A Prophecy," the main body of the work. This form is condensed in *Inhabitants*, and while in Stevens's poem the prelude is relatively tranquil, the second section moves with a sweeping onrush into an explosion of the prophetic voice.

Such a form allows Stevens to reach two intensely dramatic moments almost simultaneously. In the final stanza a voice proclaims: "I am the archangel of evening and praise / This one star's blaze." The attention is then directed to a startling conjecture: "Suppose it was a drop of blood . . ." Note that Stevens places the supposition in history; he uses the preterit *was*, not the subjunctive *were*. The ellipsis after "drop of blood" insists that one take the time to consider a supposition that links the source of light and energy with shed blood. The whole is couched in Stevens's distinctive idiom, engages in a Stevensian dialectic, and employs the familiar Stevensian iconography. If the language, logic, and images are authentically Stevensian, what then marks this poem *sui generis*, as occupying a class of its own? Why should its lexis work harder than usual to suggest multiple senses in each key term? Why does its syntax encourage extreme ambiguity, foster serious confusion as to perspective and voice? And why has Stevens sealed the final lines in end rhyme? One is asking, at bottom, how it is that *Inhabitants* resists interpretation at the same time that it positively invites it.

In *Pastoral Forms and Attitudes*, Harold E. Tolliver reads *Inhabitants* by way of Keats, rather than Blake, referring to Stevens's Medusa figures as "Lamia-like snakes." The poem's vision is devoid of moral or ethical content for Tolliver. In fact, the "text" suggests a debasement of older forms: "The divinations and the mechanism suggest that, though 'angelic,' the pastoral text is a diminished affair—a reduction of old myths."[15] Harold Bloom refers only briefly to the poem in a discussion of the "dialectical relationship between innocence and autumn,"[16] while

Frank Doggett interprets Stevens's "well-rosed two-light" as an example of Schopenhauer's "light of double knowledge" and usefully connects the Medusa figures with the "men of stone." For Doggett, the archangel of evening represents "higher understanding" and remains an "impossible pure being."[17] While each of these readings undeniably adds something to the understanding of this strange poem, one feels that *Inhabitants* has continued to elude interpretation.

Assuredly one key to the poem is the notion of a "pastoral text." One thinks of pastoral as a supremely sophisticated mode that calls up innocent eroticism in a natural setting. The Theocritan idyll is immediately established in Stevens's setting of wind and clouds. In this context, the archangel first enters the picture as the "well-rosed" star of evening, well-risen in the pastoral character of the Passionate Shepherd. But the passionate shepherd exists in *Inhabitants* as a doubled presence, a "two-light," for pastoral also refers to the ministry. Just as the evening star symbolizes erotic energy and acts as a guide to direction, so does the passionate shepherd in this poem suggest the lover of idyllic poetry and the inspired spiritual director of a human flock. Unquestionably, the superordinate character of the poem determines the nature of its "message," and Stevens has framed that character with careful precision in the opening lines: *divinatory, prophetic*. By choosing to launch the poem in oracular terms, Stevens is indicating that he has activated a mechanism—one of the "mechanisms of angelic thought"—which performs as both a messenger and a mediator and whose highly charged state is a form of divine possession. In short, Stevens has launched a prophetic body—certainly a prophetic voice.

I do not mean that *One of the Inhabitants of the West refers* to a prophet, as the opening stanza of *Like Decorations . . .* refers to Walt Whitman (as the sun-son):

> He is singing and chanting the things that are part of him,
> The worlds that were and will be, death and day.
> Nothing is final, he chants. No man shall see the end.
> His beard is of fire and his staff is a leaping flame.   (*CP*, 150)

Nor do I mean that *Inhabitants* is a prophetic poem or a poetic prophecy, though these are plainly related modes.[18] I am suggesting, rather, that the poem itself be understood as a person, a Chanter of Personality, as Whitman called his speaking poem *To a Historian*, one of the "Inscriptions" that form the opening section of *Leaves of Grass*.[19]

In *The Prophetic Moment* Angus Fletcher comments on the double perspective of the prophet: "He contemplates the eternal verities of his faith—his moral, political, and religious principles—which remain his standards of truth. At the same time he observes the tangle of human experience. . . . The method of prophecy is to hold the eternal and the ephemeral in simultaneous copresence, balancing stable principle against unstable reality." From this point of view, says Fletcher, prophetic utterance becomes an interpretation of history: "Visionary as he may be, the prophet lives with the actual deeds of men and, like the historian, studies, that he may interpret, the fragmentary, discontinuous, seemingly irrational succession of these deeds."[20] Whitman's poem *itself* addresses the historian as "you" and refers to *itself* in the first person. Like Melville's White Steed, it is an inhabitant of the Alleghanies; like Stevens's archangel, it "projects" a divination of history:

> I, habitan of the Alleghanies . . .
> . . . . .
>
> Chanter of Personality, outlining what is yet to be,
> I project the history of the future.

It is my impression that, following Whitman, Stevens has created a similar "Personality" in his own late work. Just as Whitman's *habitan* is a chanter, chanting, so is Stevens's *Inhabitant* a prophet, prophesying.

Yet in its prophetic core, its treatment of innocence and experience, its ironic reversals of conformist ideology, and in certain of its images, as well as in its formal structure, Stevens's poem summons up Blake. In his commentary on *America: A Prophecy*, Harold Bloom notes that "Blake's *America* is at once a political allegory based on the American Revolution, an introduction to the poet's mythic word, and a moral prophecy in the tradition of the Hebrew prophets."[21] Stevens's poem shares something of this complexity, this particular compound of political, mythic, and moral elements. In Blake's *America* we are introduced to Albion's Angel, a furious inhabitant of the east:

> Albions Angel; who enrag'd his secret clouds open'd
> From north to south, and burnt outstretched on wings of wrath
>   cov'ring
> The eastern sky, spreading his awful wings across the heavens.
>
> (Plate 13)

There are prefigurings of Stevens's archangel, his men of stone, the fires of war, and the sheeted Atlantic in both the Blake poems, but *Europe: A Prophecy* also contains a debased universal text—the "brazen Book" of Urizenic power:

Albions Angel rose upon the Stone of Night.
He saw Urizen on the Atlantic;
And his brazen Book,
That Kings & Priests had copied on Earth
Expanded from North to South.   (Plate 11)

A prophet, by definition, is a charismatic individual endowed with the divine gift of receiving and imparting the message of revelation. The biblical prophet is both an independent person and a metonym of God, so to speak, a divine mouth. The poem-as-prophet can similarly be understood as an independent entity, controlled by its author, that both represents and speaks for its originator. *Inhabitants* comes forth as Stevens's instrument of prophecy. It expresses dire warning and predicts overwhelming loss, catastrophe, the breaking of the covenant—but it is also the instrument of revelation. The poem-as-prophet reveals itself to an audience that is essentially a readership; each member of its congregation is a quiet reader of the text. But the poem, itself a congregation of words, becomes the living spokesman or reader for an author who no longer has a body.

The title is an index to the poem. Like Melville's "chosen star," it appears first, signals what is to come, and stands above and apart from its fellows. Semiotically, the title enacts the "progress of poesy" theme that gives the poem its essential contour: the movement of a multiform unity (one among many) through successive generations (suggested by alternating genitives: of the . . . of the) to a final beginning—the "last Alp(ha)" of the poem proper—in the west. This is not the declining west, the *Abendland*, of Geoffrey Hartman's elegant essay on the poetry of descendence,[22] but the movement of poetry seeking liberty of expression and renewal of inspiration in its historic westerly drift, arriving at its last frontier in the New World.

Stevens's prelude asserts the oracular character of the text and sets the scene of revelation as if it were a performance in a theater, a show at the planetarium, a service in a church. It frames the advent of the evening star and its pastoral text, and focuses our attention sharply on the notion of reading. Indeed, the awaited arrival is three times said to be a *reader:*

A reader of the text,
A reader without a body,
Who reads quietly

A Reader of the Text is the formal designation of the lay member of the congregation appointed to read aloud the lines from Scripture upon which the sermon is based. A reader may be the senior lecturer in a given field at a university. But *reading* is a wonderfully open term in English. Its senses include: to *look at* inscribed characters and absorb their significance; to *understand* something (I "read" you); to *speak out* as an actor utters a script; to *give an interpretation*, as a diagnosis or critical insight; to *foretell* the future. Like the prophet, a reader receives, interprets and imparts a message—a given text. But what is the text in Stevens's poem, and who reads it?

The whole meaning of the prelude can be grasped intuitively if one recognizes the kind of slippage Stevens relies on to indicate the connectedness of unlike things. Certainly in this poem he is intent on a skillful juggling of correspondences, such that several relations are always in force at any given moment. The text thus comes into focus as the firmament seen by those who divine from the stars, be they astrologers, seafarers, or astrophysicists. The text is the terrestrial globe or map as "seen" by the evening star, and it is all the events that have taken place under its gaze: history. The pastoral text in *Inhabitants* ironically calls up a history of world war as much as the peaceful "establishments" of wind and cloud. On the other hand, the text is also the covenant implied in the archangel's praise: the promise of new cycles and new life, the possibility of redemption, the certainty of return. The text is the quoted prophecy read by the quiet reader. The poem is the text. All of these readings are active in Stevens's *Inhabitants* and each one of these interlocking texts forms a scenic backdrop with a distinct perspective, an appropriate reader.

While the outer text, or prelude, is serene, peaceful, detached, the inner text, or prophecy, chants of "Horrid figures of Medusa" and its concerns are guilt and innocence, paralysis, implications of war, violence, and blazing fire. The medusa image brings back the blood-haunted murder of Duncan in *Macbeth*: "Approach the chamber, and destroy your sight / With a new Gorgon!" (2.3). But *horrid* goes back to Virgil's poem of war. Stevens's schoolboy edition of the *Aeneid* will have had a note recording the lines that opened the epic through the Renaissance: "At nunc horrentia Martis / Arma virumque cano" (But now of the horrid arms of Mars and the man I sing). In Stevens's poem, the horrid figures represent both past and potential violence; they are stony replicas of men-at-arms, statues of soldiers, memorials of war fixed around the centers of life. *Banlieu*, as Stevens knew (see *LWS*, 764), was originally a military term meaning the territory outside the walls but within the legal limits of a town or city. What one finds, accordingly, as one moves toward the center of the text within the text, is a zone of potential violence, then a neutral band of darkness falling over land and ocean, and then an inner circle of danger surrounding the proclamation of the archangel and the central point, the drop of blood.

The establishments that await an arrival, the guiding light of the star, and the announcement of the archangel all imply a wonderful coming, a blessed birth. We see, however, that themes of Advent and Nativity are paralleled by implications of violent death in the inner text; a crucifixion must follow the miraculous birth. Death appears with the stars in the "sparkling fall of night"; death moves over the morguelike figure of the "sheeted Atlantic" and superintends the burial of ancient guilt beneath a layer of innocence. Within "the rinde of one apple" we see guilt and innocence eternally folded one within the other.

The archangel of evening is a dyadic being. As Hartman observes, the evening star "both rouses and chastens the prophetic soul. A fixed yet fugitive sign . . . Hesper / Lucifer points at once toward and beyond itself."[23] As the poem points to its bodiless author, the star is a sign that points to a design—and to the intrinsic problem of dual identity: *Venus is the morning star.* The revelation of the star-angel is precisely its praise of its other face, its antithetical identity. The germ of the prophecy is in the idea—the utterance—that the great blaze of light both *was* and *is* the drop of blood, for it is *one star:*

> I am the archangel of evening and praise
> This one star's blaze.
> Suppose it was a drop of blood . . .

Is this a drop of sacrificial blood? Does the ellipsis hold open the space, reserve the time for the unspeakable feast of violence: Lamb devoured by Tyger? (Hartman tellingly notes of the daemonic *Tyger! Tyger! burning bright / In the forests of the night:* "Usually stars burn this way.")[24] Yet Blake clearly intends us to see a dread beauty and grace in Tyger.

Stevens's moral formulation in *One of the Inhabitants of the West* thus comes down from Milton and Blake, on the one hand, and from Whitman and Melville, on the other. It affirms that the source of all energy—mental, physical, moral, creative, destructive—is a single source, that the problem of evil is inseparably bound to the production of good. One is enfolded in the other, just as the fair-hair'd angel of the evening inevitably turns into the Satanic principle, the Prince of Darkness, and cannot do otherwise. Blake asks, "Did he who made the Lamb make thee?" Stevens reframes the question in *The Auroras of Autumn:*

> Is there an imagination that sits enthroned
> As grim as it is benevolent, the just
> And the unjust, which in the midst of summer stops
>
> To imagine winter?   (CP, 417)

Milton refers in *Areopagitica* to those "fabulous Dragons teeth; [which] being sown up and down, may chance to spring up armed men." In *Inhabitants*, the drop of blood also reflects the spawn of the dragon's teeth. In an earlier poem Stevens observes: "The armies kill themselves, / And in their blood an ancient evil dies" (CP, 292). It is the blood of miraculous birth and violent death, violent birth and miraculous, saving death; the germ of good and evil. It is the organic counterpart of the star blaze, the element of pure energy, pure force, pure light. Perhaps it reconstitutes that alchemical, magical, powerful drop of blood conjured up by Faustus at the moment of his reckoning: "See, see where Christ's blood streams in the firmament! / One drop would save my soul, half a drop: ah, my Christ!"

Stevens has attempted, in *Inhabitants*, to compress the energies of matter and spirit, the phenomenal and the noumenal, into a single text that reflects the oppositional extremes built into the design of things. Like Melville's great sperm whale, Stevens's archangel sounds the depths of organic life, and like Melville's all-encompassing Whiteness, the star-angel describes the full circle of being. It is female and male, the emblem of love and the emblem of the Fall; at once the blazon of creation and the architect of evil.

For all its meditative remoteness, the poem contains a true moral concern and the hot spark of prophecy. It returns to that larger text—also a prophetic vision—seen by the Large Red Man Reading. Because he is alive and breathing, because he can read, the Red Man suddenly understands what has been revealed:

> And laughed, as he sat there reading, from out the purple tabulae,
> The outlines of being and its expressings, the syllables of its law:
> *Poesis, poesis,* the literal characters, the vatic lines.   (CP, 424)

Chapter 6

Enough

Follow after, O my companion, my fellow, my self,
Sister and solace, brother and delight.   STEVENS

That light we see is burning in my hall:
How farre that little candell throwes his beames!
So shines a good deed in a naughty world.
THE MERCHANT OF VENICE

FINAL SOLILOQUY OF THE INTERIOR PARAMOUR first appeared in the Spring 1951 issue of the *Hudson Review*. Stevens liked the poem, and with the encouragement of Marianne Moore chose it to "wind up the English book" (Faber and Faber's *Selected Poems*, 1953).[1] *Final Soliloquy* is also the culminating poem of the star-candle group. In it, star blaze and candle flame are joined together simply as Light. Perhaps for the first time, in this very late poem, we are permitted to hear the poet's interior voice directly. Stevens's paramour speaks out in a vocative that is also an imperative, the first verse echoing the first spoken words in Genesis, the first sentence reenacting the first creative acts—light out of darkness, the world projected from thought into word into being:

> Light the first light of evening, as in a room
> In which we rest and, for small reason, think
> The world imagined is the ultimate good.
>
> This is, therefore, the intensest rendezvous.
> It is in that thought that we collect ourselves,
> Out of all the indifferences, into one thing:
>
> Within a single thing, a single shawl
> Wrapped tightly round us, since we are poor, a warmth,
> A light, a power, the miraculous influence.

> Here, now, we forget each other and ourselves.
> We feel the obscurity of an order, a whole,
> A knowledge, that which arranged the rendezvous.
>
> Within its vital boundary, in the mind.
> We say God and the imagination are one . . .
> How high that highest candle lights the dark.
>
> Out of this same light, out of the central mind,
> We make a dwelling in the evening air,
> In which being there together is enough.   (CP, 524)

The poem shimmers. Its exquisitely simple language, the clarity and directness of the voice, the unusually ordered syntax all suggest a piece forged slowly over a lifetime, the intensity of the refiner's fire. Not only are human and divine emblems of creation, candle and star, sacramentally collected into one thing, but *Final Soliloquy* is the only poem in the canon that resolves in complete sufficiency. As might be expected in Stevens, it is not synthesis or fusion but the precise articulation of the inner presence that is felt to be *enough*. Thus the fact of copresence appears to be the proper end, the ἐντελέχεια of the poem. In Aristotelian terms, the actualization of the paramour makes *Final Soliloquy* a final cause; a complex entity has fully become that which was in it to be.

Stevens cross-harmonizes meditative and lyric modes in this poem. It develops as a contemplative exercise or prayer, but also as a hymn of praise. The poem's sacramental character stems from the centrally located "miraculous influence" irradiating the couple with its light and power, and from the notion of a "central mind." Its secular dimension *and* the poem's ascetic quality are expressed in humble objects, the idea of poverty, the chastened lexis, and the transparency of the surroundings. A look at the schematic content and at formal structure shows how this works.

Final Soliloquy divides into eight end-stopped sentences that vary in length from one to five lines of verse. In consecutive order the pattern reads: 3–1–5–1–2–1–2–3. Very roughly, the content breaks down as follows:

Sentence one (3 verses): the scene is dusk. A voice asks another to produce a light "as in" a room where two people sit in peaceful awareness of each other's company. The light might be a candle or lamp.

Sentence two (1 verse): *This* is said to be a climactic encounter. The ostensive indicates the coordination of here-now as much as the closeness of the couple. *This* also refers to the making of the poem itself.

Sentence three (5 verses): the profound communion, which makes things seem ultimately good, unites the two beings who are distinct in themselves (*reason* and *imagination* have been introduced in the first stanza as emblems of opposition). This communion is experienced as a kind of nakedness. The sense of possessing nothing but the other's closeness becomes a sheltering knowledge. The joined pair have become "Two in a deep-founded sheltering, friend and dear friend" (*CP*, 521). To this humble state comes a miraculous inflowing of divine energy and illumination.

Sentence four (1 verse): a mystical present-Presence is established; awareness of separate identity is relinquished.

Sentence five (2 verses): the dyadic being becomes conscious of a design, a prescient order of things. This section contains the emotional center of the poem, expressed as the crossing of a boundary: "We feel . . . knowledge . . . in the mind."

Sentence six (1 verse): the visionary experience is confined within the mind. The sentence fragment is to the final full sentence as *mind* is proportionate to *central mind*, the part to the whole.

Sentence seven (2 verses): the existence of God and the imaginative faculty are asserted to be a single phenomenon. This statement, the climax of the poem, is followed by an ellipsis that suggests infinity.

Sentence eight (3 verses): resolution—the joined pair, conscious of a familial bond with the central mind, assume a transcendent being. Timespace seems enlarged. Like stars, they now make a dwelling in the evening air and find satisfaction in their relation with each other, their origin, and their surroundings. They have found, in the Stevensian idiom, what will suffice.

Just as the title of *One of the Inhabitants of the West* serves as an index to the poem, so does the title of *Final Soliloquy* suggest the structure of what follows. Certainly the title prepares us for the poem's aural, or phonic, virtuosity, its balance of flow and articulation (the title words must be said aloud to realize the flow of liquids against the distinctness of the syllables, like water pouring around rock). What is perhaps most remarkable about the title is that the five spatial relations essential to the poem are set forth in the prefixes: *fin-*, end; *sol-*, alone; *in(ter)-*, within (between); *para-*, beside. The motion of the poem is represented in the title by the generating *of the*, which serves as a copulative, or connective, between the adjective pairs.

Because of its high level of abstraction—practically touching the allegorical in the severity of its exclusions—the poem projects itself as a transparency, a luminous thing. It seems to float in the atmosphere like a snowflake. And like a snowflake or a six-pointed star, *Final Soliloquy* is built on a hexagonal model. There are six words in the title, six stanzas to the poem, and the verses are cast in a loose hexameter. Thematically, the poem explores a paralleled numerical relation. The pair, or dyad, is placed in a frame of relation to a third larger being. What the couple is, and then becomes, can be expressed as a proportion: two is to three. The two, who resolve "into one thing," relate to the trinitarian notion of the three-in-one being, also "a whole." The eighteen lines of verse are arranged in the familiar tercets of Stevens's later period, six sets of three-liners. In short, *Final Soliloquy* is a crystalline artifact that owes its structure to the first perfect number—six.

The poem shimmers because its interiority has been turned inside-out, so to speak. Stevens reveals the inner presence, not only by means of the firm but invisible voice, but visibly, in the extraordinary number of times the word *in* gleams at us from various positionings: 6 times as a free-standing preposition; 6 times as a prefix or suffix (*in*tensest, *in*differences, *in*to, *in*fluence, with*in*); and 14 times infixed (as even*in*g, th*in*k, imag-*in*ed, th*in*g, s*in*gle, m*in*d, dwell*in*g, etc.), 26 times in all. In a poem that contains only 145 words, *in* is repeated a remarkable number of times; close to 20 percent of the wordstock is deployed in pointing toward the center. Running counter to the axis of internality are the three genitive chords exploding outwards: "*Out of* all the indifferences" in the second stanza, and "*Out of* this same light, *out of* the central mind" in the sixth. For some reason, the fourth stanza is free of both *in*s and *out*s—nor does it contain a single participial *-ing* or other process term. It is clear, however, that Stevens's genitive structures—"out of all the indifferences," "Out of this same light, out of the central mind"—reach back to Whitman's "Out of the cradle endlessly rocking," focal to an earlier American poetics.

Letter and spirit are speaking together here. Stevens is pursuing not the letter of the law but the law of the letter. In this poem, the molecular morpheme *in* is reduced to its atomic value, a compound formed by two letters of the alphabet. No longer is its significance limited to a free-standing preposition that indicates interiority. All through the canon Stevens crosses easily over language boundaries, punning with Greek and Latin, running French into English, inventing language games with

Final Soliloquy of the Interior Paramour

Light the first light of evening, as in a room
In which we rest and, for small reason, think
The world imagined is the ultimate good.

This is, therefore, the intensest rendezvous.
It is in that thought that we collect ourselves,
Out of all the indifferences, into one thing:

Within a single thing, a single shawl
Wrapped tightly round us, since are poor, a warmth,
A light, a power, the miraculous influence.

Here, now, we forget each other and ourselves.
We feel the obscurity of an order, a whole,
A knowledge, that which arranged the rendezvous.

Within its vital boundary, in the mind.
We say God and the imagination are one . . .
How high that highest candle lights the dark.

Out of this same light, out of the central mind,
We make a dwelling in the evening air,
In which being there together is enough.

single letters. Just so, by microscopic boundary crossing, does he stretch poetic license in *Final Soliloquy,* so disposing the compound *in* that cryptically, and with strict economy, the *location* of the paramour attains a quietly accumulative significance. Simply put, wherever the two letters are found together they cannot help but suggest interiority, but at a level of perception that lies closer to the rhythm and tonalities of music, perhaps, than to the readings of structural analysis. Thus we can best receive the *in*-frequency as a syncopated visual iteration, qualitatively "tonic" when it fits the conventional sense of the preposition exactly and "subdominant" when it appears cryptically, half-hidden as an element in another area of meaning, another lexical context.

Like her sibylline sisters who dwelt in caves, the paramour reveals by indirection. The principles of chance are her instrument, and intuitively she uses every chance fall of the letters to shape the lexicon from within. What she reveals is her *whereness*—the place "as in a room" where the indwelling presence touches, contacts, channels the source of creative power. What we understand is that the paramour exists because the poet has given her a place to be. The stanza is her room and the poem her home. The repeated *in* makes the invisible presence graphically visible, concrete in the letter *as written.* Spirit and letter are thus gracefully joined.

It may be old-fashioned to point out that this is a finely wrought piece, but it would be thoughtless to gloss over the technical skill—the labor—that goes into the making of a poem at once so fragile and so strong. For example, the central fact of the dyadic being is reinforced by lexical doublings throughout, beginning with "Light the first light" and continued in the doubling of "evening," "rendezvous," "one," "single," "thing," "ourselves," and "mind." In place of end rhyme, Stevens has generally, and characteristically, preferred scriptive repetition, internal rhyme, morphemic twinning and echoing. These modes can produce mutation as well as reiteration in syllable, word, and idea. "Imagined" becomes "imagination," and "high" turns to "highest." "Think" rhymes initially with "thing"; "all" echoes in "small" and "shawl"; "now" is repeated in "know," while "now" and "know" both relate morphemically and conceptually to "knowledge." These doublings—especially the command for light—and the parallelism of the genitive phrases go back past Whitman to the Hebrew source of poetry, prophecy, and parataxis, the Book of Genesis.

Repetition is surely the mover in *Final Soliloquy,* an instrument upon which Stevens practices with mastery. It branches and bifurcates, provides continuity and a central core. *Light,* for instance, is made to replicate itself much as one uses a first candle to fire several others. Stevens distributes the word 5 times over three stanzas, the first, third, and fifth. The repeated pronouns form a kind of network, a verbal webbing in which the voice of the paramour is contained and its identity given both limitation and distinctness. The 7 *we's* are evenly distributed, reaffirming the sense of closeness, while the reflexive *ourselves* command the force of terminal emphasis. The epistemic axis of the poem also derives from a form of repetition, developed in sequence: "small reason, think, thought, mind, central mind." Clearly, the shaping spirit of *Final Soliloquy* is in the use of repetition rather than rhyme.

On the other hand, it should be recognized that Stevens has taken care to recall, not only Dante's terza rima stanza, but terza rima itself in the alternating terminations of the first three lines. The *a b a* rhyme scheme appears in modified form in "room-think-good," while the visual rhyme of the double vowel is carried over as slant rhyme in the "poor" of stanza three. In fact, there is more than a suggestion of end rhyme. The doubling of "ourselves" at line-end in stanzas two and four, and the repeat of "mind" as the terminus of the first line in stanzas five and six, constitute an irregular form of end rhyme. As noted earlier it seems, too, that Stevens is playing on Italian *stanza* (meaning "room") to suggest that "as in a room" has a parallel sense: "as in a poem." Taken all together, the ingenious version of terza rima, the three-line stanza, the twist on *stanza*, and the irregular end rhyme strongly signal a Dantean presence in *Final Soliloquy of the Interior Paramour.*

Stevens has tapped into three great reservoirs of the vernacular for this poem. Its stanzaic form, genitive structures, parallel phrasing, and use of repetition call up aspects of all three. The presence of Whitman assuredly is strong. The presence of the Bible and its rhythms is strong. But the presence of Dante is strongest. Only in Dante does one find the lexical instrumentation that occurs, in microcosm, in Stevens's poem. Writing in the vernacular—the *dolce stil nuova* ("sweet new style")—Dante introduces Latin into the *Vita Nuova* and the Provençal of courtly love poetry into the *Commedia.* In so doing, he indicates the historic descent of language and the evolution, or nativity, of its poetry. The inclusion of the parent Latin into the *Vita Nuova* and the *lingua materna* ("mother tongue") spoken in the *Purgatorio* by Arnaut Daniel serves, moreover, to deepen and heighten the frame of the work by including the levels of style these languages represent.[2]

"The great poems of heaven and hell have been written." Stevens declared in a talk given in 1948, "and the great poem of earth remains to be written" (NA, 142). This is a striking and rather grand statement, and it has been much quoted. What concerns us more immediately is what directly follows in the talk on "Imagination as Value," because it gives us an idea of the scale that Stevens considers appropriate, or applicable, to modern poetry and art. "One wants to consider the imagination on its most momentous scale," he notes, and adds flatly: "Today this scale is not the scale of poetry, nor of any form of literature or art. It is the scale of international politics and in particular of communism" (NA, 143). We can see that Stevens is very much aware of the larger scene. Like Dante, and like Stevens's most gifted contemporaries in literature and the arts, the modern poet is engaged in a cosmic project, the reinvoking of an authentic world picture. It is my belief that *Final Soliloquy of the Interior Paramour* can be approached as the culmination of a cosmic project, in small. On a sharply limited scale, then, we may note that *Final Soliloquy* also ranges from the humble to the lofty in style, and that its total effect depends upon a carefully orchestrated lexis.[3] To see this clearly, we shall need to examine the poem microscopically. We will return to the presence of Dante in *Final Soliloquy* after a close look at the poem's interplay of language and languages—and after considering an element significant for its absence.

The French terms *paramour* and *rendezvous* had long been absorbed into English while, as Stevens knew, they retained connotations of an earlier time. A *paramour* is the illicit partner of a married man or woman (the term can thus be applied to either sex), but Stevens was aware of its derivation from Old French *par amour*, "by (or with) love." *Rendezvous*, a romantic encounter secretly arranged, goes back to a military usage in Early French, the command to surrender: *Rendez-vous* meant "Give yourselves up!" Thus, in the old sense or the new, whether military or romantic, it bears the meaning of a complete yielding of the self to the other party. The French terms, including *reason*, are set against the plainer, rougher Anglo-Saxon words (*make, think, first, dwelling, God*) and the more euphonious members of the Latin-Greek wordstock (*ultimate, obscure, miraculous, central, influence*). A word like *poor* is paradoxically rich for Stevens—it is both etymologically and philosophically loaded. It represents a union of tongues (Middle English *poure*, and Old French *povre* from Latin *pauper*) to a poet who has reflected that "French and English constitute a single language" (OP, 178) and whose familiarity with Latin stems from both law and literature. But *poor* also means, very simply, "lacking possessions"—and Stevens has also said that "there is no wing like meaning" (OP, 162). On the one hand, he uses the word for its connotations of humility, even mediocrity (and this should not be overlooked), while on the other, the notion of poverty is, for him, the philosophical notion of the undefended soul, the unencumbered spirit, able to yield itself up at last to whatever grace exists. In his discussion of Dante's *Paradiso*, Auerbach points out that "the life of St. Francis is represented as a marriage with an allegorical female figure, the Lady Poverty."[4] It is no accident, perhaps, that in Stevens's poem the word *poor* occurs in the third stanza, itself numerically loaded, so to speak, and that this particular stanza shows the causal relation of divine influence to poverty: "since we are poor, a warmth / A light, a power, the miraculous influence."

Final Soliloquy is the soliloquy of the paramour who does not speak, as Hamlet does, in the first person singular. Stevens is deploying the plural *we* and *ourselves*, along with the final *together*, in such a way as to suggest a dual person, the grammatical dual that occurs for example in classical Greek. The voice of the paramour is clearly speaking for both, but more than that, is speaking *as* both. The first person dual—*I-and-you-together-as-one*—found in Greek lyric poetry, certainly in Sappho, conveys an intimacy, a rapport, and a unity unavailable to the plural form. It both simplifies and subtilizes discourse, which is what seems to be happening in *Final Soliloquy*, and offers a linguistic form for the experience we call communion.

Finally, one is struck by the radical absence of negation in the paramour's soliloquy. There is not a single negative. True, the poem's economy, the limitations of "small reason" and poverty, suggest a way station on the *via negativa*. But the luminousness that pervades the dusk, the warmth and power that flood the couple collected into one thing, tell us that this is no way station but the end of the journey. The path of the obscure has led somehow to order, wholeness, knowledge. Seen thus, the poem projects a special kind of elegiac love relation that appears to be the reward of emotional and spiritual relinquishment—a reward achieved, one feels, at some cost.

The one term that flirts with negation is *indifferences*. We can suppose that Stevens is playing on this term much as he plays on *inhuman*. With possible readings of *in-* (privative) or *in-* (copulative) he can indicate *apart from* humanity and *within* humanity at once. So too with *indifferences*. The crucial line in *Final Soliloquy* is worth looking at: "we collect ourselves / Out of all the indifferences, into one thing." T.S. Eliot used the noun *indifference* as Stevens did to convey remoteness, to suggest both lack of distinction (unimportance) and distinction, but also—like Stevens—to express connection and a medial value. Commenting on Dante's placement of the souls in paradise and their degree of blessedness as represented by the degrees of their distance from the Deity, Eliot observed: "It is the mystery of the inequality, and of the *indifference* of that inequality, a blessedness, of the blessed. It is all the same, and yet each degree differs."[5]

If *in-differences* in *Final Soliloquy* is taken to include both linking and contrary senses, the permutations and combinations mount exponentially—meaning really takes wing. The interior being and the exterior consciousness are pulled together in two ways: they are "collected" out of, or, possibly, away from apathy, neutrality, inconsequentiality, the lack of either desire or aversion. In this bland sense, *indifferences* refers to what is inert, inactive, neutral, neuter, and undifferentiated. *Difference* (leaving aside deconstructionist interpretations) is strong and contrastive, so that the linking sense of *in differences* yields a couple drawn together, or grown together, in spite of, perhaps because of, differentiation—with all their distinguishing characteristics, contrarieties, disputes, and disagreements intact.

As elsewhere in Stevens's poetry, the effect of the paradoxical is to free the mind from the chambers of logic and open an escape route to the irrational. However the explosion of meanings possible to *indifferences* (I have shown no more than a few), and the attendant obfuscation when one considers the myriad contrary possibilities, makes very good sense if we are aware of the numerical joke concealed in two of the poem's key words: *intensest* and *central*. In fact, they supply a clue to the identity of the paramour, or at least to a part of that composite figure.

Let us look at "in*ten*sest" (line 4) and "*cent*ral" (line 16) this way, isolating the half-hidden *ten* and *cent*. These numbers suggest the relation of a fractional part to a whole—although ten has long been accounted a mystically perfect number—and we can see an enlargement from the *ten* of the opening verses to the *cent*, or *hundred*, of the closing stanza. Stevens scholars will know immediately that the ten-cent piece, the silver dime issued by the U.S. Treasury in 1916, has a special significance for Stevens: it bore the classic profile of Elsie Kachel, Mrs. Wallace Stevens.[6] Every time Wallace Stevens looked at a dime, he saw his wife's idealized image. Perhaps the ten cents buried in the poem explains, to some extent, the wry flirtation with *indifferences*.

Miraculous Influence

"Fili mi, tempus est ut praetermictantur simulacra nostra," Love tells Dante in the *Vita Nuova*: "My son, it is time for our false images to be put aside."[7] We are in a position, now, to see that the "idealized image" of the beloved, in Stevens, is presented to us through the eyes of a scarcely hidden Dante. To understand this perspective, which is in the poem, we need to digress, to describe the strong link binding Stevens and Dante. Dante explains his allegorical concept of Love in chapter 25 of the *Vita Nuova*: "I speak of Love as if it were a bodily thing. . . . I say also that he laughed and that he spoke, which things are appropriate to a man."[8] Love also weeps in the *Vita Nuova* and appears dejected. He changes in aspect from dominating master to humble traveler, a pilgrim (*peregrino*) reminiscent of Plato's barefoot daemon, Eros, searching for ultimate good. He is the patient instructor and intermediary; Love elicits Dante's new verses and brings them to Beatrice. In the opening chapters, however, Dante's personification of Love—a classicized youthful *Amore* with wings and white dress—skirts the edge of blasphemy. "I am thy lord," he tells the young poet in a frightening vision: "Ego dominus tuus" (chap. 3). Possibly, the figure owes something to the "Lord of Love" of the medieval Florentine feast of St. John, as Charles Eliot Norton maintained.[9] But Dante is nevertheless echoing the jealous God of Moses who thunders "I am the Lord thy God," and then speaks the Ten Commandments—which begin with the command to set aside simulacra, the prohibition concerning graven images.

The *Vita Nuova* ("New Life") tells of Dante's love for Beatrice, his encounters with her in childhood and young manhood; of the "screen" loves which served to conceal his true object; of Beatrice's death. It tells, at the end, of the poet's desire to write of this love and this woman in a way never before attempted, and his request to God to enable him to do this: to transfigure his language. It records the memory of retreats to his room, and into "la secretissima camera de lo cuore" (chap. 2), "the most secret room of the heart." It relates visions, dreams, and imaginings—all carefully distinguished. It sets forth love poems; sonnets, canzonas, a ballad; and presents a simple commentary on each—a "division" of thematic material. Like Boethius' *Consolation of Philosophy*, to which it refers, it is a mixed work, containing prose and poetry and a careful balance of expository modes: narrative, lyric, exegetical. With the exception of Love's occasional pronouncements in Latin, the whole is cast in the vernacular. And in fact, the birth of a vernacular literature from the parent language is symbolically enacted in the final phrase of the opening sentence from which the book takes its title: "Incipit vita nuova" (Latin *Incipit*, "Here begins," and Italian *vita nuova*, "new life").

The book has meant many things to many people. Introducing her translation of the work, Barbara Reynolds characterizes the *Vita Nuova* as "a treatise by a poet, written for poets, on the art of poetry."[10] More recently, Jerome Mazzaro has approached the book from the point of view of its opening proposition: "Dante's concept of the *Vita Nuova* as a 'book of memory'" ("libro de la mia memoria") and situated it in the history of poetic autobiography.[11] An earlier Dante specialist, J. E. Shaw, defined it as "the story of Dante's education in love, written by himself," and noted the interaction of the "three Dantes" of the work: poet, protagonist, and author.[12] After Emerson, who published a version in 1847, Charles Eliot Norton was the first American to render the *Vita Nuova* into English, just twenty years later. Norton presented the work as revolutionary, although he chose a more moderate term to convey that idea. "In compiling and publishing the *New Life*," he wrote, Dante "was making a great innovation." Norton firmly underscored the political aspect of Dante's leap into the vernacular: "He was claiming a position of dignity for his work which had hitherto been refused to all compositions in the vulgar tongue. It was an assault on the literary supremacy, still superstitiously maintained, of the Latin language. He had to prove his right, not only as a poet, but also as a scholar; to show that his verses were productions deserving of as much consideration as if composed in a dead language."[13]

Stevens was probably familiar with Norton's point of view. As Joan Richardson points out in her survey of Stevens's Harvard years, "Though Stevens did not attend Charles Eliot Norton's classes on Dante, Russell Loines . . . a friend and housemate did. Together on long walks, they spoke about poetry, about the Middle Ages, about Dante—the 'Comedian.'"[14] We know too, from Milton J. Bates's carefully annotated checklist of Stevens's books at the Huntington Library, that texts dating from Stevens's Cambridge years included Bowen's *First Italian Readings*, Grandgent's *Italian Composition*, and Grandgent's *Italian Grammar* (all published in 1898). All three have markings in Stevens's hand, while the composition and grammar books also contain notations in his hand. Bates comments that the Bowen and Grandgent volumes "suggest that, while Stevens never took a course in Italian, he set out to acquire the language on his own."[15]

Stevens may well have learned something of Dante from Santayana during the Harvard years (1897–1900), as Glauco Cambon has noted in "Wallace Stevens's Dialogue with Dante."[16] In the preface to *Three Philosophical Poets* (1910), Santayana remarks that the little book on Lucretius, Dante, and Goethe was "based on a regular course which I had been giving for some time at Harvard College."[17] To the young Stevens, Santayana was something more than a friendly member of the Philosophy faculty. He was a poet with whom Stevens had exchanged sonnets, just as Dante had challenged responses to his own poem and received an answering sonnet from the older poet, Cavalcanti.[18] Without straining the parallel too greatly, we can say that Stevens may have entertained the thought that Santayana was to him what Cavalcanti had been to the aspiring young Dante.

In *Three Philosophical Poets* one finds the aesthetic sensibility, the rational overview, the concern with nobility of language and sweep of idea—and the intrinsic concept of a philosophical poet. In short, in this treatment of the discourse between philosophy and poetry, and certainly in Santayana's major writings—*The Sense of Beauty, The Life of Reason,* the wartime *Soliloquies,* the wonderful *Dialogues in Limbo,* the meditations on Platonism, and in Santayana's formulation of "Pure Being" so precisely reflected in Stevens's late poem *Of Mere Being*—in these writings and teachings one finds the philosophical ground of the language that Stevens would absorb and use all his life when called upon to publicly frame his ideas on poetry, philosophy, and art.

Discussing the *Vita Nuova,* Santayana focused on the "Platonic expansion of emotion" that, for him, structured the work.[19] What is particularly interesting in this context is how much of Santayana's lively appreciation of the poetry in the *Vita Nuova* is critically applicable to the poetry of Stevens. Santayana writes:

> This story is interspersed with poems of the most exquisite delicacy, both in sentiment and in versification. They are dreamlike, allegorical, musical meditations, ambiguous in their veiled meanings, but absolutely clear and perfect in their artful structure, like a work of tracery and stained glass, geometrical, mystical and tender. A singular limpidity of accent and image, a singular naïveté, is strangely combined in these pieces with scholastic distinction and a delight in hiding and hunting, as in a charade.[20]

At approximately the same time that Santayana was publishing *Three Philosophical Poets,* a young Ezra Pound was also engaged in defining the character of Love in Dante, also identifying the allegorical presence of Love in the *Vita Nuova* with the Divine Energy of the *Paradiso.* In *The Spirit of Romance,* Pound introduces the *Vita Nuova* as "the tale of Love the revealer, of Love the door and the way into the intelligence, of Love infinite 'that moves the sun and the other stars.' "[21]

Longfellow's translation of the *Divine Comedy* appeared in 1867, the same year that Norton published his version of the *Vita Nuova.* The Tuscan "poet saturnine" was thus brought with forceful impact into American letters. The generation represented by Norton, and the somewhat younger

Santayana, was challenged and excited by the idea that Dante had forwarded the cause of liberty in his time. He had participated actively in the republican politics of his native Florence and been instrumental in the emancipation of the vernacular—freeing Italian from its status as a language inferior to Latin. Longfellow's sixth sonnet in celebration of Dante's achievement takes liberty as its theme:

> O star of morning and of liberty!
> O bringer of the light, whose splendor shines
> Above the darkness of the Apennines,
> Forerunner of the day that is to be!

Longfellow had identified Dante, rather remarkably, both with Lucifer, "star of morning," and with *Phosphor*, "bringer of the light"—a mingling of the diabolical and the divinely Promethean, of pagan and Hebraic-Christian streams of power. Stevens's generation responded to these several aspects, but in very different ways. William Carlos Williams, for example, enraged by fascist power structures and the political savagery that would shortly place Frederico Garcia Lorca before a machine-gun squad, evoked "the unchristian sweep of Shakespeare, the cantless, unsectarian bitterness of Dante against his time" in a 1932 essay.[22] T. S. Eliot saw Dante differently.

Eliot had published an important paper on Dante three years earlier, in 1929. Eliot's Dante was a Catholic, a monarchist, a bastion of orthodoxy, the poet of ritual "pageantry." He was the literary bulwark of a particular spiritual edifice, a mainstay of its dogma. Curiously enough—and this is a measure, one thinks, of Eliot's continuing influence—after developing a carefully worded, highly constrained argument framing Dante as the conservator of tradition, Eliot turns in his discussion of the *Vita Nuova* to Freud. "The type of sexual experience which Dante describes as occurring to him at the age of nine years," he says, "is by no means impossible or unique." The whole meditation of the little book of memory is "simply prolonging the experience." And, the poet of *Prufrock* and *The Waste Land* goes on, "the *Vita Nuova*, besides being a sequence of beautiful poems connected by a curious vision-literature prose is, I believe, a very sound psychological treatise on something related to what is now called 'sublimation.' "[23] Had anyone talked about the *New Life* in quite this way before? Indeed, a young Wallace Stevens had been struggling with quite another aspect of Dante's love for Beatrice.

On May 14, 1909, Stevens wrote to his bride of eight months: "Dante's 'New Life' is a strange book. I have had it for a long time, looked through it often—and never read it. But I know what it is about."[24] He goes on to tell Elsie of Paul Elmer More's ideas about "Dante's adoration of Beatrice" being a culmination of the "raptures of chivalry" and the Christian idealization of the Virgin, and he quotes More's view that it represents the rise of "the distinctly feminine virtues in place of the sterner ideals of antiquity." Stevens concludes: "Thus it appears that the 'New Life' is one of the great documents of Christianity."[25]

Certainly, the young Stevens was familiar with the *Commedia* as one of the "great documents of Christianity." Just out of Harvard, in July 1900, he notes in his journal that he has moved to a new address in New York. "The room really belongs to an Italian," he writes, and catalogues the furnishings: "Oval gilt mirror on one wall, bureau with mirror on another, twenty or thirty pictures of actresses + a little set of shelves whereon I found a well-thumbed Dante in the original, Emerson's poems, somebody on the pleasures of solitude and one or two musical books."[26] In April 1907 he writes to Elsie that he has acquired "a little volume called the 'Note Books' of Matthew Arnold" which is made up of "quotations in half a dozen languages. (It gives me a sort of learned delight to guess at the Latin ones; and last night I hunted all through Dante for translations of several Italian ones)." *I hunted all through Dante.*[27]

On June 5, 1908, a year before their marriage, a twenty-nine-year-old Stevens gave Elsie a present to celebrate her twenty-second birthday.[28] It was a *Book of Verses* composed of twenty short poems. The second of these was entitled *New Life*:

> Noon, and a wind on the hill—
> Come, and I shall lead you away
> To the good things, out of those ill,
> At the height of the world today.
>
> I shall show you the mountains of sun,
> And continents drowned in the sea;
> I shall show you the world that is done,
> And the face of the world to be.

Most probably, the young Stevens had "looked through" Charles Eliot Norton's *The New Life of Dante Alighieri* (1892), and it may not be out of place to observe once more that Stevens's little poem on the "New Life" was composed in 1908—the year of Norton's death.

One marvels, in passing, that the writer of these undistinguished verses, of an age with Dante when he produced the *Vita Nuova*, bears within him the poet of *Final Soliloquy*. And this is not far from the point, which is that from the very beginning the Comedian as the Letter D must have been a shaper of Stevens's verse. Dante is credited with the invention of terza rima, and Stevens would increasingly prefer the three-line stanza for his own compositional unit. But in a more comprehensive sense, Dante is part of Stevens's poetic archaeology. "Poetry is a cemetery of nobilities," declares Stevens in "The Noble Rider and the Sound of Words" (*NA*, 35). Dante can be unearthed, so to speak, in Stevens's concept of the noble; in his relation of nobility to the spoken tongue—the power of language to change and to change things; in his primary models of obscurity and of illumination; in the riddling element that Santayana termed Dante's "delight in hiding and hunting"; in the nurture of an interior love object; and certainly—as Dante describes Love—in the "capacity to laugh." Even if it is only ten cents' worth, as in *Final Soliloquy*, we are reminded that Stevens too can combine "angelic hilarity with monastic simplicity."

Clearly, the *Commedia* and the *Vita Nuova* were both, in Angus Fletcher's felicitous phrase, "genial texts" for Stevens. What poem but the *Paradiso* is in Stevens's mind when, at the age of seventy-two, he recalls "the one poem that is unimpeachably divine, the poem of the ascent into heaven"? ("A Collect of Philosophy," *OP*, 193). In 1954, a year before his death, Stevens responded to inquiries about an influential friend of his younger days, noting a salient fact about Walter Arensburg in three words: "He translated Dante."[29]

The little poem about Saint Ursula shows that Stevens had reflected on the poetry of sacral eroticism. Dante's canzone in the *Vita Nuova* (31) lamenting the death of Beatrice expounds the notion of God's desire. In the Reynolds translation:

> For light, ascending from her lowliness,
> So pierced the heavens with its radiance,
> That God was moved to wonder at the same
> And a sweet longing came
> To summon to Him such benevolence.

> (chè luce de la sua umilitate
> passò li cieli con tanta vertute,
> che fè maravigliar l'etterno sire,
> si che dolce disire
> lo giunse di chiamar tanta salute)

Stevens's ironic echo of the passage also makes the good Lord's *dolce disire* for the beautiful girl a response to the call ascending from her lowliness:

He heard her low accord
Half prayer and half ditty,
And He felt a subtle quiver,
That was not heavenly love,
Or pity.   (*CP*, 22)

Forty-two years after Stevens presented Elsie with the poem *New Life* on her birthday, he wove the phrase into A *Discovery of Thought* (first published in 1950). This late poem voices an ancient astonishment at the event of virility, the event of new life:

The sprawling of winter might suddenly stand erect,

Pronouncing its new life and ours, not autumn's prodigal returned,
But an antipodal, far-fetched creature, worthy of birth,
The true tone of the metal of winter in what it says:

The accent of deviation in the living thing
That is its life preserved, the effort to be born
Surviving being born, the event of life.   (*OP*, 96)

One treads carefully in suggesting parallels between the poetics of Stevens and the poetry of Dante—or of any other poet. Stevens himself was supremely sensitive to the numbing and neutralizing chemistry of influence. To Richard Eberhart he wrote in 1954: "I sympathize with your denial of any influence on my part. This sort of thing always jars me because, in my own case, I am not conscious of having been influenced by anybody and have purposely held off from reading highly mannered people like Eliot and Pound so that I should not absorb anything, even unconsciously. But there is a kind of critic who spends his time dissecting what he reads for echoes, imitations, influences, as if no one was ever simply himself but is always compounded of a lot of other people" (*LWS*, 813).

We may ask, nevertheless, what precipitated the necessary "accent of deviation" into Stevens's poetic genius. What was the catalytic agent? While Stevens's temperament would quite naturally lead to a theory of detachment, some part of his philosophy was surely sparked by the great Comedian and encouraged by his break into vernacular poetry. To write in the vernacular meant a strong ultrapolitical break with the establishment, and with the past. It was an attempt to establish a broader language base for poetry and literature, to give due value to the here and now, to recognize the temporal power of the general currency, the general speech.

To return to the vernacular is to reestablish the primary force of poetry in common language. Neither Homer nor Virgil had written in a dead or ritualized language. Dante, like the epic poets, would use the *lingua materna*, the flexible, changing, living tongue. Dante's poetry, as John Freccero has pointed out, is not only couched in the vernacular but is shockingly experimental.[30] Again, as Erich Auerbach reminds us, from the very first, Dante's poems were addressed to an elite, "a group of poets who were neither nobles nor ecclesiastics and who wrote in the vernacular although what they had to say was in no sense popular." Auerbach goes on to describe a closely knit literary circle that has distinct parallels to the literary and aesthetic movements of Stevens's time. These medieval poets, says Auerbach, "opposed nobility of heart to nobility of birth, and, though actively engaged in political affairs, give the impression of a secret society of initiates. In their poems love mysticism and philosophical and political elements form a unity that is often hard to account for. They appear to have striven more clearly and consciously than the poets of any other country to create a sublime style in their native language."[31]

Stevens's generation had attempted an equivalent breaking of icons and had similarly effected a radical departure from a received aesthetic. It follows that while it is surely an impoverished criticism that must reduce the work of art to a quivering web of affiliations, no painting or music or poem is composed entirely *in vacuo*. The presence of Dante, both as a poet of the living spirit and the poet of revolution, had affected two generations of American poets. As Eliot had suggested, Dante's youthful work can easily be appreciated as a psychohistory of the love lyric. And as Pound saw, the *Vita Nuova* combines the psychological with the rational and the mystical in a unique exposition of "Love the revealer, Love the door and the way into the intelligence." We can best gauge its effect on Stevens, however, if we recognize that, apart from other considerations, Dante's *Vita Nuova* is the original Reader's Guide to the Interior Paramour.

In the *Vita Nuova* Dante shows that love is the mover and maker of poetry: this is not a revolutionary idea. What is unusual is the precision with which Dante reveals a singular dynamic of detachment and internalization—the detachment of passion inspired by the love object, and its preservation *as* inspiration within the psyche of the lover. For Dante, as for Stevens, the beloved is *ingested* in some way and transformed into "the lover that lies within me." The interiorized love object remains a protected critical mass that generates creative energy. This absorption of the beloved's essence into the self is given dramatic form in chapter 3 of the *Vita*

Nuova, where Love feeds Dante's heart to Beatrice. The experience occurs as a vision within the sleeping poet's dream:

> "In my room I seemed to see a cloud the color of fire, and in the cloud a lordly figure, frightening to behold, yet . . . he was filled with a marvellous joy. . . . In his arms I seemed to see a naked figure, sleeping wrapped lightly in a crimson cloth. Gazing intently I saw it was she who had bestowed her greeting on me earlier that day. In one hand the standing figure held a fiery object, and he seemed to say *Vide cor tuum* [Behold your heart]. After a little while I thought he wakened her who slept and prevailed on her to eat the glowing object in his hand. Reluctantly and hesitantly she did so." [32]

The first American to translate the *Vita Nuova* was singularly able to capture not only the visionary power but the ruthlessness of such a passage. "The somnambulic genius of Dante is dream strengthened to the tenth power," writes Emerson, "dream,—so fierce that it grasps all the details of the phantom spectacle, and, in spite of itself, clutches and conveys them into the waking memory, and can recite what every other would forget." [33] What we must not forget is that while Beatrice consumes the young poet's heart in the dream, it remains Dante's dream. Beatrice is actually absorbed by Dante. This dream-reversal takes place in a text, the poet's "book of memory"; the narrative of the dream occurs within the solitude of the narrator's chamber; it is received, finally, into the innermost circle, the "most secret room of the heart." Thus, Dante's heart, which has been consumed by Beatrice is reabsorbed into the "secretissima camera de lo cuore" where Dante's vital spirit dwells together with the image of Beatrice. In this way is Dante's paramour interiorized.

The *Vita Nuova* is a work of closure. It lays to rest youthful ambitions and the old life and examines the reality of death. As Mazzaro points out, it is remarkable for the "deliberate balancing or blending of sacred and profane that pervades the work from end to end." [34] *Final Soliloquy of the Interior Paramour* is, in its way, a child of the *New Life*. It too shifts delicately between the secular and the sacred. It contemplates the approach of death both as a natural closure and a spiritual enclosure. At the threshold of the elegiac it posits a serene union. Within the microcosm of a single poem, it sounds the major themes of the *Vita Nuova*: the interanimation of poetry and love; the antipodes of yearning and encounter; the fact of loss, of unutterable loneliness; the arrival at humility; the interior "rendezvous"; the miracle of light. As a final gift, it exposes a long-sealed poetic identity.

The materials we have examined lead inescapably to the conclusion that the paramour represents a dynamic, a use of desire and an aesthetic intuition, that has been sealed in Stevens since he first read and discussed Dante as a young man. The term *paramour* occurs only four times in the whole of the poetry. This leads one to believe that Stevens internalized the notion at an early stage so that the term, and what it suggests, retained an abiding power and significance for him. From *Final Soliloquy* we learn something of its sealed meaning. Stevens's paramour, like Dante's, suggests a trinity of selves, or strongly experienced aspects of the self: the male, the female, and love as a mystical energy and influence. And, much like Dante's figure of Love, whose force is subject to a continually shifting focus, Stevens's less visible paramour is outspoken yet enigmatic, complex yet curiously undifferentiated.

Let me be clear. One of the most striking things in the *Vita Nuova* is the constantly shifting character of Love. Love is amorous emotion, a consumer of thought, the companion of solitude, visitor to dreams, figure of vision and revelation. He is dominating lord, weeping youth, humble pilgrim, and messenger. Love appears as an "intermediary" in the form of sonnet and canzone. He may be bright and winged, ill-clad and desolate, young or old. He can speak with admirable directness or extreme obscurity. "I want you to compose something in rhyme," he instructs Beatrice's lover in chapter 12, "in which you will tell of the power I have over you on her account." The language is simple and clear. In the same chapter, however, Love addresses the poet not in the vernacular but in Latin, with veiled gnomic force: "Ego tanquam centrum circuli, cui simili modo se habent circumferentiae partes; tu autem non sic" (I am like the centre of a circle, to which the parts of the circumference are related in similar manner; you, however, are not).[35] The trinity of lover, love object, and love is the essence of this section of the *Vita Nuova*, and the meaning of Dante's famous riddle can be extended to illuminate Stevens's paramour as well as Dante's. Among the various readings, J. E. Shaw's approach seems particularly helpful: "Love, who had discarded his 'simulacra,' says that he is like the centre of a circle. And since Love is Dante's own love for Beatrice, the circle can be no other than Dante's affections. . . . The points on the circumference are not the centre, and Dante's other affections are not Love, but these points are all similarly related . . . to Love."[36] Shaw concludes, "Dante is not like the centre of a circle: he is like a circle. If his love for Beatrice is like the centre of a circle, it follows that he himself is like a circle that contains such a centre." Shaw's explanation permits us to see how Stevens is able to connect the voice, the presence, the poem of the paramour to the miraculous influence of the "central mind." Isn't Stevens implying that the paramour within—like Dante's love for Beatrice—is not only the center of his poetry but a spark of that divine energy that moves the sun and the other stars?

When Stevens cares about something, he tends to bury it. Yet the young Stevens's letters to Elsie show a desire to identify on a deep level with the girl he loved, a twinning urge, clearly expressed in the salutations and signatures. He writes affectionately to "Dear Buddy" or "Bud," to "Dear Bo-bo" or "Bo." Usually in another letter, one finds signatures that match these salutations: "Your Buddy" and "Bud," while "Bo" is echoed in "Sambo." [37] Thus the two are verbally doubled, twinned.

In the *Vita Nuova*, Dante deploys Love on an allegorical level to effect an interchange and merging of sexual identity, and on the anagogical level to show an identification with the Deity. Throughout, one finds mergings of (1) Love and Dante, (2) Love and Beatrice, (3) Dante and Beatrice, (4) Love and God, (5) Beatrice and God. Finally, Dante's figure of the soul's espousal by Love provides the paradigm case for Stevens's humble couple, collected together in the intensest rendezvous. Dante describes the effect of seeing the young Beatrice when he was a boy: "D'allora innanzi dico che Amore segnoreggiò la mia anima, la quale fu sì tosto a lui disponsata"—"From then on indeed Love ruled over my soul, which was thus wedded to him early in life." [38]

Stevens would have appreciated how grammatically graceful it is, in the Italian, for masculine *Amore* to marry the feminine *anima*. He might have enjoyed the idea that this linguistically compatible couple was thus aligned with the power of the Word, for "the gaiety of language is our Seigneur." Emerson, who saw Dante as the master rhetorician of his age, characterized his particular and overarching presence in a journal entry of 1849. In his assessment of Dante we can see, perhaps, the seed-ideas of some of Stevens's most cherished values—including his staunch denial of overarching influence. Emerson wrote:

> Dante knew how to throw the weight of his body into each act, and is, like Byron, Burke, and Carlyle, the Rhetorician. I find him full of the *nobil volgare eloquenza*; that he knows "God Damn," and can be rowdy if he please, and he does please. Yet is not Dante reason or illumination and that essence we were looking for, but only a new exhibition of the possibilities of genius. Here is an imagination that rivals in closeness and precision the senses. But we must prize him as we do a rainbow, we can appropriate nothing of him. [39]

Stevens is careful to avoid the possibility of appropriation. What he nevertheless inherits from Dante, most particularly, is a complex dynamics of merger and interchange. One finds in both poets the ability to merge the sexual with the spiritual and the emotional; an easy intersubjectivity, the interchange of gender identity; a remarkable internalization of what is outside and externalization of what is inside. The apparently effortless interleaving of internality and externality accomplished with exquisite art in the *Vita Nuova* is perfectly reflected in *Final Soliloquy*. Careful analysis has shown that the formal structures of *Final Soliloquy* derive from a transformational poetics of inwardness and outwardness. It should be clear, at this point, that only such a poetics—whether in Dante or Stevens—can sustain the metaphysic of an internalized paramour.

Of Stevens too one might say: *Here is an imagination that rivals in closeness and precision the senses.* In its modesty and music, its quietude and sense of sufficiency, *Final Soliloquy* conveys a delicate intuition. Like George Herbert's *Prayer (I)* it tells us that at the end there is "something understood." Milton Bates has summed it up as simply and beautifully as one could wish. The poem, he says, "modulates to a feeling of quiet satisfaction. It is as though the world has been destroyed and created anew, the light once again divided from darkness. If this is poverty, it is the poverty of the Book of Genesis, with whose Creator Stevens could affirm, on the seventh day of his poetic enterprise, it is good, it suffices, it is enough." [40]

Chapter 7

Love of Place

The known universe has one complete lover, and
that is the greatest poet.   WALT WHITMAN

Here is a region through which you move, yet which moves
through you as you make your paseo; it is as if it were receptive to
the space you bring along with you, and as if all the spaces flowed
into each other like clear, green water.
    JOHN HOLLANDER from *Asylum Avenue*

THE LOVE POEM of the interior paramour is composed at the final stage of the poetry. *Final Soliloquy* situates a starlike being in a dwelling which is in fact ethereal but which reflects psychic space and corporeal conditions—*as in a room.* It memorializes a loss sustained and a harmony achieved over a lifetime, a reconciliation of spirit with mind. Thus, it produces a rare moment in the canon when things have stopped whirling and changing, where inward and outward domains hang suspended in a peaceful balance. The poem of the paramour is unusual not only because it expresses sufficiency but because with exemplary purity it opens up private feeling. It is unusual precisely because it does reveal the interior lover. One may boldly state that Stevens directs the greater part of his love poetry, not to the interior, but to the outer, natural world—or so it would seem. "A poet looks at the world," Stevens declared, "as a man looks at a woman" (OP, 165). It is no secret that in evocations of landscape, climate, season, even weather—in Stevens's poetry of place—one finds the strongest emotion, the tenderest affection, the most playful amorousness, and the least reserve:

> For easy passion and ever-ready love
> Are of our earthy birth and here and now
> And where we live and everywhere we live.   (CP, 395)

Like Whitman, Stevens moves easily into the poetic topos of the land-as-erotic-body. But a serious consideration of his poetry of place yields a good deal more than a number of verses dedicated to "earth, / Seen as inamorata" (*CP*, 484). One thinks of Stevens's famous admission: "Life is an affair of people not of places. But for me life is an affair of places and that is the trouble" (*OP*, 158).[1] To examine poems in the canon that are deeply concerned with place is to come to understand something of what love means to Stevens.

An examination of the poetry of place suggests, too, what might be called the *templar* nature of Stevens's poetics. "The poet is the priest of the invisible," Stevens writes (*OP*, 169), yet the temple is the sacred precinct both of the godhead *and* the law. For a lawyer, the temple is the dwelling place of law in a more than figurative sense. Since medieval times, a London law student or barrister living at one of the Inns of Court was said to inhabit "the Temple" and was called a templar. As a lawyer, no less than a visionary, Stevens shared in these ancient identities. The idea of a templar poetics, and a merging of the modes of vision and method, is inherent in Stevens's forthright response to Harvey Breit in a letter dated July 29, 1942: "One is not a lawyer one minute and a poet the next." He proceeds in a most lawyerlike way to make the point entirely clear: "You say in your first letter something about a point at which I turned from being a lawyer to writing poetry. There never was any such point. . . . I don't have a separate mind for legal work and another for writing poetry. I do each with my whole mind" (*LWS*, 413–14). Stevens's poetics of place may be said to possess a templar character, in fact a doubly templar character, in that analytic elements of law—method, logic, judgment—can be seen in combination or conflict with forces of the holy and the uncanny—the powerful forces of dread.

Apart from the romantic value accorded to particular locations—at times to the planet itself—one finds aspects of place multiplying on every page of the poetry. The notion of place is all over the place in Stevens, and it becomes infinitely interpretable if *place* can be defined as "here and now / And where we live and everywhere we live." *Everywhere* we live suggests a universalized "whereness" that goes beyond mere physical or material reference and includes "crystal atmospheres of the mind," for instance, as one description of place. But the concept of place lends itself to dangerously broad interpretation, and it is crucial to narrow it down to isolate the most pertinent aspects if we hope to focus with some clarity on Stevens's templar structures.

Place, Space, Topos

In general, the concept of place, as Leonard Lutwack recently observed in *The Role of Place in Literature*, is almost depressingly ubiquitous.[2] Along with strictly geographical meanings—topography and terrain, rural and urban sites, the boundaries of nations, continental landmasses, bodies of water, stream systems, heights, depressions, canyons and caves, the rolling plain, the tropical rainforest—are the senses derived by analogy. Time becomes spatialized, as a "point in time" or "space of time."[3] Terms such as *domain, area, realm,* are used to specify orders of knowledge (domain of philosophy, area of specialization), and *kingdom* signifies the division of animal life from vegetable and mineral substances as well as the territory ruled by a monarch. Without so much as a passport one has crossed over to the "pays de la métaphore," as Stevens put it, which is also the country of poetry: "Reality is a cliché from which we escape by metaphor. It is only *au pays de la métaphore qu'on est poète*" says Stevens (*OP,* 179), sliding neatly out of English into French, out of ontological abstraction into rhetorical particular with bland facility.

One can speak of place as a position or role, as a spot on the map, a point on a chart, a setting at the dinner table, a vacancy to be filled. It can mean one's present dwelling ("my place") or a former home ("the old place"). Webster's lists twenty-five distinct meanings for place, passing from the initial "square or court in a city" through denotations of region, residence, rank, sequence, and substitution, to special uses in arithmetic, astronomy, geometry, racing (*win, place, show*), and falconry ("the greatest elevation attained by a bird in flight"). The second of Webster's twenty-five definitions—"a short, usually a narrow street"—is of particular interest if one is addressing Stevens's poetics of place, partly because of its rank in the list, but more significantly because it establishes the conditions for paradox. Of all the meanings set forth, this second definition most closely adheres to the original sense of the term from which the English word derives: Latin *platea* from Greek *plateia,* a street. Thus, contradiction is built into the notion of place because, as the etymology makes clear, the first two definitions of the term contain antithetical senses of stasis and kinesis. Place may indicate a static site, a location or building. On the other hand, a place may be a passage constructed to facilitate movement: a street, gallery, or bridge built to transport things from here to there.

In *An Ordinary Evening in New Haven,* we find Stevens engaged with these polarities of place as the poetic consciousness wanders through "the metaphysical streets of the physical town" (*CP,* 472). In the second canto of *Ordinary Evening,* "houses" take on a less substantial, more pro-

cesslike sense of "dwellings," and one is again subject to a con-fusion of
stasis and kinesis, and again transferred from physical to metaphysical
space by the instantaneous agency of metaphor:

> Suppose these houses are composed of ourselves,
> So that they become an impalpable town, full of
> Impalpable bells, transparencies of sound,
> Sounding in transparent dwellings of the self,
> Impalpable habitations that seem to move
> In the movement of the colors of the mind.   (*CP*, 466)

While Stevens plays with virtuoso ease on the ghostly tintinnabula-
tions of "Impalpable bells," on the one hand, and on the figure of mind-
as-region—"Impalpable habitations"—on the other, the mind-place
figure is itself deeply rooted in English poetry. To give a few obvious examples, it appears in romantic landscapes of desire and despair, as in Shelley's *Alastor,* or as the paralyzed sea in *The Ancient Mariner;* it supplies
the psychological dimension to Lear's blasted heath, Prospero's enchanted
island. Indeed, to give the screw another half-turn, Henry James proposed
that the incomparable Shakespearean unity of language, matter, and style
in *The Tempest* had been forged for over twenty years in "the very home
of his mind."[4] The mind-place equation fathers the pathetic fallacy. English poetry remembers well how godlike Achilles broods by the shore of
an angry black sea, its salty, storm-tossed waves bespeaking his state of
mind. Milton's fallen Angel, newly unchained from the burning lake,
assesses his surroundings: "Is this the Region, this the Soil, the Clime, /
Said then the lost Arch-Angel, this the seat / That we must change for
Heav'n, this mournful gloom / For that celestial light?" (1.242–45). We
are then given the most concise articulation of the mind-place figure,
perhaps the most bitter: "The mind is its own place, and in it self / Can
make a Heav'n of Hell, a Hell of Heav'n" (1.254–55).
    Stevens owned Coleridge's poems, but his library also contained I. A.
Richards's *Coleridge on Imagination.*[5] We can assume a more than passing
interest in the romantic predecessor who, like Stevens, was so strongly
drawn to philosophy. In *Biographia Literaria* Coleridge uses metaphors of
landscape to illustrate the difference between "philosophic consciousness"
and the more common "spontaneous consciousness natural to all reflecting beings." He develops the comparison in a wonderful passage on the
alpine topography of thought:

> As the elder Romans distinguished their northern provinces into
> Cis-Alpine and Trans-Alpine, so may we divide all the objects of

human knowledge into those of this side, and those on the other
side of the spontaneous consciousness. . . . The latter is exclu-
sively the domain of pure philosophy . . . properly entitled transcendental, in order to discriminate it at once both from mere
reflection and *re*-presentation . . . [and from] flights of lawless
speculation.[6]

Coleridge now moves from defining two modes of thought to the land-
scaping of ideas—in I. A. Richards's phrase, the "celebrated allegory" of
the first range of hills: "The first range of hills that encircles the scanty
vale of human life is the horizon for the majority of its inhabitants. On its
ridges the common sun is born and departs. From them the stars rise, and
touching them they vanish. . . . Its higher ascents are too often hidden
by mists and clouds from uncultivated swamps which few have courage
or curiosity to penetrate." The meditation draws to its conclusion with the
image and idea of a river: "But in all ages there have been a few who,
measuring and sounding the rivers of the vale at the feet of their furthest
inaccessible falls, have learnt that the sources must be far higher and far
inward."

But poetic figures and philosophic constructs approach questions of
place and space in a way alien to the imagination of the geographer, the
lexicographer, the physicist. In scientific discourse place may be used interchangeably with space, or the terms may be weighted with distinct,
even opposed, meanings (e.g., place = habitable space;[7] or, place as a
physical locus may be opposed to space as a set of cognitive conditions or
mathematical coordinates: "logical space," "geometric space"). Einstein,
in a foreword to Max Jammer's *Concepts of Space: The History of Theories
of Space in Physics*, remarks that if two authors "use the words 'red,' 'hard,'
or 'disappointed,' no one doubts that they mean approximately the same
thing, because these words are connected with elementary experiences in
a manner which is difficult to misinterpret. But," he points out, "in the
case of words such as 'place' or 'space,' whose relation with psychological
experience is less direct, there exists a far-reaching uncertainty of interpretation."[8] Einstein contrasts the earliest concepts of space—the first, "geometric," the second, "kinematic"—as follows: "(a) space as positional
quality of the world of material objects; (b) space as container of all material objects. In case (a), space without a material object is inconceivable.
In case (b), a material object can only be conceived as existing in space;
space then appears to be a reality which in a certain sense is superior to
the material world. Both space concepts are free creations of the human
imagination."[9] The man who by a free creation of the human imagination

bent Newtonian space like a great bow points to Descartes as the reconciler of the geometric and kinematic systems. These points of view, he says, "are in a sense reconciled with each other by Descartes's introduction of the coördinate system, although this already presupposes the logically more daring space concept (b)."

Descartes asserted that the mind alone could maintain an unchanging perspective, conceive a "permanent place." In *Principles of Philosophy* (13), he poses the problem of a man seated in a vessel that moves out to sea: he "preserves the same situation," yet with respect to his ports of departure and arrival he will "be found continually to change his position." Descartes concludes that, as the fixed stars are observed to change their position, "there is nothing that has a permanent place except in so far as it is fixed by our thought." Place and space are distinguished in terms of *body* and *extension*—matter and measure—and Cartesian theory contrasts both "internal" and "external" place against the notion of space: "We never distinguish space from extension in length, breadth and depth; but we sometimes consider place as in the thing placed, and sometimes as outside of it" (15).[10]

The Cartesian articulation of space—precise, analytic, elegant in its mathematical simplicity—frames emptiness. The empty slate is the prerequisite for the imposition of X, Y coordinates, but there is a feeling of something lacking when one comes to consider the space of poetry. One may ask, however, what the space frame of *The Snow Man* is, if not Cartesian. A painter may attempt to empty his frame or to draw attention to the picture plane. But *The Snow Man* seems less indebted to an aesthetic, say, of *White on White* than to the logic of the void—an emptied continuum in which positive and negative extremes can zigzag paradoxically into infinity. Surely, this is the correct space frame for an experiment that entails a subtle, impossible relocation of consciousness from a man to a man-of-snow while the reader is tricked into looking, so to speak, in the other direction. The greater part of Stevens's poetry, however, develops in a far more vital kind of space—active, energetic, almost conscious in itself. This notion of a *vital* space draws inspiration from another philosophical source.

Spinoza opposed the Cartesian separation of mind from matter. The Dutch philosopher held, heretically, that extension (physical space considered as a single concrete continuum) *and* matter are attributes of God. Unless God is understood to be manifest in physical space, he argued, all other theories of God's causality are rendered nonsensical or contradictory. Reduced to the simplest terms, God is identical with the physical universe and must be and act according to eternal and necessary laws.[11] For the anti-Cartesian Spinoza, God is matter, God is mind: God is nature.

At the age of twenty-four, Baruch Spinoza was excommunicated from the Synagogue by the rabbis of Amsterdam. His unorthodox opinion concerning the corporeality of God is stated in propositions 14 and 15 of Part 1 of *The Ethics*: "Besides God no substance can be granted or conceived" (14); and "Whatsoever is, is in God, and without God nothing can be, or be conceived" (15). Stevens found occasion to refer to these formulations. Late in the summer of 1942 he visited the Reformed Protestant Dutch Church at Kingston and wrote to Harvey Breit that it was "one of the most beautiful churches" he had come across. The congregation had at one time boasted nine judges, he recounts in an amused tone, and "often the whole nine of them were there together at a service, sitting in their separate pews." One of them—Judge Hasbrouck—had penned an article on the Dutch Church, and Stevens quotes the opening statement, setting the line apart: "Indeed when Spinoza's great logic went searching for God it found him in a predicate of substance." "Now," says Stevens, referring again to Breit's division of poets from lawyers, "if a lawyer as eminent as Judge Hasbrouck went to church because it made it possible for him to touch, to see, etc., the very predicate of substance, do you think he was anything except a poet?" What this episode makes clear, Stevens's letter concludes, "is that Spinoza's great logic was appreciated only the other day in Kingston; and, still more, that lawyers very often make use of their particular faculties to satisfy their particular desires" (*LWS*, 415–16).

Stevens carries forward both the Spinozan logic and the Spinozan heresy in a famous passage that makes the physical world seem more divine than the metaphysical notion of paradise:

> The greatest poverty is not to live
> In a physical world, to feel that one's desire
> Is too difficult to tell from despair. Perhaps,
> After death, the non-physical people, in paradise,
> Itself non-physical, may, by chance, observe
> The green corn gleaming and experience
> The minor of what we feel.   (*CP*, 325)

Although the fine edge of irony chisels these lines, it is difficult *not* to feel a sublime presence in the music—the physical music—of the passage that follows:

> The green corn gleams and the metaphysicals
> Lie sprawling in majors of the August heat,
> The rotund emotions, paradise unknown.
> This is the thesis scrivened in delight,
> The reverberating psalm, the right chorale.

Stevens's celebration of the physical world is not only Spinozan in spirit, but Emersonian, as Harold Bloom has taught us. Indeed, the opening passage of Emerson's "Nature" not only reads the above stanzas from *Esthétique du Mal* but serves as a gloss to Stevens's "Florida" poems and to the entire *Credences of Summer*. "There are days which occur in this climate," writes Emerson, "at almost any season of the year, wherein the world reaches its perfection; when the air, the heavenly bodies and the earth, make a harmony, as if nature would indulge her offspring; when in these bleak upper sides of the planet, nothing is to desire that we have heard of in the happiest latitudes, and we bask in the shining hours of Florida and Cuba." [12] Stevens will pinpoint this perfection, this epiphanic time-out-of-time in *Credences* as "The brilliant mercy of a sure repose" (CP, 375).

One might ask if such a line issues from a Cartesian or a Spinozan theory of space, and surely one will respond, from the latter. Even so, poets do not directly reproduce, or even allegorize, the concepts of the metaphysician. Instead, they mythologize such ideas. Hence, we need a somewhat different way of talking about place and space. Ernest Cassirer provides the critical language we need. In *The Philosophy of Symbolic Forms* he develops a mythographic concept of space.

Cassirer tells us that the mythic intuition of space "occupies a kind of middle position between the space of sense perception and the space of pure cognition, that is, geometry." [13] Between the sensory world—"the space of vision and touch"—and the space of pure mathematics, Cassirer postulates a zone where the sacred is divided from the profane. Mythic space is experienced, in this construct, as a qualitative "difference between two provinces of being: a common, generally accessible province and another, sacred, precinct which seems to be raised out of its surroundings, hedged around and guarded against them." [14] This precinct is the *templum*—intuitively recognized sacred space—whether applied to the Ark of the Covenant, the *omphalos ges*, a ring of oak trees, the cathedral at Chartres, or to "the natural tower of all the world," Stevens's magic mountain.

Mircea Eliade conceives profane space in much the same terms that Cassirer uses to define Euclidean space. But for Eliade the plane of human existence suffers precisely from "homogeneity," while sacred space implies a fixed point, or center, that serves to orient man to his cosmos. It is, however, Eliade's focus that casts some light on Stevens's repeated references to "the centre that I seek." "Religious man," says Eliade, "has always sought to fix his abode at the 'center of the world.' *If the world is to be lived in*, it must be *founded*—and no world can come to birth in the chaos of the homogeneity and relativity of profane space. The discovery or projection of a fixed point—the center—is equivalent to the creation of the world."[15]

Naturally, Stevens cannot be pinned securely into either one of Eliade's categories of sacred and profane space, but he has made it clear that he has given thought to these matters. The connoisseur of chaos may be a specialist in disorder, but he recognizes that disorder itself generates the directive for meaningful orientation:

> A. A violent order is disorder; and
> B. A great disorder is an order. These
> Two things are one. (Pages of illustrations.)   (CP, 215)

Pages of illustrations are not needed, either, to persuade us that Eliade's description of "crypto-religious behavior" and "privileged" locations sheds some light on Stevens's affair of places: "There are . . . privileged places, qualitatively different from all others—a man's birthplace, or the scenes of his first love, or certain places in the first foreign city he visited in youth. Even for the most frankly nonreligious man, all these places still retain an exceptional . . . quality; they are the 'holy places' of his private universe."[16]

Finally, the memorial and literary aspects of place should be mentioned, if briefly, and the vital, plastic continuum that Henri Focillon termed the "space of art." The "holy places" of one's private universe are specific sites that memory clings to. Place *as such* functions as the repository and general bank of memory—and as its specialized stimulus. Although the trigger of memory may be the scent of lime-blossom tea or freshly baked madeleines, all *récherches du temps perdu* involve recoveries of a particular configuration of terrain, a particular dwelling, a particular detail of place. Public structures provided the surface area, the background, for the formal institutes of remembrance, as Frances Yates has reminded us,[17] while the modern reader tries to recollect the place in the text, the position on the page, in order to retrieve information.

There is also the rich sense of place as a topos, a kind of literary region. The unkind lover, the evening star, solitude, autumn, are textual loci, "topics" to return to as one returns to a familiar neighborhood, subjects to be "worked" again and again. Stevens returns regularly to his own familiar topoi: "the inherited garden" (*CP*, 369), the mountain or rock, the city, the skies; to the great tree on occasion; to symbolic colors; to the directional emblems of north, south, east and west. Major topoi are the seasons—the "neurosis of winter," the "genius of summer," "The Region November"—which figure as climates and attitudes as well as planetary moods, states subject to passage. One may include among Stevens' topoi the theme of passage itself, from the early *Comedian as the Letter C* to the final *Sail of Ulysses*, and the motif of quest for the sibyl, the paramour, the partner who dwells at the mystical center.

"We live in the center of a physical poetry," Stevens writes in "The Figure of the Youth as Virile Poet," in a serious attempt to define—to "discriminate" as Coleridge might have said—the aesthetic sensibility. The passage is revealing because it tells us something of Stevens's peculiar understanding, his reading as it were, of the mind-place relation: "Few people realize on that occasion . . . when we look at the blue sky for the first time, that is to say; not merely to see it, but look at it and experience it and for the first time have a sense that we live in the center of a physical poetry, a geography that would be intolerable except for the non-geography that exists there—few people realize that they are looking at the world of their own thoughts and the world of their own feelings" (*NA*, 65–66).

This remarkable description of a bridge that connects physical and nonphysical geography—that identifies exterior surroundings with psychological terrain, "forms of life" in the mind—leads Stevens directly to the point he wants to make about degrees of perception. Calling on Henri Focillon, he defines a state he would later refer to as "extraordinary consciousness." "The experiences of thinking and feeling accumulate particularly in the abnormal ranges of sensibility," he observes, "so that, to use M. Focillon's personal language, while the 'normative type' of poet is likely to be concerned with pretty much the same facts . . . the genius not only accumulates experiences with greater rapidity, but accumulates experiences and qualities of experience accessible only in the extreme ranges of sensibility."

Stevens is talking about the poet as artist. He is moved to use "M. Focillon's personal language" because the country of metaphor implies an aesthetic. Abstract and metaphysical though the interests of the poet may be, they must finally find expression in aesthetic as well as mythographic choices.

Peter Brazeau, going through the Stevens Archive at Amherst, commented that Focillon's *The Life of Forms in Art* appears to have had a singular impact on the poet: "Though Stevens was not in the habit of extensively marking his books, Focillon's is liberally underlined on almost every page, with numerous summary notes in the margin and on the dust jacket."[18] On aesthetic grounds Stevens must have felt the rightness of Focillon's description of space as a "plastic and changing material." He must have believed that a poem, like painting, sculpture, the ornamental frieze, is to some extent an architectonic form that "treats space according to its own needs, defines space, and even creates . . . such space as may be necessary to it."[19]

"To a large extent, the problems of poets are the problems of painters," Stevens wrote, "and poets must often turn to the literature of painting for a discussion of their own problems" (OP, 160). Stevens's intuitions of order and disorder are strikingly articulated in Focillon's discussion of the "space of ornament." Two orders of shape are set in opposition, the first showing "respect for the void" while the second produces "cancellation of the void." The former is the orderly "system of the series," the latter the disorderly "system of the labyrinth." In Focillon's words: "This respect for or cancellation of the void creates two orders of shapes. For the first, it would seem that space liberally allowed around forms keeps them intact and guarantees their permanence. For the second, forms tend to wed their respective curves, to meet, to fuse, or . . . to pass into an undulating continuity where the relationship of parts ceases to be evident, where both beginning and end are carefully hidden."[20] Focillon's theory of forms is a theory of transformations. In this case, the " 'system of the series'—a system composed of discontinuous elements sharply outlined . . . defining a stable and symmetrical space . . . eventually *becomes* 'the system of the labyrinth,' which by means of mobile synthesis" causes the eye to move "across the labyrinth in confusion, misled by a linear caprice that is perpetually sliding away to a secret objective of its own."

What Focillon has set forth is an aesthetics of space that accounts for both the negations and the elaborations of Stevens's poetry. Stevens's struggle to keep things from losing their particular identities in fusion, synthesis, or cannibal devourings—what I have called his aesthetic "immune system"—finds expression in Focillon's stable order. His ascetic desire to empty out, burn away, to negate things, corresponds to Focillon's "preservation of the void." On the other hand, we see the labyrinthine system persisting in Stevens's mannerist delight in verbal gesture, wordplay, and syntactic elaboration. Verbal gestures complicate the poetic space; multiple puns fill it with multiple meanings and resonances; and the labyrinthine syntax is easily visible, as Laury Magnus has shown, in Stevens's elaborately embedded similes.[21]

We are confronted, then, with a poetics that sets up stable limits and cleared space, "hedged around and guarded," at one extreme, and a density of ornamentation and repetitive elaboration at the other. But one is also aware of a liminal metamorphic zone between the two, a zone in which an inexplicable transformation occurs—at least Focillon does not explain it. We are observing the polarities and center of a *templar poetics*. The theory of poetry that does address such a poetics is Angus Fletcher's construct of juxtaposed spatial archetypes and the liminal zone of creative tension that exists between them.

A templar poetics assumes a temple as the locus of orientation. But it is a poetics that contains an admixture of the rational and the irrational, producing conflict and opposition. The templum demands an antithetical structure, the locus of dis-orientation. These antithetical modes of temple and labyrinth are convened in Fletcher's theory of the "prophetic moment." The spatial archetypes, drawn from Frye, represent the great oppositional states of orientation and disorientation: "In essence the temple is the image of gratified desire, the labyrinth the image of terror and panic."[22] When Fletcher extends the theory to Mozart's *Magic Flute* we can begin to appreciate its significance for Stevens—in part because Fletcher sees the opera as an instrument of romantic vision, but primarily because the discussion speedily clarifies the idea of the liminal zone:

> Romantic vision, high style, employs a dialectic of Temple and Labyrinth. . . . Romanticism creates the opposite of any classical, that is, structured, construction. This is not a paradox; it simply means that romantic works create ambiences, airs, climates, inscapes, and the like. On this assumption, the ratio of Temple to Labyrinth becomes critical for the romantic poet at exactly the point of juncture *between* the two states. This betweenness is *the threshold*, its technical name should be *the liminal*.[23]

In this discussion Fletcher characterizes the Temple—the space of gratified desire—as "a sacred, fixed, shapely, quiet, solemn, absolute structure," while "the Labyrinth, or maze, is a profane, shifting, tortured, twisting, barriered and always opening 'way.' We can think of the threshold as "the erring yet templar experience" while the liminal condition may be understood as a ritual passage: "the initiating experience in its pure uncertainty and indeterminacy." This oscillation between the poles of gratification and anxiety, this threshold experience of uncertainty and indeterminacy is familiar. One recognizes the contour of indeterminacy in Stevens's poetry. It recurs in tentative constructions of word and phrase, in fugal syntax, and inevitably in the visionary perception that sees each extreme transforming into its opposite. Within the liminal margin where extremes of disorder and order meet, Stevens can say: "These two things are one." The prophetic moment becomes the momentous ground of poetry. And in fact, these archetypal forms and their critical point of juncture accurately describe Stevens's poetics of place—but from two quite different points of departure.

First, the forms and the states they represent point to an erotic model—although the conditions of cause and effect are necessarily reversed. Instead of Temple and Labyrinth producing between them the liminal zone, we will suppose the liminal zone is itself the generating power. *If the liminal zone is taken to indicate the experience of libidinal energy, it would naturally generate conflicting states of desire and fear.* Secondly, the temple-labyrinth theory posits that each image, and each state, may be found embedded in the other, like Blake's states of innocence and experience. At the center of the temple one finds a maze; at the very midpoint of the labyrinth, a templum. It would be hard, I think, to bring a more fitting critical instrument to Stevens's poetics, for it addresses the structures of fear and desire on the one hand, and on the other permits the intricate infolding of opposites that is so much a part of Stevens's way of looking at things.

Chapter 8

Native Passion

How good it was at home again at night
To prepare for bed, in the frame of the house, and move
Round the rooms, which do not ever seem to change . . .

STEVENS

WITHIN THE PROFUSION of notions having to do with place and space, three ideas stand forth as having the most direct bearing on Stevens's poetry: (1) the seduction of landscape; (2) nativity, in the sense of belonging to a region; and (3) Stevens's treatment of metaphor both as "region" in itself and as a method of transport. The first primarily calls up sensuality; the second, rootedness; the third, motion. These appear to have a correspondence with the three ontological premises of Stevens's promised land—the modes of pleasure, abstraction (what remains the same), and change (what moves). As three musical themes may be woven together and yet retain their original melodic form, so each of these "place" themes governs a conceptual area distinct from the others while each is capable of acting upon or with the others. The *transport* of metaphor, for example, suggests the motion of a figural vehicle in Stevens's poetics of place, but also the ecstatic stillness of rapture.

The sense of affectionate relation between poet and planet is particularly explicit in the final canto of *Notes*. Stevens names the great round globe of earth "my green, my fluent mundo," and addresses the circular and encircling beloved teasingly: "Fat girl, terrestrial, my summer, my night" (*CP*, 406). Is Stevens's apostrophe to earth, one wonders in passing, a half-revealed notice of identification with the "Fat girl"? For "my fluent mundo" can be read "my fluent *world*" or "my fluent *mind*"—both revolving, and both creatively, voluptuously green. The analogy of turning world and turning mind will be set forth explicitly in *The Sail of Ulysses*:

> Round summer and angular winter and winds,
> Are matched by other revolutions
> In which the world goes round and round
> In the crystal atmospheres of the mind.   (*OP*, 102)

In *Description without Place*, the mind-world analogue occurs in its most concise form: "Her green mind made the world around her green" (*CP*, 339). It would appear that Stevens's "Fat girl," his Marvell-ous Green Queen, and his "fluent mundo" are a gracefully linked triad. In *An Ordinary Evening in New Haven*, a brilliant orchestration of blowing winds, changing color and light, "eloquent" mountains, and a shivering dark-gleaming sea is again summed up in amorous terms: "These lineaments were the earth, / Seen as inamorata, of loving fame" (*CP*, 484).

While "lineaments" suggests a courteous nod in the direction of Blake (the famous "lineaments of desire"), Stevens's sense of intimacy with the physical world goes deeper than rhetoric. There is evidence that it begins in early boyhood. "He possessed a familiarity with his region that a discerning native alone can boast," observes Thomas F. Lombardi in an account of Stevens's Pennsylvania years. Lombardi describes the young man's solitary rambles over miles of country, noting his affinity for the mountains. When we think of Stevens's great emblem of the rock, as well as poems like *Valley Candle*, the passage is illuminating: "Many of the country roads that Stevens traveled wound high into the mountains. . . . At times, he would climb the Pinnacle. . . . alone or with friends he would scale Pulpit Rock . . . afterward meandering downward through hillsides thick with spruce. When Stevens was not hiking to the tops of mountains or hills, he was trekking below them . . . or simply wandering down the Great Valley."[1]

Impressions from the Pennsylvania years crop up in the poetry, particularly (as Holly Stevens notes in *Letters*) in poems of the 1940s. Stevens often imparts to these scenes a simple warmth that is unique in the canon. Here one finds the "inherited garden" of childhood, the home attached to the land, the ground where one's ancestors are both buried and remembered:

> The mother ties the hair-ribbons of the child
> And she has peace. *My Jacomyntje!*
> *Your great-grandfather was an Indian fighter.*   (*CP*, 369)

Under the most unlikely titles one is introduced to the particulars of rural Pennsylvania at the turn of the century: "The cool sun of the Tulpehocken" (*CP*, 369); the bass that "lie deep" in the Perkiomen, "looking ahead, upstream" (*CP*, 356); the "puddles of Swatara / And Schuylkill" (*CP*, 455); the hay "Baked through long days" and "piled in mows" in the Oley Valley (*CP*, 374). The "natural tower of all the world" in *Credences* owes something, surely, to the "Tower" of Mount Penn that Stevens climbed when he was nineteen,[2] while the chilled retrospect of *The Auroras of Autumn* contains more than Stevens's "master of the maze" and the nest "where the serpent lives." It contains scenes of ghostly warmth: "The mother's face, / The purpose of the poem, fills the room. / They are together, here, and it is warm" (*CP*, 413). This is Stevens's version of "memory mixed with desire," remembrance tinged with nostalgia. It is genuine sentiment, genuinely devoid of sentimentality.

"These lineaments were the earth, / Seen as inamorata . . ." Stevens's sense of intimacy with the physical world bespeaks an affair of long standing, and an intensely private affair. A letter to Elsie some eighteen months before their marriage describes a "before breakfast" tramp in the woods near East Orange. "There was pussy-willow everywhere—and mud and mist, today. The wind drove the mist in sheets over the fields. . . . Once I stopped and smelled the earth and the rain and looked about me—and recognized it all as the face of my dearest friend." What strikes one is that Stevens presents this muddy ground, this March weather, to his bride-to-be, not merely as seductive but as a serious rival for his affections: "The sheets of mist, the trees swallowed up at a little distance . . . the driving cold wind, the noisy solitude, the clumps of ice and patches of snow— the little wilderness all my own, shared with nobody, not even with you— it made me myself. It was friendly, so much deeper than anything else could be" (*LWS*, 98–99). This full-hearted communion in the "noisy solitude" of a March woods can be "shared with nobody, not even with you," Stevens tells the girl he plans to marry. It is a possessive passion, the claiming of a "little wilderness all my own."

What should not be passed over in Stevens's letter to Elsie are his impressions of friendliness and of ownership. Here we see the conjunction of two major themes, for precisely these attributes of the seductive landscape—possession and friendliness—constitute the primal sense of belonging in, or to, a place. The feeling that a place is one's own and friendly is the essential condition of nativeness, and, it may be, a precondition of identity. To the young Stevens at least, the experience of the terrain as "all my own"—even temporarily—seems to have been enough to have "made me myself."

The idea of nativity opens out in Stevens's poetry from a pointlike center into expanding rings or ripples, changing as it does from a stabilizing to a dynamic force. Native feeling moves from the boyhood world to the idea of existence on the planet as a thinking human being to the adopted region of the mature years. And always, thoughts of place initiate dynamic transfers: the notion of *where one lives* skips in and out of the physical world and glides into the geography of metaphor. At the heart of things is the almost animal sense of *home*. There is a strength, a folklore, a powerful mythology that attaches to the particular region, a visceral relation to home territory. John N. Serio has discerningly cited Stevens's appreciation of the poems of John Crow Ransom. Taking into account Stevens's usual reserve and lawyerlike neutrality, it is almost unnerving to enter into the passion of his attachment to place: "One turns with something like ferocity toward a land that one loves, to which one is really and essentially native, to demand that it surrender, reveal, that in itself which one loves. . . . One's cry of O Jerusalem becomes little by little a cry of something a little nearer and nearer until at last one cries out to a living name, a living place, a living thing" (*OP*, 260). One is reminded that while the poem is always the "cry of its occasion" for Stevens, the maker of the poem remains "the intelligence of his soil."

Stevens's poetry is studded with place-names that are part of the map of America. Many refer to the eastern seaboard, from Monhegan and Pemaquid down to Indian River and Key West. The ranging walks of the young man exploring the Pennsylvania countryside—hiking in the Canadian Rockies during college vacation—are paralleled in maturity by the travels of the insurance lawyer sent to investigate bond claims in various states. Stevens loved to vacation in Florida where the tropical heat and color, flora and fauna, sea surface and cloud structures presented a stimulating contrast to northern scenes: "rings in the nets around the racks by the docks of Indian River," and "the red-bird breasting the orange-trees" (*CP*, 112); "pine and coral and coraline sea" (*CP*, 117); "lights in the fishing boats at anchor" off Key West (*CP*, 130); "The big-finned palm / And green vine angering for life . . . the young alligator" (*CP*, 95). The early poem *O Florida, Venereal Soil* adds an ominous note to the catalogue of the South: "Convulvolus and coral / Buzzards and live-moss," "crayfish," and "corpses," alternate with "bougainvilleas" and "the guitar." [3]

Much as he loves the South, home territory exerts an intense pull on the poet. In 1955, the year of his death, Stevens wrote a short piece about his adopted region. A trip by rail from Hartford to Boston stands in contrast to all things tropical, but Stevens describes the austerity, and the monotony, of the late winter landscape with the same precision he accords its fragile beauty: "Everything seemed gray, bleached and derelict. . . . The soil everywhere seemed thin and difficult, and every cutting and open pit disclosed gravel and rocks in which only the young pine trees seemed to do well" (*OP*, 295). But he begins to see farms, cow barns, apple and peach orchards, and to reflect upon the approach of the "spare" New England spring: "The man who loves . . . the spare region of Connecticut, loves it precisely because of the spare colors, the thin light, the delicacy and slightness and beauty of the place. The dry grass on the thin surface would soon change to a lime-like green and later to an emerald brilliance in a sunlight never too full" (*OP*, 295). Stevens concludes, "It is not that I am a native, but that I feel like one," and he observes that "coming home" is an experience that "nothing can ever change or remove" (*OP*, 296).

John Malcolm Brinnin, introducing Stevens at a reading of his poetry at the YMHA in 1954, observed that one had to read Wallace Stevens to know what America was like. Peter Brazeau records Brinnin's remarks: "When you're very young and you come to Wallace Stevens and you begin to look at those sources, they seem all to come out of a European connection—except for a few little programmatic jars in Tennessee, or whatnot. But after a while . . . I began to see that this guy was as American as Walt Whitman or Frank Lloyd Wright or Gertrude [Stein]—or any of our home-grown, impossible people. That cranky, marvelous genius is really an American thing." Brinnin concludes that "it has something to do with both inheriting Europe and getting rid of it."[4]

In this, Brinnin is absolutely on target. For Stevens, the richly diverse European inheritance must be absorbed into the cranky American genius before it can be transmuted, or turned away from. Certainly for the young Stevens, the idea of nativity continues to expand. "Belonging" ripples out from a regional to a global sense of citizenship. This notion of expanded citizenship, with its socioeconomic overtones of independence and free exchange between nations, is expressed in Goethe's notion of *Der Weltbürger* in *Hermann und Dorothea* (1797)—the "citizen of the world."[5] It is a citizenship framed in the French Revolution's triad of *liberté, égalité, fraternité*. Its code was not "God and Country" but "Humanity"; its ethic, a civilized, humane commerce with others.

But the notion of world citizenship extends from purely political and military issues to the idea of an international fraternity of art and thought. Stevens reflects this latter meaning, although it is my impression that he intends the other senses as well, in *The Man with the Blue Guitar* (1936) when he claims the right to think as a "native in the world":

> I am a native in this world
> And think in it as a native thinks,

Gesu, not native of a mind
Thinking the thoughts I call my own,

Native, a native in the world
And like a native think in it.   (*CP*, 180)

Is this a dialectic involving the right to live where one pleases and think
as one chooses? Or does it, perhaps, take up a Heideggerian kind of challenge—that a thinking being must strive to attain an authentic being-in-
the-world? From such a position, the very fact of *dwelling* necessarily
conducts one to the act of *thinking*. On the other hand, Stevens may be
strumming a variation on a theme by Coleridge in these verses from *Blue
Guitar*, the belief that great poetry requires serious thought. The romantic
compressed this idea into a phrase: "native Passion." "The truth is," wrote
Coleridge, reassessing a poet of whom he had once thought highly,
"Bowles has indeed the *sensibility* of a poet; but he has not the *Passion* of
a great poet. . . . He has not native Passion, because he is not a
Thinker."[6]

Perhaps Stevens's verses on belonging and thinking, in *Blue Guitar*,
should not be ascribed to any single philosophic stance. What remains
perfectly clear is that the word *native* is repeated six times in as many
lines, while the changing forms of *to think* ("think . . . thinks . . . thinking . . . thoughts") occur with almost the same frequency. Here we may
recognize another thematic nexus, as the sense of nativity moves between
the "Cis-Alpine" and "Trans-Alpine" ranges of thought, although Stevens's thinker is blessed with synoptic vision: "The pensive man . . .
He sees that eagle float / For which the intricate Alps are a single nest"
(*CP*, 216).

Coleridge's "native Passion," the philosophical poet's ferocity of response, skyrockets into an "exhilaration of changes," Stevens's motive for
metaphor. This is the mode of transport, of delight, and of vision. The
sense of belonging becomes detached from "a living name, a living place,
a living thing"—from the physical, phenomenal universe—and attaches
to familiar topoi or to unfamiliar "things beyond resemblance." One has
arrived at the realm of metaphor, the poet's country of invisible bridges,
where nativity no longer means stability, rootedness, the Home Office,
but instantaneous motion, lightning-flash conversion; where a thing exists
as itself at the same precise moment it transforms into another thing, and
continues its primary existence. One is in a *paysage*, that is to say, where
ordinary continuities of time and space are suspended, where the command to "Beam me up, Scottie!" effects an instantaneous transfer and

reformation of particles. It is a place of formidable creative energies, disciplined by an elementary "A B C" proposition and remaining, eerily, a mystery. "We laymen have always wondered greatly," Freud remarked, "how that strange being, the poet, comes by his material. What makes him able to carry us with him in such a way and to arouse emotions in us of which we thought ourselves perhaps not even capable?"[7] Stevens's country of metaphor suggests a ground where this happens, a place where "nativity" truly means bringing to birth in the wonderful; a place, says Stevens in *The Motive for Metaphor,*

> Where you yourself were never quite yourself
> And did not want nor have to be,
>
> Desiring the exhilarations of changes:
> The motive for metaphor, shrinking from
> The weight of primary noon,
> The A B C of being,
>
> The ruddy temper, the hammer
> Of red and blue, the hard sound—
> Steel against intimation—the sharp flash,
> The vital, arrogant, fatal, dominant X.   (*CP,* 288)

Vendler has recorded the sense of loss felt in the opening measures, and the "harshness" of this poem[8]—but not the exhilaration of change that closes *The Motive for Metaphor* on a *dominant* chord. This is the hardware of the uncanny—"Steel against intimation"—a universe hammered out of syllable and sound. It seems to me, although I do not know exactly why, that an anecdote recounted by Delmore Schwartz serves as the best gloss of Stevens's motivations for metaphor. Perhaps because it is as far from the "weight of primary noon" as one can get. Perhaps because it records the quality of experience that Stevens spoke of as "accessible only in the extreme ranges of sensibility"—the sensibility of genius. "In 1936," the younger poet recalls, "I first heard Wallace Stevens . . . read his poetry at Harvard: it was the first time Stevens had ever read his poetry in public, and this first reading was at once an indescribable ordeal and a precious event to Stevens. . . . Before and after reading each poem, Stevens spoke of the nature of poetry . . . and he said, among other things, that the least sound counts, the least sound and the least syllable. He illustrated this observation by telling of how he had awakened after midnight the week before and heard the sounds of a cat walking delicately and carefully on the crusted snow outside his house."[9]

This record of the occasion shows that Delmore Schwartz was himself finely tuned, not only to the delicacy of Stevens's acoustical perception, but to the stress of the older man's "indescribable ordeal." How good it must have been for Stevens, at home again at night, to prepare for bed in the frame of the house and move round the rooms, which do not ever seem to change.

Chapter 9

Six Significant Landscapes

Not Chaos, not
The darkest pit of lowest Erebus,
Nor aught of blinder vacancy, scooped out
By help of dreams—can breed such fear and awe
As fall upon us often when we look
Into our Minds, into the Mind of Man—
My haunt, and the main region of my song.   WORDSWORTH

I have a rendezvous with Death
At some disputed barricade . . .   ALAN SEEGER

EACH OF THE SIX POEMS in this chapter presents a significant emblem of place. Each addresses place under a different aspect; each develops a distinct setting; and each suggests a particular form of desire. None are simple evocations of place; that is, they all possess phenomenological presence and transcendental resonance. (1) *Holiday in Reality* moves from an art gallery to a garden; it demonstrates the leap of transport as an escape route, the engineering of an invisible bridge between worlds. (2) The stanzas of the Rock from *Credences of Summer*, taken together with (3) *The Poem That Took the Place of a Mountain*, exemplify the templar character of Stevens's poetics of place; they will be read as bold iconic representations of a theory of metaphor. (4) *The Man on the Dump* supplies a gently parodic countervailance to the templar mode—a "poetics of trash"—but also probes the question of the necessary ground, in Heideggerian language, of the poetic object. (5) *Celle Qui Fût Héaulmiette* is a subtle meditation on place-as-cradle. The New World is posited as the snow-blanketed receiving room of Old World art, thought, prophecy, language—but with a twist, as the title suggests.

Together, these poems constellate a theory of place, while the outline of the entire constellation is visible in the last poem: (6) *The River of Rivers in Connecticut*. To my mind, the *River of Rivers* is a fitting culmination to the canon, but especially so for this cluster of emblem poems. It gathers the others within its compass, expresses the whole of Stevens's spatial poetics, accords a place to each mode of desire, and intimates that the single most primal fear is itself part of the current of desire. Examined as such a gathering, *River of Rivers* becomes the map of a mythic region—a region of regulated motion where all things flow together as in a music, not in a dissolution, but in a total organization of being.

---

1   *Holiday in Reality*

I

It was something to see that their white was different,
Sharp as white paint in the January sun;

Something to feel that they needed another yellow,
Less Aix than Stockholm, hardly a yellow at all,

A vibrancy not to be taken for granted, from
A sun in an almost colorless, cold heaven.

They had known that there was not even a common speech,
Palabra of a common man who did not exist.

Why should they not know they had everything of their own
As each had a particular woman and her touch?

After all, they knew that to be real each had
To find for himself his earth, his sky, his sea.

And the words for them and the colors that they possessed.
It was impossible to breathe at Durand-Ruel's.

II

The flowering Judas grows from the belly or not at all.
The breast is covered with violets. It is a green leaf.

Spring is umbilical or else it is not spring.
Spring is the truth of spring or nothing, a waste, a fake.

These trees and their argentines, their dark-spiced branches,
Grow out of the spirit or they are fantastic dust.

> The bud of the apple is desire, the down-falling gold,
> The catbird's gobble in the morning half-awake—
>
> These are real only if I make them so. Whistle
> For me, grow green for me and, as you whistle and grow green,
>
> Intangible arrows quiver and stick in the skin
> And I taste at the root of the tongue the unreal of what is real.

Above all, this poem forces one to question the placement of "reality." *Holiday* is concerned with contrasting worlds, with public and private space, and the commerce between them. The poem is so designed that the juxtaposition of its two sections demonstrates the leap of metaphor as it moves between two poles. The first stanza concentrates on immediate perception and critical evaluation, while the second develops the theme of erotic emotion experienced in solitude—a theme echoed in the garden scene of *Notes* ("bethou me in my glade"), in the passion of *Madame Ste Ursule*, and in the enclosed garden of *The Hand as a Being*.

Holiday in Reality illustrates another Stevensian theme, the paradoxical embedding of opposites, but in this poem it becomes a meditation on types of space. Not only are contrasting worlds—art and nature, self and cosmos, Europe and America—housed one within the other, but so also are the fluid and the fixed, external and internal geography, perception and memory. The Old World gives birth to a new kind of painting; an artist's singular vision of light and motion is fixed on canvas; an Old World landscape is housed in a New World gallery.

Stevens's own deployment of pigment is notable. He uses color to distinguish between worlds, but also plays upon one color term—argentine—to suggest their intrinsic connection. At Durand-Ruel's, an art dealer, the new impressionists are on display. The critical eye moves from painting to painting, observing the capture of light, the startling whites and pale yellows—the vibrancy of the Argenteuil palette.[1] Each painting opens a window on the world, a world of the artists' "own thoughts and the world of their own feelings." Each painter "had a particular woman and her touch." Each had to find his own inamorata: "To find for himself his earth, his sky, his sea." Drawn into one alien vision of reality after another, the viewer finds it suddenly "impossible to breathe at Durand-Ruel's" and the poetic consciousness breaks out of the gallery with its painted scenes.

Although the gallery is an enclosed structure, it is designed to facilitate passage—like the *plateia*, or narrow street. It presents a realm of fixed perspectives. Each landscape, literally fixed on canvas, hangs motionless on the wall. Each view is separated from the others, just as each is stylistically distinct. While each scene represents a natural landscape, it is more importantly the rendering of a personal aesthetic. Hence, flight from the gallery is flight from an aesthetic conceived and fixed outside the self.

Stanza 2 creates an atmosphere in which one can breathe. The reader is transported from the south of France to North America, from pale January to full-flowering spring, from an enclosed public space to an imaginary garden where vision and logic, sensuality and metaphoric play, are marvelously interwoven: "The breast is covered with violets. It is a green leaf. / Spring is umbilical or else it is not spring." This "little wilderness all my own" is alive with motion, fragrance, sound: "The bud of the apple is desire, the down-falling gold, / The catbird's gobble in the morning half-awake." Stevens gives the stanza a warm coloration. Against the strident whites and pale yellow of the painted scenes are set the deep rose of the flowering Judas, violet, argent, and gold, shades of brown and green. There is the dappling of shadow and sunlight, and a rich texture of allusion. The Judas tree, for example, growing from the omphalos of earth, reflects the World Tree, or Cosmic Tree, and with the "down-falling gold" adds a mythic dimension to the poem.[2] The parts of the earth represented in the first stanza are paralleled in the second by the most amorously suggestive parts of the human body: "belly," "breast," "skin," "tongue." The silence of the gallery is exchanged for birdcalls and whistling, while the closing lines, erotic and seemingly mystical, bring us to the final spatial aspect to be considered here—the correspondence that obtains in this stanza between the image of the World Tree and the sense of *tongue* as language:

> Whistle
> For me, grow green for me and, as you whistle and grow green,
> Intangible arrows quiver and stick in the skin
> And I taste at the root of the tongue the unreal of what is real.

When the canto arrives at its final destination—"the root of the tongue"—we see that a lingual image has risen from the conjunction of *tree* and *spring* (with its double meaning of "season" and "fountain"). The Great Tree, with roots spreading deep beneath the earth and uppermost branches supporting the heavens, is a paradigm of the cosmos as a living organism. Northern mythologies locate a wellspring at the roots of the tree, signifying the source of life and sometimes the source of wisdom. Tree and spring, together, form what may well be the predominant spatial emblem of being. But in what way is this emblem a "lingual image" in the poem?

The Judas tree of the opening verse finds a microcosmic correspondence in the "tongue" of the closing line, with its roots in the throat, its buds of taste, and its wellspring of salivary ducts. The erotic, phallic character of the tree is carried into the intimate physical functions of the tongue, an instrument of tactility. But the tongue is also the instrument of speech, so that the macrocosmic aspect of the World Tree is reflected in the sense of tongue as "language."

The flowering of the tree thus transposes into the flowering of language which, in its many-branching forms, reaches out to the metaphysical and deep into the fictive—to "the unreal of what is real."

---

2   From *Credences of Summer*

III

It is the natural tower of all the world,
The point of survey, green's green apogee,
But a tower more precious than the view beyond,
A point of survey squatting like a throne,
Axis of everything, green's apogee.

And happiest folk-land, mostly marriage-hymns.
It is the mountain on which the tower stands,
It is the final mountain. Here the sun,
Sleepless, inhales his proper air, and rests.
This is the refuge that the end creates.

It is the old man standing on the tower,
Who reads no book. His ruddy ancientness
Absorbs the ruddy summer and is appeased,
By an understanding that fulfills his age,
By a feeling capable of nothing more.

VI

The rock cannot be broken. It is the truth.
It rises from land and sea and covers them.
It is a mountain half way green and then,
The other immeasurable half, such rock
As placid air becomes. But it is not

A hermit's truth nor symbol in hermitage.
It is the visible rock, the audible,

The brilliant mercy of a sure repose,
On this present ground, the vividest repose,
Things certain sustaining us in certainty.

It is the rock of summer, the extreme,
A mountain luminous half way in bloom
And then half way in the extremest light
Of sapphires flashing from the central sky,
As if twelve princes sat before a king.

The mountain of *Credences* is a Rock of Words. The most luminous of Stevens's spatial emblems, the "rock of summer," is a framed templar image, its form constrained in a kind of dynamic tension. Full of energy, it appears to be living and motionless at once. In figural terms, it may be understood as an allegory of metaphor—the Rock dynamically embodies, illustrates, and contains an extremely complex abstraction. But it is equally the expression of a credo: it stands forth in the canon as an article of poetic faith. This spiritual dimension of the Rock is manifest not only in its parallel to the Rock of Ages, impossible to overlook, but in its seamless continuity and aspects of change within permanence.

Unlike Whitman's endlessly rocking cradle of generation and corruption, the rock of summer satisfies the principle of the temple, the place of desire's ultimate gratification. Because the architect is Stevens, however, desire splits into separate and contradictory trajectories, toward stability and toward stimulation. The Rock is accordingly various. It is a geological formation, a "natural tower." It is summer, "green's green apogee"; it evokes "mostly marriage-hymns," and is the place of refuge and repose. It is the "final mountain." It is not, we are told, an isolated "hermit's truth" as in Wordsworth, nor mere "symbol in hermitage" (though one notes the pointed doubling of the first syllable in *herm*it and *herm*itage, and its reminder that the herm is a sacred rock—both a fertility emblem and boundary stone). Most strikingly, however, and most simply: it is. Through repeated declarations of the impersonal construction, the poem urges that the Rock in all its avatars is an ontological fact: "The rock cannot be broken. It is the truth."

Bloom calls the high rock "uniquely Stevens' own, the most original of his major tropes," and treats the theological aspect with delicacy: "We have seen the culmination of the image in *Credences*, VI, where the rock is made equal to, but not the same as, the Christian emblem of truth."[3] Thomas Hines selects the rock of summer as "the most important example of metaphor in the poetry," and from a phenomenological point of view, "one of the final images of Being itself."[4] I believe that the Rock illustrates

Stevens's quintessential fiction: the idea that metaphor, as such, constitutes not only the ever-renewing ground of language but the material and
philosophic substance of being.

What does this mean? Paul Ricoeur has spoken of metaphor as the
"rhetorical process by which discourse unleashes the power that certain
fictions have to redescribe reality."[5] Stevens himself suggested such a re-
description in a statement that is both revealing and more than usually
problematic. "There is no such thing as a metaphor of a metaphor," he
remarks. "One does not progress through metaphors. Thus reality is the
indispensable element of each metaphor." He appends an example:
"When I say that a man is a god it is very easy to see that if I say that a
god is something else, god has become a reality" (*OP*, 179). All other
considerations apart, both statements imply that the formation of a metaphor is a method of directly structuring reality—although neither one
defines reality.

Stevens's poetic sermon on the mount is not, in fact, a metaphor of
metaphor. It allegorizes this figure, classically expressed as the "perception
of similitude in dissimilitude." The conditions of transformation and passage that obtain in the poem derive, in a way, from the word itself (Gr.
meta-, over, and *pherein*, to bear), literally "to carry over"—transference,
transport. The stanzas on the rock convey the utterly stable and the subtly
changing, all the way from the domain of sense perception to the plane
of the sublime, from "the visible" and "the audible" to "Things certain
sustaining us in certainty." The Rock is the great connector; and, in its
way like the Cosmic Tree, it is the slowly revolving "axis of everything":

> It rises from land and sea and covers them.
> It is a mountain half way green and then,
> The other immeasurable half, such rock
> As placid air becomes.

Like the visionary Rock that forms its subject, the canto—the Rock
of Words—moves from a physical to a metaphysical plane and continues
into a realm of light. Each stage is a demarcation and a threshold. But the
Rock "cannot be broken." It solidly connects the earth and sea below to
the sky above. Just as solidly, it holds them apart and divides the green
half from the other immeasurable half. In Focillon's terms, the emblem
"treats space according to its own needs, defines space, and even creates
. . . such space as may be necessary to it." Like metaphor itself, then,
Stevens's Rock joins together and holds apart dissimilar elements: the "axis
of everything" is a *bridge*. In one continuous figure, the Rock reproduces

the most extreme outreach, "The extreme of the known in the presence of the extreme / Of the unknown" (*CP,* 508).

At the farthest threshold one passes beyond the metaphysical and is drawn into a living icon:

> It is the rock of summer, the extreme,
> A mountain luminous half way in bloom
> And then half way in the extremest light
> Of sapphires flashing from the central sky,
> As if twelve princes sat before a king.

At the apex of the canto the promise of "brilliant mercy" is fulfilled. In remarkably controlled images, in a burst of radiance, the final stanza expresses a Dantean vision: the throne of Paradise.

---

3   *The Poem That Took the Place of a Mountain*

> There it was, word for word,
> The poem that took the place of a mountain.
>
> He breathed its oxygen,
> Even when the book lay turned in the dust of his table.
>
> It reminded him how he had needed
> A place to go to in his own direction,
>
> How he had recomposed the pines,
> Shifted the rocks and picked his way among clouds,
>
> For the outlook that would be right,
> Where he would be complete in an unexplained completion:
>
> The exact rock where his inexactnesses
> Would discover, at last, the view toward which they had edged,
>
> Where he could lie and, gazing down at the sea,
> Recognize his unique and solitary home.

Were it not so calm, the opening of this poem would have the effect of an explosion. Were it not so matter-of-fact, it would suggest a rhetorical equivalent to the theory of the big bang, the singular event. As its title declares—right up front—*The Poem That Took the Place of a Mountain* is *the* textbook example of Stevens's theory of metaphor. In it, place figures as the locus of transfer, substitution, re-placement. And, unlike any other poem in the canon, *The Poem* serves both as literary autobiography and as an allegorical narrative of ascent.

An allegory is clearly in progress as the poet-pilgrim climbs the mountain, arriving finally at "The exact rock" "Where he could lie and, gazing down at the sea, / Recognize his unique and solitary home." While the poem is a model of order, its diction beautifully restrained, its sequence a measured progress, it comes as close to a revelation of the *un-canny* as a Stevens poem will get. It embodies Freud's reading of *Unheimlich:* the emergence of the unfamiliar from what was once familiar; the sudden, creepy presence of the alien and unaccountable, sprung from an earlier substratum of the homelike, the warm and familial, which has been repressed or forgotten.[6] Indeed, the idea of home is central to Stevens's poem, almost literally its alpha and omega. *Home* is the last word of the poem, but what a strange double image it raises: Is it the place one has come to? Or the place one gazes back at?

The poem feels uncanny because it mixes elements of strangeness with ordinary things. What sort of labor is it to have "recomposed the pines, / Shifted the rocks and picked his way among clouds"? The temporal coloration reinforces the sense of the uncanny: memory figures in a sharply immediate present, while the central symbol—the book within the poem—suggests a timeless continuity.

A literal reading (the tautology is meant to underscore the sense of "the letter" in *literal*) derives from the book on the dusty table. It directs one not only to a reader but to a reading. The overturned book can be thought of as the interior *object* of the poem, its inner meaning or point. Certainly, the book-within-the-poem is a carefully positioned device or emblem—a work of art within the work of art. Like the shield of Achilles, or the "wroughten cup" of the Idyll, or the painting in Longus, or the play within the play in *Hamlet*, it contains the surrounding work in microcosm.

At the same time, the book on the table is the object that seems most real, the one thing we tend to think "true." What would be more natural than for a poet like Stevens to reflect awhile on the book he has been reading, after turning it face-down to "save the place"? Leslie Tucker, a business associate, recalls the site of Stevens's late-night readings: "He had a bedroom area that was furnished up like a library and a sitting room, and he spent most of his time in there, reading nights. He had a nice desk in there, lamps and a sitting chair . . . loads of books; he read almost all the time."[7] Peter Brazeau adds that, according to his daughter, "at home the poet did not compose at a desk but, rather, wrote sitting in an easy chair." The overturned book on the table next to the chair must have been a common sight in Stevens's study. But the table in the poem is *dusty*, which points to the past and to memory.

The book in the poem is related, I think, to a real emblem and a real book. The seal of Harvard University is composed of three books with the legend VE-RI-TAS inscribed upon them, syllable by syllable. Until 1885 the central, lower book of the triangle was sometimes shown overturned.[8] It was probably at Harvard that Stevens first came upon a book which is also a poem that—word for word—takes the place of a mountain: Dante's *Purgatorio*. Touching Hell below and Heaven above, Dante's Purgatory is a mountain made of earth with the Earthly Paradise at its summit. The *Purgatorio* is the central book of the three that comprise the *Commedia*.

With gentle but deliberate irony, John Sinclair noted that Dante's "Purgatory is his own," but amplified: "His imagination of Purgatory as a great mountain rising from the sea into the sunshine and bearing a garden on its summit . . . departed from all the traditions of his time."[9] Stevens's purgatorial mountain is also his own, but the ascent is lonelier. In Dante's poem, Virgil is right there, spurring the poet on. At the foot of the mountain, Dante asks him for directions. In Allen Mandelbaum's translation, "I said: 'My master, what way shall we take?'" (4.36). If Dante is the spiritual ancestor of a modern poet who also breaks with tradition—and yet observes the continuity of poetry—he is visible in Stevens's poem only by way of his work: the open book. And Stevens says of the book: "It reminded him how he had needed / A place to go in his own direction." In the *Purgatorio* Dante's spiritual father is the poet who acts as his guide and companion. "O gentle father," Dante calls as he begins the ascent, "turn around and see—/ I will be left alone unless you halt." Virgil responds, and the two climb together to the ledge, the exact rock, where Dante can gaze down at the sea and up at the sun:

> His words incited me; my body tried;
> on hands and knees I scrambled after him
> until the terrace lay beneath my feet.
>   There we sat down together, facing east,
> in the direction from which we had come:
> what joy—to look back at a path we've climbed!
>   My eyes were first set on the shores below,
> and then I raised them toward the sun.   (4.49–56)

It is true that by the time they reach the Earthly Paradise, Virgil has made his last speech and that after Beatrice appears, in canto 30, Virgil disappears, while Dante weeps and trembles at his loss. Dante is never to remain unaccompanied throughout the visionary ascent, however. By contrast, the climber in Stevens's poem is alone, except for the overturned book. Beyond all differences of scope, monumental epic to meditative lyric, it is the solitude of the protagonist that accounts for the difference of emotional tone in the two works. Where Beatrice comes to lead the poet who has loved her in every way a human being can love—but one, the pilgrim in Stevens's poem arrives at a "completion" as inexplicable as his father-poet is invisible. He comes to an overview, "Where he would be complete in an unexplained completion."

The poem, for Stevens, is a place as concrete as a mountain. What must not be overlooked is that the mount of Purgatory *originated in Dante's imagination*, as Sinclair has pointed out. Until Dante, Purgatory was conceived as a suburb of Hell; the poet created the idea of a labored, even tortuous ascent toward salvation. It remained essentially an abstraction—pure idea—until Dante realized the mountain in words. The poem that takes the place of a mountain, whether Dante's or Stevens's, rises in the country of metaphor. Its "oxygen" is the air of poetry, the sharply vivid, life-giving inspiration of the great poem. In the same period that Stevens composed *The Poem*, he wrote in the little essay on Connecticut about region, tradition, the difficult ascent, the inspiriting breath: "Now, when all the primitive difficulties of getting started have been overcome, we live in the tradition which is the true mythology of the region and we breathe in with every breath the joy of having ourselves been created by what has been endured and mastered in the past" (*OP*, 295).

Stevens's poem posits a place of rest, and a peaceful outlook. But the perspective also seems quizzically resigned. While a lifelong habit of reading and the shadows of other poets, other mountains, other books, are surely woven into the substance of *The Poem*, it is just as surely elemented of Stevens's own experience: his rift with his father; the self-imposed separation from his childhood home; the privateness of his marriage. It is not inconceivable that the invisibility of the poetic predecessor—in this poem and in general—is related to Stevens's repudiation of his father. The objection to filial influence may in reality be an objection to filial interference and may well be connected with young Stevens's impassioned refusal to allow the paternal point of view to govern his choice of a wife.[11] If this is so, the emergence of a father-figure as a ghostly presence in *The Poem* would account for a measure of its uncanny quality, at least according to Freud's reading.

But a poem can do what life cannot, as a poem can take the place of a mountain. And, as a stanza may constitute a room, for Stevens, a poem may be a home-away-from-home, or within the home, or it may be an activity, a process, a place to come home to. The shimmering replacements of metaphor, the dynamics of the uncanny, the invisible presence of the father, the absence of the love object, the solitary ascent—all come to a focus in the singular notion of *home*. As Stevens remarks in the essay about returning to Connecticut, the return to familiar scenes is more than the external aspect of coming home. For him the physical landscape corresponds to a strongly felt aesthetic, a bond with self-made origins: "To return to these places," Stevens explains, "is a question of coming home to the American self in the sort of place in which it was formed. . . . a return to an origin" (OP, 296).

4   *The Man on the Dump*

Day creeps down. The moon is creeping up.
The sun is a corbeil of flowers the moon Blanche
Places there, a bouquet. Ho-ho . . . The dump is full
Of images. Days pass like papers from a press.
The bouquets come here in the papers. So the sun,
And so the moon, both come, and the janitor's poems
Of every day, the wrapper on the can of pears,
The cat in the paper-bag, the corset, the box
From Esthonia: the tiger chest, for tea.

The freshness of night has been fresh a long time.
The freshness of morning, the blowing of day, one says
That it puffs as Cornelius Nepos reads, it puffs
More than, less than or it puffs like this or that.
The green smacks in the eye, the dew in the green
Smacks like fresh water in a can, like the sea
On a cocoanut—how many men have copied dew
For buttons, how many women have covered themselves
With dew, dew dresses, stones and chains of dew, heads
Of the floweriest flowers dewed with the dewiest dew.
One grows to hate these things except on the dump.

Now, in the time of spring (azaleas, trilliums,
Myrtle, viburnums, daffodils, blue phlox),
Between that disgust and this, between the things
That are on the dump (azaleas and so on),
One feels the purifying change. One rejects
The trash.

That's the moment when the moon creeps up
To the bubbling of bassoons. That's the time
One looks at the elephant-colorings of tires.
Everything is shed; and the moon comes up as the moon
(All its images are in the dump) and you see
As a man (not like an image of a man),
You see the moon rise in the empty sky.

One sits and beats an old tin can, lard pail.
One beats and beats for that which one believes.
That's what one wants to get near. Could it after all
Be merely oneself, as superior as the ear
To a crow's voice? Did the nightingale torture the ear,
Pack the heart and scratch the mind? And does the ear
Solace itself in peevish birds? Is it peace,
Is it a philosopher's honeymoon, one finds
On the dump? Is it to sit among mattresses of the dead,
Bottles, pots, shoes and grass and murmur *aptest eve:*
Is it to hear the blatter of grackles and say
Invisible priest; is it to eject, to pull
The day to pieces and cry stanza my stone?
Where was it one first heard of the truth. The the.

A character with critical know-how in Henry James pronounces his era the "age of trash triumphant." Stevens's dump reduces human eras and geological ages to one spatial emblem: the world as trash heap. On the sociological plane, as well as from the individual point of view, the poem is concerned with the leveling of values, the layering of time, the separation of fact from the images of truth. The dump represents the site of nostalgia and of unanswerable questions, but it is also the site of future archaeological finds. It is, in effect, the burying ground of daily life.

The dump is the most local of Stevens's spatial archetypes, the most stratified, and the most specific. In fact, in this poem of Stevens's earlier period—as in actual life—the dump is the institution of a paradoxical economics. Its use is to provide a place for the useless—which, again, may take on a half-life as a "used" article. It is, of course, a peculiarly American dump, with "foreign" exotica posed against local things: "The cat in the paperbag, the corset, the box / from Esthonia: the tiger chest, for tea."

In contrast with the sublime iconic mountain, the dump frames a poetics of trash, a satiric latter-day *Peri Bathous.* Two centuries of mock-heroic, negative, Gothic imagery, including that of the Graveyard School, separate Alexander Pope from Stevens.[12] A major source of these developments is the art of the grotesque. Pope introduces *The Art of Sinking in Poetry* by proclaiming himself a demonic Virgil who will guide "the promising Geniuses of this age . . . [to] the bottom, the end, the central point, the *non plus ultra*, of true modern poesy!" He formulates the poetics of the dump: "[The poet] is to consider himself a Grotesque painter, whose works would be spoiled by an imitation of nature, or uniformity of design. He is to mingle bits of the most various, or discordant kinds, landscape, history, portraits, animals, and connect them with a great deal of flourishing."[13] Stevens's Cornelius Nepos (a minor historian most of whose heroic portraits are no longer extant), the cat, and the tiger chest fit the requirements for "mingled bits" of history, portraits, real and unnatural animals. One also sees, in the "flourishing" of the grotesque style, the choking out of clear space that Focillon attributes to the ornamental "system of the labyrinth." And indeed, Pope sums up his depressive poetic tactics with a graphic suggestion that might well entail the disappearance of the promising genius: "His design ought to be like a labyrinth out of which nobody can get clear but himself." Stevens, however, as always, acts as his own guide—even to the bottom, or to the center of the labyrinth.

The poem moves through three stages, or landscapes: a pantomime; the dismantling of illusions; the search for facts. Beyond all else, the dump is the scene of rejection. It is the repository of the cast-off, and the man who finds himself on the dustheap, musing about outmoded "images," has a similarly cast-off character. The Chaplinesque genius loci, the deity of the place, is the custodian—not of poesy or the refinements of philosophy—but of stolid fact. The janitor's poems *are* the corset, the dead cat, the outworn tires. The man on the dump seems as downcast as the consciousness that observes him appears perplexed, but the man and the observer, one feels, are very closely related.

There is an energy in this poem, a wildness, a sense of unrequited emotion, and a layer of erotic language just under the surface—coupled with words like *disgust* and *trash*. Is it anger or self-loathing that prompts such a thought as "One rejects / The trash"? One thinks of the charming Valentine Stevens wrote for his wife five months after their marriage, in February of 1910:

> Willow soon, and vine;
> But now Saint Valentine,
> To whom I pray: "Speed two
> Their happy winter through:

> Her that I love—and then
> Her Pierrot . . . Amen."[14]

The huge scorn heaped on romantic images, the moon, the pantomime of courtship seems as much attached to a personal retrospective as to the retrospect of modernist poetics. Both the man and the poetic conscious-ness may properly ask: "Did the nightingale torture the ear, / Pack the heart and scratch the mind?"

The instrumentation of the poem includes punning and grotesquely divergent sound effects. The "corny" prose of Nepos transposes into the "bubbling of bassons"; the green that "smacks the eye" becomes the "smack" of the sea on cocoanut, drumming on a tin pail, the raucous "peevish birds." These sounds lead into the equally intricate instrumenta-tion of identity, in this poem, and to the question of belief. After all the shedding of "images" and copies, poses and attitudes—what *is* one to be-lieve, to be?

> That's what one wants to get near. Could it after all
> Be merely oneself, as superior as the ear
> To a crow's voice?

Out of the bathos, the depression, the anxiety, the fury, comes the tenta-tive thought that the self is *superior*—"as the ear / To a crow's voice." The identity that begins to emerge from the dump—the little wilderness of junk—is superior in the sense of an instrument that receives and identifies sound, resonates in rhythmic conjunction with it, but remains intact when the sound has ceased. At this turn, man and mind no longer seem detached from each other like articles left on the dump, and the emergent consciousness is impelled, like a very young child, to ask continual ques-tions.

Finally, one should note that the multidimensional character of the poem involves more than its tonalities. As a meditation, *The Man on the Dump* is structured by the intercalation of man-made waste between lay-ers of organic matter. The year's fresh azaleas will become "blown" like roses, and spring flowers alternate their layers with the dead articles of man's manufacture. It is a lacustrine image, geologically speaking, a "core" of time perceived in stratifications of the organic with the metallic and mineral: a stanza of stone alternating with parentheses of azaleas.

The dump is the parodic scene of time, the graveyard of outmoded styles. It is the place in which one regards the economies of change, whether diurnal, seasonal, or attitudinal. But it is also the communal place where one leaves the trash and retrieves useful parts. Whatever else one may take the final "The the" to mean, it is clear that the second word is the "spit and image" of the first; that the sounds reduce language to a stammer, or a babble (like the bubbling of bassoons). Above all, the repeated articles suggest a whimsical revelation of particular value, the unique identity of each article that comes to the dump—each *definite article.*[15]

Of Stevens's spatial archetypes, the dump is the most closely linked to a sense of private community and to personal affairs. Perhaps it is not ever in images of the moon that the poet arrives at the germ of identity, but rather, as Yeats declared, in the "rag and bone shop of the heart."

---

5   *Celle Qui Fût Héaulmiette*

Out of the first warmth of spring,
And out of the shine of the hemlocks,
Among the bare and crooked trees,
She found a helping from the cold,

Like a meaning in nothingness,
Like the snow before it softened
And dwindled into patches,
Like a shelter not in an arc

But in a circle, not in the arc
Of winter, in the unbroken circle
Of summer, at the windy edge,
Sharp in the ice shadow of the sky,

Blue for all that and white and hard,
And yet with water running in the sun,
Entinselled and gilderlinged and gone,
Another American vulgarity.

Into that native shield she slid,
Mistress of an idea, child
Of a mother with vague severed arms
And of a father bearded in his fire.

The title of this late poem refers directly to François Villon's beautiful Armoress, the celebrated "belle qui fut hëaumière." The medieval poem opens in an ironic vein, for the "beauty" is now a very old woman:

> Advis m'est que j'oy regretter
> La belle qui fut hëaumière,
> Soi jeune fille souhaiter.

In rough translation:

> It so happened that I heard the lament
> Of the beauty who was the helmet-maker's wife,
> Wishing for her girlhood.

Villon's beautiful Armoress is surely the woman on the dump, but she is also a character with a genuine history. Wyndham Lewis has dramatized the young poet's encounter with the old woman in mid-fifteenth-century Paris in *François Villon* (1928):

> And of a sudden the student observes a ragged, hag-like figure shuffling past him, and turns his curious gaze on her. The old woman is known throughout the Quarter as the Belle Heaul-mière. She was a famous beauty and courtesan in the early part of the century and the mistress of Messire Nicholas d'Orgemont, Master of the Chambre des Comptes, who very scandalously installed her in his house in the precinct of Notre-Dame, whence she was evicted by the Canons. In Villon's day she is a mumbling witch of eighty; her lover has died long ago, in 1416, in the prison of Meun-sur-Loire, where Villon himself will be cast. . . . In the Lament for her hot, sweet youth which Villon will write in a few years, the figure of this poor old scarecrow is preserved like a mummy for ever and ever.[16]

Lewis's point, although fictionalized, is well taken. Nostalgia for the ephemeral, rage and despair over loss, become the permanent material of art. But while Villon's celebrated "snows of yesteryear" are indeed preserved "in this black ink," the scarecrow figure of la Belle Hëaulmière is cast in bronze as well as words. Auguste Rodin's 19½-inch model of *The Helmet-Maker's Wife*—known also as *Old Woman, Dried-up Springs, The Old Courtesan*, and *Winter*—was thrown in a Paris foundry in the early 1880s.[17] Running molten metal poured into a waiting mold, and the grotesque body of the armoress, twisted into painful angles, defeated, aged, and ashamed, materialized in a shape of extraordinary force and beauty. Wallace Stevens saw the cast of the figure that was given in 1910 to the Metropolitan Museum of Art in New York. James Baird has noted the evidence, in *The Dome and the Rock*, that Stevens's tribute to the helmet-maker's wife was suggested by Rodin's sculpture, and pointed out that the title, both of Rodin's bronze and Stevens's poem, derives from the second line of Villon's poem: "La belle qui fut hëaumière."[18]

What must be underscored is Stevens's change in the title: "Celle" (this one, that one, the one) replaces "La belle" (the beauty); the subjunctive imperfect *fût* (could be, might be, could become) replaces the past tense *fut* (was); and the epithet "Hëaumière" assumes a diminutive inflection, "Héaulmiette." Hence Villon's ironic line, "the beauty who was the helmet-maker's wife" becomes, virtually, "that one who could be the little (child of the) Hëaumière."

Stevens's title expresses a wish, almost a prayer, that becomes visually explicit in the final stanza of the poem, the envoi. The armoress is reflected in the armorial bearings of "shield" and "arms," but also in the presence of the "mistress" who becomes a "child" at line's end. In this final stanza the poem's *heraldic*—that is, its genealogical—significance is made evident both in its emblematic terms and in its pointed reference to the child's parentage: "a mother with vague severed arms," "a father bearded in his fire."

Celle Que Fût Héaulmiette emerges as a double-headed emblematic of place: place as cradle and place as conduit. On the one hand, it posits the New World as a cradle of rebirth for classical art; on the other, it becomes the crucible or furnace where inspired thought takes fire again. One cannot miss the Hellenic Venus, or its Roman marble copies, in "a mother with vague severed arms." (Nor should we overlook the allusion to a million images of the *Venus de Milo* stamped on as many wooden pencils by an American manufacturer: "another American vulgarity"?). And nothing less than a prophetic utterance, surely, can issue from a "father bearded in his fire."

The poem opens with spare allusions to the two great divisions of poetry in the New World, the branch of Whitman and the branch of Longfellow. While the prophetic strain *and* the notion of the rocking cradle are expressed in Whitmanian genitives, the equally virtuoso but more conventional strain appears almost immediately in the Evangelinical "shine of the hemlocks." Longfellow's "forest primeval" echoes in "bare and crooked trees," but Stevens's tree image concurs also with the angular crooked limbs of the Old Courtesan, Rodin's naked *Winter:*

> Out of the first warmth of spring
> And out of the shine of the hemlocks
> Among the bare and crooked trees,
> She found a helping from the cold.

The note of the cradle is the note of Whitman, and the cadence of the opening lines is the cadence of Longfellow. Stevens is writing strongly in the American grain, in sharp contrast with the French of the title. On the other hand, the poem acts as a conduit to Europe; it becomes a bridge between worlds. It brings from the old into the new and so refreshes and renews the old. Precisely because it is a conductor of thought, a construct of passage, the poem itself and *as such* acquires a special significance as *place*. *Celle Qui Fût Héaulmiette* creates a liaison between past and present art, Old and New Worlds. In it, a medieval French poem that has been transfigured in bronze is turned, once again, into verse. The molten metal poured in a Paris foundry miraculously joins the new-melted ice of North American streams: "water running in the sun, / Entinselled and gilderlinged and gone." Thus the poem acts as a form of elision, but the bridging that for Hart Crane assumes epic dimensions is miniaturized in Stevens.

The center of *Héaulmiette* is the *arc* within the *circle*, for as Baird has noted, a geometric image governs the poem.[19] The Euclidean forms are shapes in space emptied of subjective meaning. They are mathematical relationships—place reduced to pure form—the visible images of a strict order. The new being in this poem develops from a point within zero, grows "like a meaning within nothingness" and finds shelter "not in an arc / But in a circle." The subsequent repetition of the terms *arc* and *circle* suggest enlargement, an added dimensionality, as a solid figure may be formed by the extension and repetition of a plane. The naming of the seasons adds a further, temporal, dimension:

> the arc
> Of winter, in the unbroken circle
> Of summer, at the windy edge,
> Sharp in the ice shadow of the sky.

While a cradle takes the shape of an arc—as does a rainbow—and while *ark* is rich with connotations of protective covenant and sheltering vessel, Stevens places the new creature not in a wedge but in the unbroken whole. The geometry of the poem suggests the imminence of birth, on the one hand, and the intermingling of the sexes on the other. A shield is also protective, and is often round. Although the arc and the circle, like the heraldic helmet and shield, divide into masculine and feminine sexual symbols, the geometric frame of the poem tends to support a subtle androgyny. While the arc *penetrates* the circle, the arc is also *contained within* the circle as, for example, the child is contained within the mother. For a finite season, two sexes may exist within a single round.

Again, infants and the very old both seem sexually undifferentiated. In *Héaulmiette*, the governing geometric forms, perhaps the oldest descriptions of space, cast a peaceful neutrality over the old woman's lament.

What this poem accomplishes is the granting of the impossible wish transcribed by Villon: "Soi jeune fille souhaiter." After many transformations the old woman has become a child again, as the title suggests. Winter is moving into the first warmth of spring; the old courtesan is restored to the time of her girlhood, and to purity. Héaulmiette, for all her commercialism, her tinsel and golden-tongued glitter, is a virgin. A true American, her emblematic colors repeat the French tricolore: blue, white, and fiery red. Like Atalanta, she runs swift and free as the melting streams—at least for a while.

---

6   *The River of Rivers in Connecticut*

> There is a great river this side of Stygia,
> Before one comes to the first black cataracts
> And trees that lack the intelligence of trees.
>
> In that river, far this side of Stygia,
> The mere flowing of the water is a gayety,
> Flashing and flashing in the sun. On its banks,
>
> No shadow walks. The river is fateful,
> Like the last one. But there is no ferryman.
> He could not bend against its propelling force.
>
> It is not to be seen beneath the appearances
> That tell of it. The steeple at Farmington
> Stands glistening and Haddam shines and sways.
>
> It is the third commonness with light and air,
> A curriculum, a vigor, a local abstraction . . .
> Call it, once more, a river, an unnamed flowing,
>
> Space-filled, reflecting the seasons, the folk-lore
> Of each of the senses; call it, again and again,
> The river that flows nowhere, like a sea.

At the threshold of *The Temple*, George Herbert warns the reader that he is about to enter a sacred space: "Avoid, Profaneness, come not here: / Nothing but holy, pure, and clear." While Herbert's *Superliminare* marks the point of crossover into a temenos made of words, there is no question that one is moving from unhallowed to hallowed ground. Cassirer notes the mythic significance of the liminal zone: "A primordial mythical-religious feeling is linked with the fact of a spatial 'threshold,'" and he underscores the relation of the *temporal* to the spatial crossing: "Transition from one mythical religious sphere to another involves *rites of passage . . .* [which] govern moves from one city to another, from one country to another, and changes from one phase of life to another.[20]

Like George Herbert's book, *The River of Rivers in Connecticut* is a poem that takes the place of a temple. As a meditation on the threshold between life and death, Stevens's poem is both templar and transitional. Defining the poetics of liminality, Fletcher theorizes on the interpenetration of modes within the liminal zone: "If temple and labyrinth provide the models of sacred stillness and profane movement, the threshold is the model of the transitional phase that links these two fundamental modes of being."[21] The *River of Rivers* is a poem of the threshold that combines these fundamental modes of being. A templar work, it includes a rich secular vein. In itself it performs an exquisitely modulated ritual of passage.

Between its opening and closing lines—"There is a great river this side of Stygia," and "The river that flows nowhere, like a sea"—is compressed the larger part of Stevens's experience in carefully chosen symbols. This includes the experience of a lifelong habit of reading and study, while the poem also acts, so to speak, as a showcase for Stevens's keenly trained perceptions, his clairvoyant eye. One has the impression of an entire lifetime "flashing and flashing in the sun" like pictures going by. The towns of Farmington and Haddam bring to mind Stevens's domestic life and business career as well as his poetry: the young couple's first home in Connecticut was in the village of Farmington; their next address, both in West Hartford and Hartford, was Farmington Avenue. Haddam is the town of commuters, the famously "thin men" of *Thirteen Ways of Looking at a Blackbird*. Extremes of youth and age also are represented. The glistening church steeple may recall the surpliced choirboy who looks so gravely at one, music in hand, in plate 3 of the *Letters* (p. 54). The "first black cataracts," along with falls, mean darkened vision—the near-blindness of the poet's old age.

River of Rivers is a culminating work, abundant in spirit, grave and gay and moving as the river it describes. It is Stevens's final great psalm, its music deep and lovely and many-leveled. Indeed, it is the comprehensive genius of this poem to join its opening with the sacred river of Psalm 46, a prototype of sacred rivers: "There is a river, the streams whereof shall make glad the city of God, the holy place of the most high." The first line of Stevens's poem describes a visionary circle: the Psalmist's river of eternal life is joined to the actual, particular river of the present time, which *becomes* "after the first black cataracts" the timeless mythic river "this side of Stygia"—the river Styx. Apart from its suggestions of "Stygian darkness" and final crossing, Stevens's oblique reference to the Styx may well be a reference to contracts and bonds. As Stevens knew, the Styx is the first legal site in Greek mythology: to swear by the goddess Styx, as the gods did, was to swear an unbreakable oath. Thus, the poet-lawyer introduces the templar mode of law into his poem at *both* ends of the opening verse—Hellenic at the end of the line, Judaic at the beginning—for the Psalm that "feeds into" Stevens's poem continues: "God is in the midst of her: she shall not be moved."

The *River of Rivers is* the Connecticut and is *more than* the Connecticut River. In a way it resembles a metaphor of a metaphor, over Stevens's own objection to such a metafigure. In this poem, however, the river is confidently itself—and not itself:

> It is the third commonness with light and air,
> A curriculum, a vigor, a local abstraction . . .
> Call it, once more, a river, an unnamed flowing.

The poem resumes the Heracleitan meditation on being and becoming that is made explicit in the earlier *This Solitude of Cataracts:* "He never felt twice the same about the flecked river, / Which kept flowing and never the same way twice" (*CP,* 424). Into the local currents of the *River of Rivers* pour ghostly waters from Stevens's past—the Swatara, Schuylkill, and Perkiomen of his Pennsylvania years, the Indian River of Florida vacations—all present in the poetry. In *The Countryman* the Swatara becomes a stream as darkly enigmatic as Heracleitan flux, a "place" as mythic as Stygia:

> Swatara, Swatara, black river,
> Descending, out of the cap of midnight,
> Toward the cape at which
> You enter the swarthy sea.
> . . . . .
> Being there is being in a place,
> As of a character everywhere,
> The place of a swarthy presence moving,
> Slowly, to the look of a swarthy name. (*CP,* 429)

Stevens's *River of Rivers* joins other river poems. Like the Thames in Sir John Denham's *Coopers Hill,* it "hastens to pay its tribute to the Sea, /

Like mortal life to meet Eternity." With Coleridge's sacred river Alph, or Eliot's "strong brown god" of a Mississippi, the Connecticut River in Stevens's poem radiates the power of a great spatial emblem. Conjointly, the poem itself performs a sacrament of passage, moving through a liminal zone with ritual intensity. The *River of Rivers* graphs the essentials of one life onto one map: the actual and imaginative, the philosophic, mythic, and spiritual regions of being.

Helen Vendler has rightly brought attention to the presence of Keats in the Stevens canon,[22] and surely the combined topography of nature and mind, the branched river, the templar character and epiphanic flashings of Stevens's poem are prefigured in the "Ode to Psyche":

> Yes, I will be thy priest, and build a fane
>   In some untrodden region of my mind,
> Where branched thoughts, new-grown with pleasant pain,
>   Instead of pines shall murmur in the wind.

Charles Berger has observed that "when Keats proposed 'Here lies one whose name was writ in water' as his epitaph, he was lamenting evanescence, but Stevens chooses to sign his name in the river of rivers because it will continue to flow after his death."[23] As we will see, Stevens has indeed left his signature "writ in water" at the conclusion of the poem. It is hidden, however, "beneath the appearances / That tell of it."

On April 19, 1954, Stevens wrote to his friend Thomas McGreevy about local things: "This is Easter Monday, a quiet day at the office. . . . All the snow that you saw when you were here is gone long since—and yet something of it remains." As usual, the poet's mind refuses to be confined to Hartford: "Mrs. Church reaches Gibraltar tomorrow. . . . She is one of the marvels of my experience, which, after all, has taken place in a very limited space. It means a lot to me to know a man in Dublin, to receive letters from a friend in Italy, to look at the map of Spain and to find that it suddenly becomes as significant as the map of Connecticut." *As significant as the map of Connecticut.* Stevens goes on in his methodical, ironical language to add time travel to his mental journeys in space—although this time he gets as far as Ceylon. A colleague has acquired a farm about an hour's drive from Hartford: "When I visit him there, in a fairly mountainous neighborhood, being in his old-fashioned house in which he has made no changes transports me in time as Mrs. Church's movements transport me in space. The difference is that once I lived in just such a time. My life in Europe is the same as your own life in India, or, better still, at Nuwara Elyia, in the highlands of Ceylon" (*LWS,* 827–28). Clearly the escape hatch is well-oiled, and Stevens can slip from the hills of Connecticut to the highlands of Ceylon—or back fifty years to a Pennsylvania farmhouse—in a twinkling. *Once I lived in just such a time.* Like Ariel, the magical inhabitant of *The Planet on the Table* (*CP,* 532), the poet takes delight in transport, instantaneous and limitless.

The significant map of Connecticut, on the other hand, is a study of *limits.* The map shows the Connecticut River dividing the state in two. Haddam is on the west bank; East Haddam on the opposite side. Farmington cannot be seen from the river, *except* on the map. While the river splits the state into east and west sectors, on the north-south axis it joins Connecticut with its northern neighbor, Massachusetts; commerce can pass freely between the states. The river empties into Long Island Sound and thence into the Atlantic. Like the Thames, running softly past the Temple and more forcefully under London Bridge, the Connecticut River brings commercial shipping, fishing vessels, and pleasure craft to the open sea. If we look at the river as a boundary maker *and* as an instrument of dissection as it travels from place to place, it becomes a method by which space, place, and direction can be clearly defined.

The map of Connecticut illustrates with graphic clarity a point that Stevens insists upon again and again as critical: it is the modes of separation that preserve identity and particularity—although boundaries and limitations naturally serve to connect as well as to define. It is the thinking of a poet trained in law. In Stevens's *River of Rivers* the code of mapping permits us to read one significant level of thought, starting with the title.

River of Rivers, like King of Kings, Lord of Lords, Song of Songs, and the Class of all Classes, is a superlative abstraction, a unique universal commanding all the particulars of its class. The title *River of Rivers* also indicates by doubling the idea of repeated *riving,* or cutting in two, which is what a river does to the land. As a Latin scholar (and inveterate dictionary user), Stevens will have known that the terms for *river* and *river bank* are intimately related (both "riparian"), and that *rivus* is a stream or brook. He knew too that French *rive* means river bank, and that the *Riviera* is a region adjacent to the sea.

By ignoring language boundaries in this title, as elsewhere, Stevens can suggest the interchangeability of incommensurates: the one and the many, the hieratic and the commonplace, the universal and the particular, the stream and its bank. Contradictory extremes do not merge in this poem. They emerge, separately, like separate images in a "duck-rabbit" picture. The reader is subtly disoriented, subject to deliberate dislocation, as in the first stanza. (Are we moving across or downstream? Is it the river Styx? Or the region Stygia?) In effect, Stevens has brilliantly conveyed the intense "border" experience described by Fletcher: "the special, painful uncertainty of thresholdness."[24] The poem's title encodes this element along with the less labyrinthine, more templar modes. As the map shows, the Connecticut River joins together and rives apart at the same time—and so is able to *connect* and *cut* at once.

As Helen Vendler points out in her discussion of the poem, the Indian name Connecticut means "land of many rivers." Stevens's great river is both a geological fact and a parable of existence. It springs from the sublime, passes into history, and falls in cataracts into the unknowable. The title, by "working" language for maximum yield, is able to suggest the poem's essential content while it alerts the reader that something of grandeur is about to unfold. *The River of Rivers in Connecticut* is, then, a title that playfully extends the Heracleitan riddle, the paradox of change at the heart of the unchanging, the riddle of a "local abstraction." But *River of Rivers* also serves a visionary purpose. *Because* it rives, cuts, severs, sets apart, separates, encircles, and establishes limits, the river is a templar instrument. It encodes the idea of divinity for Stevens; it embodies the phenomenology of a religious form. It creates a temenos.

Temple, templum, and *temenos* all indicate a sacred enclosure. They all derive from τέμνειν: to cut, sever. Partridge says, "The Latin *templum* . . . was originally that space 'cut off' or demarcated, by the augur . . . in which he collected and interpreted omens, hence a space consecrated to the gods, a precinct, hence the edifice in which they were worshipped" (*Origins,* 701). A *temenos,* according to Liddell and Scott, may be a river valley: "from the worship offered to the Nile, the valley of the Nile is called Τέμενος Νείλοιο" (temple of the Nile).

The *River of Rivers* is a natural temple and a terrible threshold. The poem itself is a luminous sacred precinct and a liminal zone—a zone of semidarkness where one feels the oscillations of fear and desire. In its symbolic aspect, the river in Stevens's poem can be understood as the purest *metaphor of threshold.* Metaphor, as Fletcher points out, is not only the dynamic agent of transfer but the preserver of boundary: "Metaphor has always been the figure of threshold, of passing over. Its symbolic function has always been transfer, transference, metamorphosis, shifting across, through, and over. Metaphor is a semantic process of balancing at the threshold. Metaphor draws the limen with surgical exactness."[25] Stevens's poem connects and cuts—*draws the limen with surgical exactness*—balances between maze and temple, accomplishes a passage. It breathes the Baudelairean correspondence between the templar aspect of nature and the labyrinthine "forest of symbols" at the heart of the phenomenal temple. It contains—and limits—fear.

The current of fear becomes evident in *River of Rivers* with "the first black cataracts" and the grotesque trees that "lack the intelligence of trees." We are permitted to experience the anxiety that wells up at the thought of old age, illness, death—loss of intelligence. Thus Stevens's opening stanza, echoing Luther's great hymn, begins darkly "amidst the flood of mortal ills prevailing." The deepest current in *River of Rivers* is knowledge of imminent mortality—although fear of death, fear that one may cease to be, does not in this poem predominate over desire. With Keats, Stevens intimates that one may fall "half in love with easeful death." These maze elements not only are present, but are so strongly present that only the structure of the poem—classical, serenely open, proportionate, balanced and stable—is able to confine fear and desire, both, within proper bounds.

A moment to admire the beautiful edifice. *River of Rivers* reduplicates the structure of *Final Soliloquy of the Interior Paramour*: six words in the title; six stanzas of tercets; verses cast loosely in hexameter. Like *Final Soliloquy*, it contains rhyme ("black," "cataracts," "lack"); doublings ("flashing and flashing," "again and again"); and significant repetition ("river" for instance is doubled in the title, and then placed in five of the six stanzas). Such doublings and repetitions recall liturgical responses, but are more than mere echoings. They act as linguistic parallels of return. Again, as in *Final Soliloquy*, built into the microstructure of a deeply serious poem is a half-hidden joke—in this case, a delicate piece of self-parody and a delightful signature. Finally, the threefold stanza reveals the presence of Dante. But the divine Comedian may be found too in the strength of Stevens's poem, in its acknowledgement of loss and death, above all in its fierce affirmation of life. Stevens's river reflects many rivers flashing and flashing in the sun. Surely it draws into itself something of the great river at the apex of Purgatory—also a threshold that inspires fear and desire, and a bridge that inspires hope.

The *River of Rivers* is at once a drawing of the limen and a prevision of crossing. Like metaphor itself, it constitutes a form of bridge. The poem's *structure* suggests the gracefully repeated arches and linearity of an aqueduct, a channel of measured flow engineered in conformance with the modulations of landscape. Yet the poem seems to indicate that a region may in itself be understood as a kind of bridge. In similar fashion, Dr. Donne turned his homeland into a metaphor of passage. In his sermon to the Virginia Company, England becomes "this *Iland* which is but a *Suburbs* of the old world, [and which becomes] a Bridge, a Gallery to the new; to joyne all to that world that shall never grow old, the Kingdome of Heaven."[26] Typically, Donne here Christianizes metaphors from nature; elsewhere in his sermons and sacred poems—as in his life—he could be led by his Christian beliefs to a morbid and sepulchral fascination with death. Stevens is more at home in mere nature. He elevates his adopted region to the same status, however, that Donne accords to England. In *River of Rivers,* Connecticut becomes a suburb of the old world, a bridge to the new.

The springs of affirmation in this poem derive precisely from the maze elements, the currents of dislocation and fear. If the Connecticut becomes the Styx, if the bank *is* the stream, if the river *is* the sea—if mortal being is propelled beyond mortality—then the emergent occasions are indeed meaningful. No *shadow walks* the opposite bank because it is not the region of shades but the bright world of the living. The river goes "nowhere" because it is everywhere—"As of a character everywhere." Things glisten, shine, are full of light and air. The steeple points upward to a region of pure idea, mere being beyond "appearances." The River of Rivers effects a labor, a passage, a bringing to birth, a bridging over and into the source of things.

In August of 1951, two years before Stevens composed the river poem, Heidegger developed a notion of the bridge as a model of conscious being. In the following passage from "Building Dwelling Thinking" (*Bauen Wohnen Denken*), the philosopher whom Fletcher called the chief theorist of betweenness describes the "gathering" power of the bridge:

> The bridge swings over the stream "with ease and power". . . .
> The banks emerge as banks only as the bridge crosses the
> stream. . . . [The bridge] brings stream and bank and landscape
> into each other's neighborhood.

The steeple at Farmington
Stands glistening and Haddam shines and sways

The bridge *gathers* the earth as landscape around the stream. Thus it guides and attends the stream through the meadows. The water may wander on, quiet and gay . . .

The mere flowing of the water is a gayety

the sky's floods from storm or thaw may shoot past the piers in torrential waves—

He could not bend against its propelling force

the bridge is ready for the sky's weather and its fickle nature. Even where the bridge covers the stream, it holds its flow up to the sky by taking it for a moment under the vaulted gateway and setting it free once more:

> It is the third commonness with light and air,
> A curriculum, a vigor, a local abstraction . . .
> Call it, once more, a river, an unnamed flowing

Now in a high arch, now in a low, the bridge vaults over glen and stream—whether mortals keep in mind this vaulting of the bridge's course or forget that they [are] always themselves on the way to the last bridge. [27]

The vaulting bridge, the unnamed flowing, are words of the final threshold—*Words of the fragrant portals, dimly-starred*—and images of passage. In Stevens's poem a kind of tuning is taking place, as at the entrance to Donne's memorable "Holy roome":

> Where, with thy Quire of Saints for evermore,
> I shall be made thy Musique; As I come
> I tune the Instrument here at the dore.

Winding horizontally along like a shining serpent, the River of Rivers passes wide and blue through the spare New England landscape to enter "caverns measureless to man." It does not flow, however, into a sunless sea. Stevens's stately poem of exodus is signed with a punning grace note by the jongleur: the river flows nowhere, *like a "C."* The Comedian as the Letter C has come to the end of a journey begun may years before, and the black cataracts of the opening verses are exchanged, in the closing line, for vision—*like a "see."* Tuning the instrument in readiness for the music to come, Stevens sounds his "middle C" and signs off—with just the suggestion of a smile.

NOTES

INDEX

Notes

Introduction

1. Wallace Stevens, *Opus Posthumous* (New York: Knopf, 1957), p. 161 (hereafter cited in text as *OP*).
2. Helen Vendler, *Wallace Stevens: Words Chosen out of Desire* (Knoxville: Univ. of Tennessee Press, 1984), p. 4.
3. *The Collected Poems of Wallace Stevens* (New York: Knopf, 1954), p. 108 (hereafter cited in text as *CP*).
4. *Scenes from the Drama of European Literature: Six Essays by Erich Auerbach* (Gloucester, Mass.: Peter Smith, 1973), p. 49.

Chapter 1: The Spirit's Own Seduction

1. Holly Stevens, *Souvenirs and Prophesies: The Young Wallace Stevens* (New York: Knopf, 1977). See esp. p. 16 and pp. 29–36, which reproduce Stevens's juvenile sonnets. Holly Stevens comments of Sonnet 6 ("If we are leaves that fall upon the ground") that Harold Bloom called it "pure Shelley" (p. 31).
2. *Letters of Wallace Stevens*, ed. Holly Stevens (New York: Knopf, 1966), p. 438 (hereafter cited in text as *LWS*). Stevens writes to Hi Simons: "When the sparrow begins calling bethou: *Bethou me* . . . he mocks the wren, the jay, the robin. . . . Bethou is intended to be heard; it and the ké-ké, which is inimical, are opposing sounds. Bethou is the spirit's own seduction." Holly Stevens notes that her father has written "tutoyez-moi" in the margin opposite *"Bethou me."* A. Walton Litz related Stevens's use of *bethou* to Shelley in *Introspective Voyager: The Poetic Development of Wallace Stevens* (New York: Oxford Univ. Press, 1972), pp. 197–98.
3. Angus Fletcher, *The Transcendental Masque: An Essay on Milton's Comus* (Ithaca: Cornell Univ. Press, 1971), p. 234. Fletcher points to the meanings of triplicity in Renaissance iconography and classical thought and reminds us of the tradition of the Pythagorean triad as a symbolic "marriage number" (quoting Alistair Fowler). These concepts involving unity in diversity shed light on Stevens's "spirit" and his construct of an Interior Paramour, as does

Fletcher's observation that, in these terms, "the self can be the child of one's double being" (p. 234).

4. R. P. Blackmur, *Language as Gesture: Essays in Poetry* (London: Allen & Unwin, 1954), p. 456. This collection includes Blackmur's better-known early essay "Examples of Wallace Stevens."

5. See, for example, Frank Kermode, *The Romantic Image* (New York: Macmillan, 1957); and Harold Bloom, *The Ringers in the Tower: Studies in the Romantic Tradition* (Chicago: Univ. of Chicago Press, 1971). For the conflict of influence, see esp. Bloom's *Anxiety of Influence: A Theory of Poetry* (New York: Oxford Univ. Press, 1973), *Poetry and Repression: Revisionism from Blake to Stevens* (New Haven: Yale Univ. Press, 1976), and *Wallace Stevens: The Poems of Our Climate* (Ithaca: Cornell Univ. Press, 1977). More recently there is Margaret Peterson's *Wallace Stevens and the Idealist Tradition* (Ann Arbor: UMI Research Press, 1983), esp. pp. 5–15.

6. See Adalaide Kirby Morris, *Wallace Stevens: Imagination and Faith* (Princeton: Princeton Univ. Press, 1974) for the pioneer study of theological elements in Stevens's poetry, approached from a rationalist standpoint.

7. See Peterson, *Stevens and the Idealist Tradition*, pp. 12–14. This study follows Ivor Winters in reading Stevens as an atheist and hedonist. Although the readings are often valuable, the approach is reductive: a negative "reality" component posed against a positive "imagination." Peterson's survey of the critical background is succinct, however, and her study of Stevens's relation to Coleridge and the romantics particularly useful.

8. Vendler, *Wallace Stevens*, p. 6.

9. Origen, *The Song of Songs: Commentary and Homilies*, trans. R. P. Lawson (Westminster, Md.: Newman Press, Longmans, Green, 1957), pp. 29–30.

10. Ibid., bk. 3.8, p. 198.

11. For the emblems and hagiography of Saint Ursula of Cologne, see George Ferguson, *Signs and Symbols in Christian Art* (New York: Oxford Univ. Press, 1959), p. 87.

12. Although Stevens quips "This was not writ / In any book," the incursion of a pagan eros principle into Christian theology has been traced in detail. See Anders Nygren, *Agape and Eros: A Study of the Christian Idea of Love* (Philadelphia: Westminster Press, 1935), esp. p. 583. Here, Bishop Nygren disapprovingly quotes from Dionysius the Areopagite: "Ecstatic love causes God to be drawn down to the lower world from the heavenly height where He is enthroned in absolute isolation from all else."

13. The history of speculative theology is set forth with great clarity in Evelyn Underhill's *Mysticism: A Study in the Nature and Development of Man's Spiritual Consciousness* (New York: Noonday, 1955); see esp. pp. 139–40.

14. I am indebted to Professor Jerome Mazzaro for the valuable suggestion that Stevens's connection to the ideas of speculative theology would be found in his Harvard years. His study *The Figure of Dante: An Essay on the Vita Nuova* (Princeton: Princeton Univ. Press, 1981) deals with issues that parallel the concerns of this chapter.

15. William James was on the faculty of Harvard University while Stevens attended the college as a special student (1897–1900). *The Varieties of Religious Experience*, first delivered as the Gifford Lectures in Edinburgh in 1901–2 was published in New York in the Modern Library edition in 1902, when Stevens was just two years out of Harvard. (See *LWS*, pp. 476, 704, for references to James. In the letter to Sister Bernetta Quinn, Stevens responds to her query respecting the influence of Alfred North Whitehead: "There was an entirely different generation of philosophers when I was at college: William James, Josiah Royce, and so on.") For an excellently focused study of the joint influence of William James and Emerson on Stevens's poetry, see David M. La Guardia, *Advance on Chaos: The Sanctifying Imagination of Wallace Stevens* (Hanover, N.H.: Brown Univ. Press, 1983).

16. Joseph Riddel, *The Clairvoyant Eye: The Poetry and Politics of Wallace Stevens* (Baton Rouge: Louisiana State Univ. Press, 1965), p. 247. Louis Martz, in "Wallace Stevens: The World as Meditation," *Yale Review* 47 (1958):517–36, saw this poem as a departure from Stevens's earlier sensualist values, imputing to the poet a new-blossomed admiration for the power of thinking. Most recently Frank Lentricchia has touched on desire in *The World as Meditation* as part of a neo-Marxist approach to gender and poetic identity in *Ariel and the Police: Michel Foucault, William James, Wallace Stevens* (Madison: Univ. of Wisconsin Press, 1988). See esp. pp. 228–29.

17. Eleanor Cook's recent book, *Poetry, Word-Play, and Word-War in Wallace Stevens* (Princeton: Princeton Univ. Press, 1988) fills a long-standing critical need. Cook notes Stevens's cross-linguistic punning: "Stevens' sophistication in etymological word-play . . . is extraordinary. So is his multilingual punning. When I argue for a pun on Homer's Greek in *An Ordinary Evening in New Haven* (V), I trust my readers to accept the possibility of such punning. It may help to know that Stevens copied Greek passages into his notebook, but it helps more to listen to the words of Stevens' poems" (p. 7).

18. See Gaston Bachelard, *The Poetics of Space*, trans. Maria Jolas (New York: Orion, 1964), esp. pp. 202, 211, 215.

19. See *LWS*, p. 17, n. 5: In 1897–98 Stevens took "History and Development of English Literature" at Harvard (a two-semester course). In April 1953 Stevens wrote to Renato Poggioli, thanking him for a copy of Donne sent to him: "It is . . . a book of both elegance and dignity and will tempt me to read Donne again whom I haven't read for fifty years" (p. 775).

Chapter 2: Ambiguous Birds and Quizzical Messengers

1. *Aucassin and Nicolette and Other Medieval Romances and Legends*, trans. Eugene Mason (New York: Dutton, 1910), p. 53; see also *Of the Tumbler and Our Lady and Other Miracles* (New York: Cooper Square Publishers, 1966), pp. 3–33, and esp. the introduction for historical background and textual information.

2. *Aucassin and Nicolette*, pp. 55–56.

3. Erich Auerbach, discussing the use of the vernacular in conveying sacred texts, notes the performance of jongleurs for this purpose: "It seems that on certain holidays, at certain services . . . the vulgar tongue was occasionally

used in the liturgy itself; in any event vernacular compositions were read in close connection with it in the church or outside it or in cloisters, by clerics and also by *jongleurs*. Although most ecclesiastical pronouncements on the subject express undiminished disapproval of *mimi et ioculatores*, a collaboration seems to have developed . . . between the clergy and the *jongleurs* by the eleventh century, so much so that *the two functions were sometimes combined in one person* [my emphasis]" (*Literary Language and Its Public in Late Latin Antiquity and in the Middle Ages*, trans. Ralph Mannheim [New York: Pantheon, 1965] pp. 284–86).

4. I am indebted to Joan Richardson's "By Their Fruits: Wallace Stevens, His Poetry, His Critics," Ph.D. diss., CUNY, 1977, pp. 482–85, for documentation of Stevens's knowledge of the story, and for his reference in the December 8, 1908, letter to Elsie. Richardson traces Stevens's reading of the tale to Alonso de Berceo, *Miracles of Our Lady*, and suggests that Stevens's use of the tale "informs us that his vision of himself is no . . . contemporary vision" but as a "troubadour poet, as 'juggler,' even if it is an ironic vision" (pp. 484–85).

5. *LWS*, p. 114.

6. For readings of the theological nuances in *The Bird with the Coppery, Keen Claws*, see Daniel Fuchs, *The Comic Spirit of Wallace Stevens* Durham, N.C.: Duke Univ. Press, 1963), pp. 62–93; and Louis H. Leiter, "Sense and Nonsense: Wallace Stevens' 'The Bird with the Coppery, Keen Claws,'" *College English* 26 (Apr. 1965):551–54.

7. *LWS*, p. 428; *OP*, p. 172; and *LWS*, p. 763.

8. M. M. Bakhtin, "From the Prehistory of Novelistic Discourse," in *The Dialogic Imagination*, trans. Caryl Emerson and Michael Holquist (Austin: Univ. of Texas Press, 1981), pp. 41–83.

9. Ibid., p. 59. Bakhtin notes that "alongside the great and significant models of straightforward genres and direct discourses . . . there was created in ancient times a rich world of the most varied forms and variations of parodic-travestying, indirect, conditional discourse," which "far from expresses the full richness of types, variants, nuances of the laughing word."

10. Ibid.

11. Gilbert Highet, *The Anatomy of Satire* (Princeton: Princeton Univ. Press, 1962), p. 69. Also see *The Stuffed Owl: An Anthology of Bad Verse*, ed. D. B. Wyndham Lewis and Charles Lee (London: Dent, 1948), which includes, besides Wordsworth's self-parody, some wonderfully dreadful numbers of Crashaw, Cowley, Byron, and Poe.

12. Eleanor Cook comments on the sexual punning in *Bantams*: "Why commentators have been so singularly abstemious about the funny phallic subtext here, I do not know, especially when it has been barely submerged at all" (*Poetry, Word-Play, and Word-War*, p. 70).

13. Stevens, incidentally, owned an edition containing both Southey's *Vision of Judgment* and Byron's parody, printed back-to-back by Maynard and Bray in 1932. See Milton J. Bates, "Stevens' Books at the Huntington: An Annotated Checklist," in *Wallace Stevens Journal* 2 (Fall 1978):60. Holly Stevens,

in *Souvenirs and Prophecies*, records that Stevens showed a tendency toward parody and irreverence, and a knowledge of the classics, as a young student. A friend remembers that "at high school Wallace was a whimsical, unpredictable young enthusiast, who lampooned Dido's tear-stained adventures in the cave, or wrote enigmatic couplets to gazelles" (p. 11).

14. Fuchs, *Comic Spirit*, p. 2.

15. Stevens's *Negation* (CP, 97–98) is a parodic reflection of Coleridge's poem of the same name; the blind God of Stevens's poem becomes the parody of a parody if it is understood to echo Coleridge's sightless Watcher. For a useful commentary on Stevens's *Negation*, see Morris, *Wallace Stevens*, pp. 102–3.

16. Sigmund Freud, *Jokes and Their Relation to the Unconscious*, in *The Standard Edition of the Complete Psychological Works of Sigmund Freud*, trans. James Strachey, 24 vols. (London: Hogarth, 1953), 8:108–9.

17. Leiter, "Sense and Nonsense."

18. See Glen G. MacLeod, *Wallace Stevens & Company: The Harmonium Years 1913–1923* (Ann Arbor: UMI Research Press, 1983), for a view of a probable living model for Stevens's "uncle" in *Le Monocle de Mon Oncle*. MacLeod suggests Donald Evans, who wore a monacle, died at the age of thirty-nine, and whose "Sonnets from the Patagonian," says MacLeod, manifest the "pose of the dandy-aesthete, which informs 'Le Monocle de Mon Oncle'" (p. 72).

19. Richardson, "By Their Fruits," p. 531.

20. Bloom, *Wallace Stevens*, p. 37.

21. Helen Vendler, *On Extended Wings: Wallace Stevens' Longer Poems* (Cambridge: Harvard Univ. Press, 1969), p. 58.

22. OP, p. 178.

23. *Le Testament Villon*, ed. Jean Rychner and Albert Henry (Geneva: Librairie Droz, 1974), 1:79. The ballade is subtitled *Ballade: Que Villon feit a la requeste de sa mère, pour prier Nostre Dame*. I should point out the connection, too, between the old French liturgical forms and the opening of Baudelaire's *Le Balcon* in *Les Fleurs du Mal*, both of which have a bearing on the invocation in Stevens's *Monocle*: "Mère des souvenirs, maîtresse des maîtresses, / O toi, tous mes plaisirs! o toi, tous mes devoirs!"

24. Bakhtin, *Dialogic Imagination*, p. 78. Bakhtin notes the prevalence of *parodia sacra* in medieval France, observing that quotations from the Bible, Gospels, Church Fathers, etc., "continually infiltrate medieval literature . . . beginning at one pole with the pious and inert quotation that is isolated and set off like an icon, and ending at the other pole with the most ambiguous, disrespectful, parodic-travestying use of a quotation" (p. 69).

25. See Ruth Z. Temple, *The Critic's Alchemy: A Study of the Introduction of French Symbolism into England* (New York: Twayne, 1953), pp. 93–97, for a discussion of Swinburne's translations of Villon.

26. See Underhill, *Mysticism*, pp. 136–40 and passim. Also see Saint Bernard, *Bernard, Abbot of Clairvaux: The Steps of Humility*, trans. G. B. Burch (Cambridge: Harvard Univ. Press, 1950), esp. introduction.

27. François Villon, *The Complete Works of François Villon*, trans. Anthony Bonner (New York: Bantam, 1960), p. 35. The "Angelus" lines are as follows:

> *J'ois la cloche de Serbonne,*
> *Qui tousjours a neuf heures sonne*
> *Le Salut que l'Ange predit.*

> *(I heard the bell of Sorbonne*
> *That each day at nine sounds*
> *The Salute that the angel announced.)*

Stevens's long familiarity with Villon, and his fascination with medieval French forms of verse, has not been given formal treatment to date. Evidence is plentiful, however, and a few observations may be useful here. In March 1948 Stevens wrote to his art buyer in France, "The only thing I want at the moment is Les Oeuvres de François Villon for 700 francs" (*LWS*, 582). His Harvard years produced *The Ballade of the Pink Parasol*, its refrain ("But where is the pink parasol?") a sophomoric parody of Villon's most well-known refrain. In "Wallace Stevens at Harvard," in *The Act of the Mind: Essays on the Poetry of Wallace Stevens*, ed. Roy Harvey Pearce and J. Hillis Miller (Baltimore: Johns Hopkins Univ. Press, 1965), Robert Buttel notes the prevalence of the Pre-Raphaelite translations of Villon at the time, and observes: "For Stevens' use of the ballade form itself there were many precedents, ranging from Villon's ballades to several by E. A. Robinson. . . . with the help of Swinburne and Rossetti, the vogue for Villon and the ballade form passed over to England. Rossetti translated Villon's "Ballade des Dames du Temps Jadis" in 1869 . . . and Swinburne wrote his double ballade of tribute to Villon, "A Ballade of François Villon, Prince of all Ballade-Makers" (p. 54).

In July 1909, just two months before their marriage, Stevens wrote to Elsie Moll that he had "spent the whole day—a gorgeous, blue day—in my room, reading some of the French poets of the sixteenth century. . . . In fact, I have spent the afternoon, translating a sonnet by Joachim du Bellay" (*LWS*, 150–51). Finally there is Stevens's late lyric *Celle Qui Fût Héaulmiette* (*CP*, 438) which, as James Baird has pointed out in *The Dome and the Rock: Structure in the Poetry of Wallace Stevens* (Baltimore: Johns Hopkins Univ. Press, 1968), is taken from the second line of Villon's dramatic lyric *Les regrets de la belle Hëaumière* (p. 87).

Chapter 3: Something for Nothing

1. Frank Doggett, *Stevens' Poetry of Thought* (Baltimore: Johns Hopkins Univ. Press, 1966), pp. 71–72.

2. In 1952 C. Roland Wagner introduced "The Idea of Nothingness in Wallace Stevens." J. Hillis Miller dealt with the negative mode head-on in "Wallace Stevens' Poetry of Being" (1964), and in 1976 introduced deconstructionist readings of Stevens with the well-known "Stevens' Rock and Criticism as Cure." In *Stevens' Poetry of Thought* (1966), Frank Doggett related *The*

Reader to the second law of thermodynamics, while Helen Vendler analyzed the "resolutely impoverished poem" of the later poetry in *On Extended Wings* (1969) and his "brutality of style" in "Apollo's Harsher Songs" in *Wallace Stevens* (1984). Edward Kessler isolated the wintry images of negation and nothingness in *Images of Wallace Stevens* (1972); Adalaide Kirby Morris traced the spiritual vacuum indicated in Stevens's early *Negation*, in *Wallace Stevens* (1974). Throughout *Wallace Stevens*, Harold Bloom's major work on the poet, are references to themes of absence and disjunction (1977). More recently there has been Roy Harvey Pearce's "Toward Decreation: Wallace Stevens and the 'Theory of Poetry'" (1980); Paul Bové's reading of *The Snow Man* in *Destructive Poetics: Heidegger and Modern American Poetry* (1980); and David M. La Guardia's treatment of decreation and destruction in *Advance on Chaos: The Sanctifying Imagination of Wallace Stevens* (1983).

3. Sigmund Freud, "Negation" (1925), *Standard Edition*, 5:185.

4. For an extremely useful discussion of this passage in *Credences of Summer*, see Joseph N. Riddel, "The Climate of Our Poems," *Wallace Stevens Journal* 7 (Fall 1983):59–75.

5. Frank Doggett, "Wallace Stevens' Later Poetry," *ELH* 25 (1958):138.

6. Rosalie L. Colie, *Paradoxia Epidemica: The Renaissance Tradition of Paradox* (Princeton: Princeton Univ. Press, 1966), p. 6. Colie is referring to the classical "Cretan Liar" paradox: "Epimenides the Cretan says that all Cretans are liars."

7. Ibid., p. 38.

8. Cleanth Brooks, "The Language of Paradox," in *The Language of Poetry*, ed. Allen Tate (Princeton: Princeton Univ. Press, 1942), p. 37.

9. W. V. Quine, *The Ways of Paradox and Other Essays* (New York: Random House, 1966), p. 11. Quine's very readable discussion surveys the progress of paradox from Zeno through Gödels.

10. W. B. Yeats, *The Collected Poems of W. B. Yeats* (New York: Macmillan, 1974), p. 125.

11. See J. Hillis Miller, *Poets of Reality: Six Twentieth-Century Writers* (Cambridge: Harvard Univ. Press, 1965), p. 219; and Vendler, *On Extended Wings*, p. 265.

12. Henri Bergson, *Creative Evolution*, trans. A. Mitchell (New York: Modern Library, 1944), p. 124.

13. Bloom, *Wallace Stevens*, pp. 214–15.

14. Plotinus, *The Enneads*, trans. Stephan MacKenna (London: Faber and Faber, 1962), p. 616 (*Enn.* 6.9.3).

15. Saint John of the Cross, "Concerning the Direction of Contemplative Souls," in *Renaissance Philosophy: The Transalpine Thinkers* (New York: Modern Library, 1969), p. 384.

16. C. G. Jung, *The Archetypes and the Collective Unconscious*, trans. R. F. C. Hull (New York: Pantheon, 1959), p. 15.

17. Compare T. S. Eliot's opening lines in "A Game of Chess" in *The Waste Land* with its Satanic echoes of *Paradise Lost* (2.1–10) and the Sapphic echo of Aphrodite's golden chair in the *Ode to Aphrodite*. Eliot's stanza begins:

> The Chair she sat in, like a burnished throne,
> Glowed on the marble, where the glass
> Held up by standards wrought with fruited vines
> From which a golden Cupidon peeped out. . . .
> . . . . .
> The glitter of her jewels rose to meet it,
> From satin cases poured in rich profusion

18. Wallace Stevens, "Imagination as Value," in *English Institute Essays, 1948*, ed. D. A. Robertson, Jr. (New York: Columbia Univ. Press, 1949), p. 9.

19. See Angus Fletcher, " 'Positive Negation': Threshold, Sequence, and Personification in Coleridge," in *New Perspectives on Coleridge and Wordsworth*, ed. Geoffrey Hartman (New York: Columbia Univ. Press, 1972), pp. 133–64, for a seminal discussion of the "threshold poem" and the zone of liminality.

20. Sigmund Freud, "The Antithetical Meaning of Primal Words" (1910), *Standard Edition*, 2:155–61. See also 13:67; 15:79, 229–30; 23:169.

21. Ibid., 2:156.

22. Ibid., 2:61; see also *Totem and Taboo* for Freud's discussion of "taboo" as a prohibition "to be understood as consequences of an emotional ambivalence" (13:67).

23. Ibid., 2:155. A much later paper shows Freud still considering the play of contraries and the absence of the negative in dreams, and the apparent linkage between linguistic and oneiric structures: "The dream language forms part of a highly archaic system of expression. . . . there is no special indication for the negative in the language of dreams. Contraries may stand for each other. . . . concepts are still ambivalent in dream language, and unite within themselves contrary meanings—as is the case, according to the hypotheses of philologists, in the oldest roots of historical languages" (ibid., 13:176).

24. Ibid., 5:185.

25. Fletcher, " 'Positive Negation,' " p. 159; discussing personification as the created "phantom" of the threshold poem, Fletcher argues: "To envision and realize the phantom person poetically the poet must empty his imagery of piety and sense, allowing in their place some measure of daemonic possession. The one necessary act will be to utter, to speak, nothingness." He adds, referring to Coleridge's *Negation*, that to achieve "this defining negativity, the poem . . . seeks to *posit* negation as the ultimate daemon" (p. 159).

26. *LWS*, p. 636.

27. This is not a Coleridgean Limbo, a topos of horror, blank, blind, and grotesque in its travesty of reverence, but a Stevensian lower-case limbo, a muted, neutral zone, set as a seasonal allegory of bad housekeeping.

28. *Neutral Tones*, in *Selected Poems of Thomas Hardy*, ed. John Crowe Ransom (New York: Collier, 1966), p. 2.

29. Lewis Thomas, *The Lives of a Cell: Notes of a Biology Watcher* (New York: Viking, 1974), p. 126.

30. Ibid., p. 10. It may be of interest here to note that Thomas refers to Stevens in a later essay on "Humanities and Science" in *Late Night Thoughts on Listening to Mahler's Ninth Symphony* (New York: Viking, 1980). Speaking of the engrossing strangeness of nature, he remarks: "There are more than seven-times-seven types of ambiguity in science, awaiting analysis. The poetry of Wallace Stevens is crystal-clear alongside the genetic code" (p. 150).

31. Freud, *Standard Edition*, 5:182.

Chapter 4: A Woman with the Hair of a Pythoness

1. Michel Benamou, "Art, Music, Angels and Sex: A Note on the Shorter Poems of *Auroras of Autumn*," *Wallace Stevens Journal* 2 (Spring 1978):3–9.

2. Edward Kessler, *Images of Wallace Stevens* (New Brunswick: Rutgers Univ. Press, 1972), pp. 16–17.

3. Ibid., p. 22.

4. Litz, *Introspective Voyager*, p. 118.

5. See Holly Stevens's reference to her mother's hair in "Holidays in Reality" in *Wallace Stevens: A Celebration*, ed. Frank Doggett and Robert Buttel (Princeton: Princeton Univ. Press, 1980), pp. 105–6.

6. Bloom, *Wallace Stevens*, pp. 45–46.

7. Stevens's figure of the "abstract, the archaic queen" as the embodiment of a cognitive principle has antecedents in the history of Western thought. To find the intellective principle in female form, however, one must travel by way of Christian Platonism to the *Noys* (Mind) of Bernard Silvestris in the 12th century, and to the Nous of Plotinus in the 3d, noting Plotinus' exposition of the nature of Aphrodite Ouranos. In the classical period, one notes the continuity of Plato's Diotima in the *Symposium* with a pre-Socratic intellective principle: Parmenides' Goddess of Truth in the proem to *The Way of Truth*. One should also consider the figure of the Divine Tetractys in this context, the holy triangle that formed the core of Pythagorean mystical mathematics. See George Economou, *The Goddess Natura in Medieval Literature* (Cambridge: Harvard Univ. Press, 1972), p. 152; also see Ernst Robert Curtius, *European Literature and the Latin Middle Ages*, trans. Willard R. Trask (Princeton: Princeton Univ. Press, 1953), pp. 108–11; and Theodore Silverstein, "The Fabulous Cosmogony of Bernardus Silvestris," *Modern Philology* 66 (1948):95–98.

8. C. G. Jung, "The Syzygy: Anima and Animus," in *Aion: Researches into the Phenomenology of the Self*, vol. 9, pt. 2, of *The Collected Works of C. G. Jung* (Princeton: Princeton Univ. Press, 1968), pp. 12–13.

9. Ibid., p. 14.

10. Jung, *Collected Works*, 17:198.

11. Mary Arensberg, "Wallace Stevens' Interior Paramour," *Wallace Stevens Journal* 3 (Spring 1979):3–7.

12. Ibid. The reference is to Michael Beehler's "Meteoric Poetry: Wallace Ste-
     vens' 'Description without Place,'" *Criticism* 29 (1977):241–59.

13. Bloom, *Wallace Stevens*, pp. 110–11.

14. See John Hollander, *The Figure of Echo: A Mode of Allusion in Milton and
     After* (Berkeley and Los Angeles: Univ. of California Press, 1981), p. 98.
     Also see Angus Fletcher's discussion of the acoustical principle of echo in
     The Transcendental Masque, esp. pp. 198–99.

Chapter 5: The Archangel of Evening

1. Herman Melville, *Moby-Dick*, ed. Harrison Hayford and Hershel Parker
    (New York: Norton, 1967), p. 165.

2. Samuel Taylor Coleridge, *The Poems of Samuel Taylor Coleridge* (London:
    Oxford Univ. Press, 1935), p. 486. See n. 3 for Coleridge's comment on
    the background of the piece. Stevens, as we know, owned editions of Cole-
    ridge's poetry and a copy of I. A. Richards's *Coleridge on Imagination*; he
    referred to Richards's book in "The Noble Rider and the Sound of Words"
    (Bates, "Stevens' Books," pp. 57, 60). I am indebted to Professor Geoffrey
    Hartman for drawing attention to *Coeli Enarrant* during a seminar he con-
    ducted at CUNY in July 1986. Alan D. Perlis considers the "problematic of
    metaphor" in a deconstructionist reading of Stevens's "Reader" poems, based
    on formulations of metonymy and metaphor by Roland Barthes and Paul
    De Man, in which the poems seem to disappear and the critic is left observ-
    ing himself reading an "effaced text" (Alan D. Perlis, "Wallace Stevens'
    Reader Poems and the Effacement of Metaphor," *Wallace Stevens Journal*
    10 (Fall 1986):67–75.

3. Ronald Sukenick, *Musing the Obscure* (New York: New York Univ. Press,
    1967), pp. 50–51.

4. Bloom, *Wallace Stevens*, p. 63. In a discussion of *Tea at the Palaz of Hoon*,
    Bloom comments that Stevens, Whitman, and Pater are "Epicurean-
    Lucretian in their ultimate metaphysics." Also see Bloom's essay on Stevens
    in his *Figures of Capable Imagination* (New York: Seabury, 1976), esp. pp.
    118–19, where Stevens is presented as an "American Lucretius."

5. For an illuminating analysis of Stevens's strategic use of repetition in *Valley
    Candle* and other poems, see Laury Magnus, "Wallace Stevens: 'And Things
    beyond Resemblance . . . ,'" chap. 7 of *The Track of the Repetend: Syntac-
    tic and Lexical Repetition in Modern Poetry*, AMS Ars Poetica, no. 4 (New
    York: AMS Press, 1989), pp. 193–243.

6. See esp. *LWS*, pp. 92, 96, 146, 378, 481–82, 635, 637, 722, 761–62, 771,
    820, 822. In January 1945 Stevens writes to José Rodriguez Feo of Santay-
    ana's "interest and sympathy" when he visited with him at Harvard: "I always
    came away from my visits to him feeling that he made up in the most
    genuine way for many things I needed. He was then still definitely a poet"
    (*LWS*, 482).

7. George Santayana, "Cross-Lights," in *Soliloquies in England and Later So-
    liloquies* (New York: Scribners, 1922), pp. 23–24. See Doggett, *Stevens' Po-*

etry of Thought for a full discussion of Santayana's influence on Stevens's poetry and thought.

8. For Sumerian hymns to Inanna as the Lady of Evening, see Diana Wolkstone and Samuel Noah Kramer, *Inanna: Queen of Heaven and Earth* (New York: Harper & Row, 1983), p. 101. The Evening Star hymn begins:

> At the end of the day, the Radiant Star, the Great Light that fills the sky
> The Lady of the Evening appears in the heavens.

Also see Mary Ackworth Orr, *Dante and the Early Astronomers* (1913; reprint, Port Washington, N.Y.: Kennikat, 1969), pp. 66–67, for a discussion of the names used for the planet in antiquity. Orr notes that the Greek names—Hesper (meaning "western" for the evening star) and Phosphor (meaning "light-bringer" for the morning star)—were changed in classical times to conform to the Babylonian denominations of the deity: "Greek descriptive names of the planets were changed for names of Greek deities . . . believed to correspond with the Babylonian gods and goddesses who presided over the planets. Thus Plato . . . is the last to use commonly the name of Phosphor for the planet which henceforth was known as Aphrodite among the Greeks, and Venus among the Romans, corresponding to the Babylonian Ishtar."

9. William Blake, *The Poetry and Prose of William Blake*, ed. David V. Erdman with a commentary by Harold Bloom, rev. ed. (Garden City, N.Y.: Doubleday, 1970), p. 402.

10. *To Aphrodite*, in *Hesiod: The Homeric Hymns and Homerica*, Loeb Classical Library, 1964, pp. 410–11.

11. Ibid.

12. Helen Vendler argues that *Parts of a World* finds Stevens split by two modes of rhetoric as well as "the obtrusive fact of war" (*On Extended Wings*, p. 144. See "Abecedarium of Finesoldier," pp. 144–67).

13. Bakhtin, *Dialogic Imagination*, pp. 84–158.

14. Enjoying a walk on the Palisades overlooking the Hudson River in April 1904, Stevens writes, "No doubt, if it had been a bit nearer sunset, the particular hills I gazed at so long would have been very much like the steps to the Throne. And Blake's angels would have been there with their 'Holy, Holy, Holy'" (*LWS*, p. 71).

15. Harold E. Tolliver, *Pastoral Forms and Attitudes* (Berkeley and Los Angeles: Univ. of California Press, 1971), p. 301.

16. Bloom, *Wallace Stevens*, p. 277.

17. Doggett, *Stevens' Poetry of Thought*, p. 153.

18. For a full discussion of the prophetic poem, see Angus Fletcher, *The Prophetic Moment: An Essay on Spenser* (Chicago: Univ. of Chicago Press, 1971).

19. Walt Whitman, *Leaves of Grass*, ed. John Valente (New York: Macmillan, 1929), p. 3.

20. Fletcher, *Prophetic Moment*, p. 5.
21. Erdman, ed., *Poetry and Prose of William Blake*, p. 815.
22. Geoffrey Hartman, "Evening Star and Evening Land," in his *The Fate of Reading and Other Essays* (Chicago: Univ. of Chicago Press, 1975), pp. 147–78.
23. Ibid., p. 178.
24. Ibid., p. 154.

Chapter 6: Enough

1. *LWS*, pp. 733–34.
2. See Ezra Pound, *The Spirit of Romance* (Norfolk, Conn.: New Directions, n.d.), pp. 30–31. Pound notes: "In Canto 26 of the *Purgatorio* Dante's Provençal lines which do not rime with other lines in Italian, contain only ten syllables. And the single line—
   Ai fals ris! per qua traiz avetz
   with which he begins the 'desacoart,' usually styled Canzone XXI, should show that either 't's and 'z's had in Provençal a different sound from that which is usually imagined, or that Dante believed certain things to be fitting in the *lingua materna* which were not laudable in *lingua Toscana*" (pp. 30–31).
3. For a description of the "lowly" style, or *sermo humilis*, see Auerbach, *Literary Language*, pp. 27–66.
4. Auerbach, *Scenes from the Drama of European Literature*, p. 82.
5. T. S. Eliot, *Dante* (1929, reprint London: Faber and Faber, 1965), p. 46 (my emphasis).
6. See *LWS*, p. 155n; plate 9, facing p. 182, is a photograph of the prize-winning head sculpted by Adolph Alexander Weinman. Also see Peter Brazeau, *Parts of a World: Wallace Stevens Remembered* (New York: Random House, 1983), pp. 87n, 91; and Joan Richardson, *Wallace Stevens, a Biography: The Early Years, 1879–1923* (New York: William Morrow, 1986), p. 360. Most recently, see the discussion of Sandra M. Gilbert and Susan Gubar in *Critical Inquiry* 14 (1988):393–94.
7. Dante Alighieri, *La vita nuova* (Milan: Lerici, 1965), p. 71; English trans. by Barbara Reynolds (New York: Penguin, 1969), p. 42.
8. Dante, *La vita nuova*, trans. Reynolds, pp. 72–73.
9. See Charles Eliot Norton's commentary in "Essays and Notes" following his translation of *The New Life of Dante Alighieri* (Boston: Houghton, Mifflin, 1892), p. 97. Norton writes: "The chroniclers tell of constant festivals and celebration. 'In the year 1283, in the month of June, at the feast of St. John, the city of Florence being in a happy and good state of repose . . . there was formed a company of a thousand men or more, all clothed in white dresses, with a leader called the Lord of Love, who devoted themselves to games and sport and dancing, going through the city with trumpets and other instruments of joy and gladness, and feasting often together. And this court lasted two months, and was the most noble and famous that ever was held in

Florence or all Tuscany, and many gentlemen came to it, and many jongleurs, and all were welcomed and honorably cared for.' "

10. Reynolds, trans., *La vita nuova*, Intro., p. 11.

11. Mazzaro, *Figure of Dante*, p. 3.

12. J. E. Shaw, "Ego Tanquam Centrum Circuli," in *Essays on the Vita Nuova*, cited by Mazzaro, p. 29.

13. Norton, *New Life*, p. 142.

14. Richardson, *Wallace Stevens*, p. 61; see also *LWS*, p. 588 (letter to William Carlos Williams, April 26, 1948). Also helpful is Ashley Brown's "A Note on Dante and Stevens," *Wallace Stevens Journal* 2 (Summer 1977):66–68; and, more recently, Glauco Cambon's excellent discussion of "Wallace Stevens's Dialogue with Dante," in *Dante among the Moderns*, ed. Stuart Y. McDougal (Chapel Hill: Univ. of North Carolina Press, 1985), pp. 102–27. Both Brown and Cambon cite the stanza from *Esthétique du Mal*:

> His firm stanzas hang like hives in hell
> Or what hell was, since now both heaven and hell
> Are one, and here, O terra infidel.

Most recently, Laury Magnus has drawn attention to Stevens's "expanded similes" which, she notes, follow "a pattern first discernible in Dante" ("'And Things beyond Resemblance': On Stevens' Embedded Similes," *Wallace Stevens Journal* 11 (Spring 1987):12–20, esp. pp. 12, 13 and n. 3. Magnus amplifies: "Dante's simile embeddings are certainly less elaborate than Stevens', but they, too, seem to flirt with the reader, evading the original context of simile-making and enhancing the similes' digressiveness by invoking a metapoetic dimension . . . at the tail end of a simile; Dante will seem to be terminating a comparison and to be coming back to his 'point,' only to slip in another comparison. See for example, *Inferno* III.112–117, XVI.94–105, or XVIII.19–24."

15. Bates, "Stevens' Books," p. 48.

16. McDougal, ed., *Dante among the Moderns*, esp. pp. 123–25.

17. George Santayana, *Three Philosophical Poets* (1910, reprint Garden City, N.Y.: Doubleday Anchor, n.d.), p. 5.

18. See Stevens, *Souvenirs and Prophecies*, pp. 32, 68. Stevens's poem was the ninth in a sequence of fourteen Petrarchan sonnets: "Cathedrals are not built along the sea." Also see chap. 5, n. 6.

19. Santayana, *Three Philosophical Poets*, p. 86.

20. Ibid., p. 87.

21. Pound, *Romance*, p. 120.

22. Paul Mariani, *William Carlos Williams: A New World Naked* (New York: McGraw-Hill, 1981), p. 335.

23. Eliot, *Dante*, pp. 60–61.

24. Stevens, *Souvenirs and Prophecies*, p. 223.

25. Ibid. A study of the "moral approach to literary criticism" in the work of Paul Elmer More has recently been published. See Stephen L. Tanner,

Paul Elmer More: Literary Criticism as the History of Ideas (Albany: SUNY Press, 1987). In this connection, it is of interest that Paul Elmer More edited the complete poetical works of Byron—Stevens's "corsair of hearts, le grand Byron" (*LWS*, 177)—for The Cambridge Poets series (1905). The collection included *The Prophecy of Dante*, a fragment composed in terza rima, comprising some 670 lines of verse.

26. *LWS*, pp. 43–44.
27. Ibid., p. 101.
28. Stevens, *Souvenirs and Prophecies*, p. 190.
29. *LWS*, p. 822.
30. See John Freccero, *Dante: The Poetics of Conversion* (Cambridge: Harvard Univ. Press, 1986).
31. Auerbach, *Literary Language*, p. 296.
32. Dante, *La vita nuova*, trans. Reynolds, pp. 31–32.
33. Stephen E. Whicher, ed., *Selections from Ralph Waldo Emerson* (Boston: Houghton, Mifflin, 1957), pp. 318–19. I am indebted to Professor Fletcher for bringing these passages on Dante in the Emerson journals to my attention.
34. Mazzaro, *Figure of Dante*, Preface, p. xv.
35. Dante, *La vita nuova*, trans. Reynolds, pp. 42–43.
36. Shaw, "Ego tanquam," pp. 90–91.
37. See Stevens, *Souvenirs and Prophecies*, pp. 199, 226, 241, 243; also *LWS*, pp. 185–90.
38. Dante, *La vita nuova*, trans. Reynolds, p. 30.
39. Emerson, *Selections*, p. 318.
40. Milton J. Bates, *Wallace Stevens: A Mythology of Self* (Berkeley and Los Angeles: Univ. of California Press, 1985), p. 302.

Chapter 7: Love of Place

1. See John N. Serio's finely focused discussion in "Stevens' 'Affair of Places,'" *Wallace Stevens Journal* 2 (Spring 1978):26–32.
2. Leonard Lutwack, *The Role of Place in Literature* (Syracuse, N.Y.: Syracuse Univ. Press, 1984). In the preface, Lutwack notes that "no one has examined in a single study more than one or two aspects of the subject, perhaps because it appears presumptuous and foolhardy to encompass an element of literature that is so ubiquitous" (p. vii).
3. Max Jammer amplifies on the space-time analogue in language in *Concepts of Space: The History of Theories of Space in Physics* (Cambridge: Harvard University Press, 1957): "Probably the category of space preceded that of time as an object of consciousness" and he points to language as the repository of such a sequence: "before" and "in front of" become temporal terms, for example; Jammer notes similar analogues in Hebrew and ancient Sumerian (pp. 3–4).

4. See Henry James, *The Tempest*, Intro. to vol. 16 of the Renaissance Edition of *The Complete Works of William Shakespeare*, ed. Sidney Lee, 1907.

5. Bates, "Stevens' Books," pp. 57, 60. For a comprehensive discussion of Stevens's relation to both Coleridge and Richards, see B. J. Leggett, *Wallace Stevens and Poetic Theory: Conceiving the Supreme Fiction* (Chapel Hill: Univ. of North Carolina Press, 1987), esp. chap. 2, "Why It Must be Abstract: Stevens, Coleridge, and I. A. Richards." Noting Stevens's preparations for the talk in 1941 at Princeton on "The Noble Rider and the Sound of Words," Leggett says, "There can be no question as to the care with which Stevens followed Richards' argument. His copy of *Coleridge on Imagination*, now in the . . . Huntington Library, is more heavily marked and annotated than was Stevens' usual practice. Beginning on page 5 and continuing almost to the last page, a great number of passages have been marked or bracketed, and on the back flyleaf and the back inside cover," adds Leggett, Stevens has set a detailed index (p. 27).

6. Samuel Taylor Coleridge, *Biographia Literaria* (London: Dent, 1965), pp. 136–38.

7. Lutwack, *Role of Place*, p. 27.

8. Jammer, *Concepts of Space*, pp. xii–xiii.

9. Ibid., p. xiv.

10. René Descartes, "The Principles of Philosophy," in *The Philosophical Works of Descartes*, vol. 1, trans. Elizabeth S. Haldane and G. R. T. Ross (1931, reprint, New York: Dover, 1955), pp. 260–61.

11. See *The Philosophy of Spinoza*, Intro. Joseph Rattner (New York: Modern Library, 1927), p. xxxiii. Spinoza has been considered from many points of view and his philosophy called atheistic, pantheistic, materialist, and mystical. Rather than suggest a preference in Stevens's approach to Spinoza, I wish simply to juxtapose Spinoza's frame of space against Stevens's poetry. The propositions quoted here are from the R. H. M. Elwes translation, *The Chief Works of Benedict de Spinoza*, 2 vols. (New York: Dover, 1951), 2:54–55.

12. Ralph Waldo Emerson, "Nature," in *Essays: Second Series, The Complete Essays and Other Writings of Ralph Waldo Emerson* (New York: Modern Library, 1940), p. 406.

13. Ernst Cassirer, *The Philosophy of Symbolic Forms*, vol. 2, *Mythical Thought*, trans. Ralph Mannheim (New Haven: Yale Univ. Press, 1955), p. 83. For a presentation of the relation of landscape to the architecture of the temple, see Vincent Scully, *The Earth, the Temple, and the Gods: Greek Sacred Architecture*, rev. ed. (New Haven: Yale Univ. Press, 1969).

14. Cassirer, *Mythical Thought*, p. 85.

15. Mircea Eliade, *The Sacred and the Profane: The Nature of Religion*, trans. Willard R. Trask (New York: Harcourt, 1957), p. 22. See esp. chap. 1, "Sacred Space and Making the World Sacred," pp. 20–65. For an excellent discussion of the concept of center, as it relates to Stevens, see La Guardia, *Advance on Chaos*, pp. 21–48.

16. Eliade, "The Sacred and the Profane, p. 24.

17. See Frances A. Yates, *The Art of Memory* (Chicago: Univ. of Chicago Press, 1966). On the general principles guiding the use of mnemonics, Yates observes: "The first step was to imprint on the memory a series of *loci* or places. The commonest, though not the only, type of mnemonic place system used was the architectural type . . . given by Quintilian. . . . a building is to be remembered, as spacious and varied a one as possible. . . . The images by which the speech is to be remembered . . . are then placed in imagination on the places which have been memorized in the building" (p. 3). Also see p. 23.

18. Peter Brazeau, "Wallace Stevens at the University of Massachusetts: Checklist of an Archive," *Wallace Stevens Journal* 2 (Spring 1978):50–54. Leggett, in *Wallace Stevens and Poetic Theory*, believes that "Focillon is the presiding spirit of 'The Figure of the Youth as Virile Poet,'" and thinks "Focillon's conception of art, more than any other theoretical influence, was responsible for the shift in Stevens's aesthetic after *Notes toward a Supreme Fiction* and 'The Noble Rider'" (pp. 148–49). See chap. 6 for an extended discussion of "Stevens, Focillon, and the Life of Forms" (pp. 142–72).

19. Henri Focillon, *The Life of Forms in Art*, trans. Charles Beecher Hogan and George Kubler (New York: George Wittenborn, 1948), p. 17.

20. Ibid., p. 18.

21. Laury Magnus, "'And Things beyond Resemblance,'" pp. 12–20.

22. Fletcher, *Prophetic Moment*, p. 13.

23. Angus Fletcher, "On Two Words in the Libretto of *The Magic Flute*," *Georgia Review* 29 (1975):128–53; for the "dialectic of Temple and Labyrinth," see pp. 142–43.

Chapter 8: Native Passion

1. Thomas F. Lombardi, "Wallace Stevens: At Home in Pennsylvania," *Wallace Stevens Journal* 2 (Spring 1978):13–17.

2. See *LWS*, pp. 398, 719, for commentary on the Oley Valley; also see Stevens, *Souvenirs and Prophesies*, p. 24, for Journal entry dated December 27 (1898): Stevens writes, "Yesterday afternoon I took a walk alone over Mount Penn starting from Stony Creek and going through the trees to the Tower and down from that to the city, avoiding paths as much as possible." He was nineteen at the time.

3. Also see Brazeau, *Parts of a World*, pp. 100–102, for recollections of Stevens's first stays in Florida.

4. Ibid., pp. 193–94. For an illuminating discussion of the poet's attachment to American soil and his American literary roots, see Joseph N. Riddel's early essay "Walt Whitman and Wallace Stevens: Functions of a 'Literatus,'" *South Atlantic Quarterly* 61 (1962):506–20.

5. See Johann Wolfgang von Goethe, *Hermann and Dorothea*, trans. Daniel Coogan (New York: Frederick Ungar, 1976), pp. 72–73. For Stevens's acknowledgment of the powerful influence on him of Goethe, see *LWS*, p. 457.

6. Coleridge's letter is quoted by M. H. Abrams, "Structure and Style in the Greater Romantic Lyric," in *From Sensibility to Romanticism: Essays Presented to Frederick A. Pottle*, ed. Frederick W. Hilles and Harold Bloom (New York: Oxford Univ. Press, 1965), pp. 548–49. In the *Collected Letters of Samuel Taylor Coleridge*, ed. Earl Leslie Griggs (Oxford: Oxford Univ. Press, 1956), 2:864, the letter is dated September 10, 1802.

7. Sigmund Freud, "Relation of the Poet to Daydreaming," trans. I. F. Grant Duff, *Collected Papers* (London: Hogarth Press, 1950), 4:173.

8. Vendler, *Wallace Stevens*, pp. 23–26. Opposed to this view of Stevens as solely a pessimist and an ironic, indeed to the general capture of Stevens by the deconstructionist school is Bloom, who examines Stevens as the poet of the American sublime, of "imperishable bliss." In *Figures of Capable Imagination*, Bloom observes that the Stevens of "solipsistic bliss" has little in common with the poet of "decreation" that "most of his better critics have described for us. There is indeed a Stevens as seen by Hillis Miller," Bloom goes on, "a poet of the almost Paterian flux of sensations, of a cyclic near nihilism returning always upon itself. There is also truly a Stevens as seen by Helen Vendler: Stevens the venerable Ironist, the apostle of 'the total leaflessness.' I do not assert," Bloom continues, "that these are merely peripheral aspects of the poet, but . . . aspects only, darker saliences that surround the central man, shadows flickering beyond that crucial light cast by the single candle of Stevens' self-joying imagination" (p. 110).

9. Delmore Schwartz, "The Present State of Poetry," in *American Poetry at Mid-Century* (Washington, D.C.: Library of Congress, 1958), pp. 18–19. Stevens refers to the delicacy of the cat's footsteps on snow, too, in "The Irrational Element in Poetry" (*OP*, 217).

Chapter 9: Six Significant Landscapes

1. Stevens's pun on *argentine-Argenteuil* is directly related to the color-play noted in the poem. Kenneth Clark in *Landscape into Art* (Boston: Beacon Press, 1949) helps to gloss the pun: "In the pictures of Argenteuil by Monet and Renoir, done between 1871 and 1874, the painting of sensation yielded its most perfect fruits." He notes "the excitement with which the impressionists conquered the representation of light," and remarks of Monet and Renoir: "A comparison of the pictures they painted together at Argenteuil shows that Monet still renders sparkle by contrasts of light and dark; whereas Renoir dissolves the whole scene in broken touches of pure colour" (pp. 92–93). Clark quotes Van Gogh on his passion for yellow: "Un soleil, une lumière, que, faute de mieux, je ne peux appeler que jaune soufre pâle, citron pâle, or," and observes that Van Gogh was "driven to use lighter and lighter colours, ending almost in yellow monochrome" (p. 110).

2. The Cosmic Tree appears more than once in Stevens's poetry. In *Owl's Clover* the onset of evening is imagined as a great yew tree:

> It would become a yew
> Grown great and grave beyond imagined trees

> Branching through heavens heavy with the sheen
> And shadowy hanging of it, thick with stars.   (*OP*, 45–46)

In the very late poetry, the great Tree is, of course, the Palm at the End of the Mind that "stands on the edge of space." The "down-falling gold" and the bird of *Holiday* are represented in the Yeatsian bird, in *Palm*, whose "fire-fangled feathers dangle down"—both birds are sun emblems, mythically connected with the Tree.

3. Bloom, *Wallace Stevens*, p. 343.

4. Thomas J. Hines, *The Later Poetry of Wallace Stevens: Phenomenological Parallels with Husserl and Heidegger* (Lewisburg, Pa.: Bucknell Univ. Press, 1976), pp. 236–37. See Hines's discussion (pp. 216–37) for a useful phenomenological approach to *Credences*.

5. Paul Ricoeur, *The Rule of Metaphor: Multi-Disciplinary Studies of the Creation of Meaning in Language*, trans. Robert Czerny (Toronto: Univ. of Toronto Press, 1977), p. 7. I have found the following studies useful with respect to Stevens's deployment of metaphor in the poetry, and in reading *his* understanding of metaphor as such. W. K. Wimsatt, "Symbol and Metaphor," in *The Verbal Icon* (Lexington: Univ. of Kentucky Press, 1967); Allen Tate's essay "Tension in Poetry," reprinted in *On the Limits of Poetry* (New York: Morrow, 1948); Ernst Cassirer, "The Power of Metaphor," chap. 6 of *Language and Myth*, trans. Susanne K. Langer (New York: Dover, 1953). Deconstructive studies, such as Derrida's *La mythologie blanche* or Paul de Man's notions of aporia and rhetorical substitution, the "figuration of doubt" as Bloom calls it, have appealed to large numbers of Stevens's readers. One aim of the present study has been to cast doubt, precisely, on the "figuration of doubt" in Stevens.

6. Freud, *Standard Edition*, 17:220–22. Charles Berger, in *Forms of Farewell: The Late Poetry of Wallace Stevens* (Madison: Univ. of Wisconsin Press, 1985), comments on the spatial metaphors which "express the yoking together of the farfetched and the ordinary in Stevens's late poetry, the homely and the *unheimlich*" (p. 144).

7. Brazeau, *Parts of a World*, p. 32.

8. Mike Raines, Curatorial Assistant of the Harvard University Archives, notes of the book in the lower half of the seal that the "open-face approach would have been in use during the time Wallace Stevens attended Harvard (Class of 1901). The design of the seal might have differed, but the books would have been open-faced." The archivist adds, "Prior to the 1885 adoption of this design, the seal had several incarnations—including face down books" (Letter dated September 1, 1987). The photographs of the seals from plate 3 of the Sept. 1933 issue of *Harvard Graduate Magazine* (vol. 42, no. 165) illustrates the article by Samuel Eliot Morison on "Harvard Seals and Arms," an article that Stevens, the Harvard graduate, may well have seen.

9. See John D. Sinclair, *Dante: The Divine Comedy: Purgatorio* (1939, reprint New York: Oxford Univ. Press, 1978), p. 27.

10. *Purgatorio*, vol. 2 of *The Divine Comedy of Dante Alighieri*, 3 vols., trans. Allen Mandelbaum (New York: Bantam Books, 1984), p. 33.

11. Brazeau, *Parts of a World*, pp. 254–62. Stevens's niece, Mary Catherine Sesnick, recalls: "They didn't accept Elsie. That's when he brought her home. I remember Mamma saying she had on one of those great big hats they wore in those days, and dressed beautifully. All set to make a royal entrance. Mamma said that Wallace was so proud. She came in, so elegant-looking dressed that way. Just didn't work out too well. Wallace said, 'I'll never come back. I'll never come back into this house!'" (p. 262).

12. Geoffrey H. Hartman, writing on "Wordsworth, Inscriptions, and Romantic Nature Poetry," in *From Sensibility to Romanticism*, isolates the "graveyard" strain that feeds into the romantic poets: "There is . . . a general convergence of elegiac and nature poetry in the eighteenth century. Poems about place (loco-descriptive) merge with meditations on death, so that the landscape becomes dramatic in a quietly startling way. . . . Not only is the graveyard a major locus for the expression of nature sentiment, but Nature is herself a larger graveyard inscribed deeply with evidences of past life" (p. 392).

13. Alexander Pope, *Peri Bathous: or, of the Art of Sinking in Poetry*, in *Alexander Pope: Selected Poetry and Prose*, ed. William K. Wimsatt, Jr. (New York: Holt, Rinehart, Winston, 1951), pp. 307, 313.

14. See Stevens, *Souvenirs and Prophesies*, p. 248.

15. J. L. Austin comments on C. S. Peirce's study of the different senses of the word *word*, noting Peirce's list of sixty-six divisions of signs: "The textual critic's sense in which the 'the' in l. 254 *has been written twice* [emphasis added]" (*Philosophical Papers* by the late J. L. Austin [Oxford: Clarendon, 1961], p. 87, n. 1. Stevens's interest in C. S. Peirce is on record.

16. D. Wyndham Lewis, *François Villon* (Garden City, N.Y.: Garden City Pub. Co., 1928), p. 42.

17. See John L. Tancock, *The Sculpture of Auguste Rodin* (Philadelphia: Philadelphia Museum of Art, 1976), esp. chap. 7, "The Helmet Maker's Wife," pp. 141–47.

18. James Baird, *The Dome and the Rock: Structure in the Poetry of Wallace Stevens* (Baltimore: Johns Hopkins Univ. Press, 1968); see p. 87, n. 11; also p. 304.

19. Ibid., pp. 86–87.

20. Cassirer, *Philosophy of Symbolic Forms*, 2:103–4.

21. Fletcher, "Positive Negation," p. 135.

22. Helen Vendler, "Stevens and Keats's 'To Autumn'" in *Part of Nature, Part of Us: Modern American Poets* (Cambridge: Harvard Univ. Press, 1980), pp. 20–40.

23. Berger, *Forms of Farewell*, pp. 183–84.

24. Fletcher, "Positive Negation," p. 141.

25. Ibid., p. 161.

26. I am quoting Donne's sermon to the Virginia Company, *The Sermons of John Donne*, 10 vols, ed. John T. Shawcross (New York: Doubleday, 1967), 4:x, 280–81, as set forth in Jeanne Shami's useful essay "John Donne: Ge-

ography as Metaphor," in *Geography and Literature: A Meeting of the Disciplines*, ed. William E. Mallory and Paul Simpson-Housley (Syracuse: Syracuse Univ. Press, 1987), p. 164. Shami observes: "More often than not, the bridge is built over perilous seas or straits, water often being used by Donne to convey danger or afflictions. . . . Donne's efforts to connect the old with the new, whether England and Virginia, the medieval and the modern, or this world and the next, are given form and clarity through his geographical metaphors of maps, with their straits and passageways" (p. 164).

27. Martin Heidegger, "Building Dwelling Thinking," in *Martin Heidegger: Basic Writings from Being and Time (1927) to The Task of Thinking (1964)*, ed. David Farrell Krell (New York: Harper & Row, 1977), pp. 323–39; the passage quoted is from p. 330 of Heidegger's meditation on the bridge. For a full study of the relation of phenomenology to Stevens's poetry, as noted above, see Hines, *The Later Poetry of Wallace Stevens*. See also Paul Bové, *Destructive Poetics: Heidegger and Modern American Poetry* (New York: Columbia Univ. Press, 1980). Also see the comment of Berger in *Forms of Farewell*, referring to Frank Kermode's essay "Dwelling Poetically in Connecticut," in Frank Doggett and Robert Buttell, eds., *Wallace Stevens: A Celebration* (Princeton: Princeton Univ. Press, 1980). Berger notes that Kermode's essay "demonstrates the importance of the 'dwelling' in both Stevens and Heidegger" (p. 144).

Index

Allegory, xxiv, 6, 12, 23, 34, 80, 88, 93, 95, 97, 105, 111, 131, 134, 136

Ambivalence (contraries), 13, 24, 27, 30, 32–33, 42, 46–47, 48–49, 52–53, 57, 83, 84, 88, 104, 119, 130, 151, 166 n. 23

America: A Prophecy (Blake), 80

Aphrodite (Venus), 71–74; *see also* Evening Star

Archetype, xxiv, xxv, 59; spatial emblems, 119, 131–32, 132–35, 133–39, 140–43, 148–55; *see also* Cosmic Tree, Temple and labyrinth

Arensberg, Mary, 60

Arensburg, Walter, 100

Aristotle, 26, 86

Arnold, Matthew, 99

Asceticism, xxiv, xxvi, 2, 36, 37, 85–86; as chastened lexis, 38, 51, 75; as nakedness, 33, 35, 37–38, 40–41; as poverty, 35, 45, 92–93; as quest for the plain, 49–50; *see also* Speculative theology

Asylum Avenue (Hollander), 107

Auerbach, Erich, xxiv, 93, 102, 161 n. 3

Bachelard, Gaston, 17

Baird, James, 144, 164 n. 27

Bahktin, M. M., xxv, 23, 24–25, 30, 75, 162 n. 9

Bates, Milton J., 96, 106

Baudelaire, Charles, 36, 59, 152, 163 n. 23

Beehler, Michael, 60

Being, 43, 48–49, 75, 84, 87, 120, 125, 133; as Cosmic Tree, 116, 131–32; as Coleridgean "I AM," 34; Heideggerian, 125; metaphor as, 134; as mountain, 116, 138; as "pure being," 97, 154; as river, v–vi, 111, 129, 148–49, 152; *see also* Center

Benamou, Michel, 54

Berger, Charles, 150, 176 n. 6

Bergson, Henri, xxv, 17, 37, 41–42

Bernard of Clairvaux, Saint, xxiv, xxvi, 12, 57

Blackmur, R. P., 2

Blake, William, 42, 48, 57, 73–74, 78, 80–81, 83, 119, 121, 169 n. 14

Bloom, Harold, xxiii, 3, 27, 28, 30, 42, 55, 56, 62, 68, 78, 80, 114, 133, 175 n. 8

Boethius, 95

Boundaries, 14, 17, 47, 52–53, 87, 90, 117, 151; *see also* Language, Liminality

Bové, Paul, 165 n. 2, 178 n. 27

Brazeau, Peter, 117, 124, 136

Bridge (passage), 109, 116, 123, 125, 128, 134, 146, 148, 150, 153–55; *see also* Cosmic Tree, Metaphor

Brinnin, John Malcolm, 124

Brooks, Cleanth, 39

Buttel, Robert, 164 n. 7

Byron, George Gordon, Lord, 25, 67, 172 n. 25

Canbon, Glauco, 96
Cassirer, Ernst, 114, 148
Center, 37, 38, 69, 88, 104–5, 115
Clark, Kenneth, 175 n. 1; *see also*
    Impressionists
Coeli Ennarant (Coleridge), 67
Coleridge, S. T., 27, 34, 110–11,
    125, 150, 163 n. 15, 168 n. 2
Colie, Rosalie, 39
Color symbolism, 10, 56–57, 121,
    130, 131, 147, 175 n. 1; black
    and white, 35, 56, 60–61, 64,
    68, 84; lack of, 80; *see also*
    Light, Negation
Comedic, xxvii, 24, 25, 27, 31, 94,
    155; *see also* Jongleur, Parody
Cook, Eleanor, 161 n. 17, 162 n. 12
Cosmic Tree, 131–32, 134, 175
    n. 2
Crane, Hart, 146

Dante, xxv, xxvi, 12, 63, 91, 94–
    106, 137–38, 153
Denham, Sir John, 149
Descartes, René, 14, 43, 112
Desire, xxiv, 1–2, 3–4, 11–12, 13,
    18, 19, 72, 133; and asceticism,
    xxvi, 117 (see also *via negativa*);
    and aesthetic experience, 3, 13–
    14, 42, 59, 104, 113–14, 131,
    139; for belief, 27, 30; as *be-
    thou*, 2, 4, 5, 8, 18, 19; as drive
    (libido), xxv, 4, 13, 66, 79, 119;
    as elegiac, 93; as erotic, 3–4, 8,
    10, 18, 61–62, 72, 74, 131; in
    landscape, 10–11, 61, 108,
    121, 122, 123, 128; as play, 12,
    107, 120; as primary good, 4,
    12, 19; as sacral eroticism, 6–9,
    11, 100; in solitude, 10, 13, 18,
    202, 266; sublimated, xxiv, 3,
    4, 13, 14, 98, 104, 113; as
    thanatos, 10, 19, 62, 103, 129,
    153; as violence, 2, 4, 10, 43;
    see also Eros, Seduction
Dickinson, Emily, 50
Directional emblems, 47, 56, 62,
    65, 116
Divina Comedia (Longfellow), 98
Doggett, Frank, 35, 38
Donne, John, 11, 18, 38, 153–54,
    155, 177–78 n. 26

Einstein, Albert, 111–12
Eliade, Mircea, 114–15
Eliot, T. S., 13, 68, 93, 98, 101,
    150, 166 n. 17
Emerson, Ralph Waldo, 96, 99,
    103, 105, 114
Enigma (riddle), 40, 58, 77, 104–5,
    151–52; *see also* Paradox
Eros (love), xxiv, 4, 18, 97, 104–5;
    in Dante, 94–95; Jungian, 59;
    see also Allegory, Aphrodite,
    Desire
Europe: A Prophecy (Blake), 81
Evening Star, xxvi, 65–66, 76, 79,
    98, 169 n. 8; double nature of,
    83–84; mythic dimension, 72–
    73

Fletcher, Angus, xxv, 2, 50, 79–80,
    100, 118, 148, 152, 154, 166
    n. 25; *see also* Liminality,
    Temple and labyrinth
Focillon, Henri, 115, 116–17, 134,
    141
Freccero, John, 102
Freud, Sigmund, xxiv, 3–4, 14, 27,
    37, 47–49, 53, 98, 126, 136,
    138, 166 n. 23
Frost, Robert, 50
Frye, Northrop, 118
Fuchs, Daniel, 26

Garden, 2, 7, 10–11, 60, 116, 130,
    131
Geometric images, 17–18, 36–37,
    88, 104–5, 121, 146
God (gods), 4, 7–8, 9, 10, 12, 23,
    26, 43, 81, 87, 95, 100, 105,
    112–13; death of, 41; as *genius
    loci*, 63, 90, 141
Goethe, Johann Wolfgang von, 96,
    124, 174 n. 5
Good and evil, poetics of: 4, 12, 26,
    42, 48, 64–65, 74, 75, 80, 83–
    84, 87; *see also* Evening Star

Hardy, Thomas, 51
Hartman, Geoffrey, 81, 83, 168 n.
    2, 177 n. 12
Heidegger, Martin, 125, 154, 178 n.
    27; *see also* Hines, Bové
Heracleitus, 5, 149, 152

Herbert, George, 106, 147, 148
Highet, Gilbert, 24–25
Hines, Thomas, 133, 178 n. 27
Hollander, John, 63, 107
Homer, 15, 18, 19, 55, 102, 110
Homeric hymn, *To Aphrodite*, 74
Hymn to God My God in My Sicknesse (Donne), 155

Impressionists, 130–31, 175 n. 1; *see also* Rodin
Interior paramour, xxiv, xxvi, 2, 18, 54–58, 62–63, 90, 107; as androgynous, 32–34, 104; dynamics of, 102–3, 106; as erotic object, 15–16, 32–34, 55, 60–61, 105; locus of, 55, 60, 63, 90, 103; noetic aspect, 58, 167 n. 7; as self, 41, 56, 57; as sibyl, 40–41, 44–45, 58, 62–63; theological aspect, 33, 105; as the uncanny, 58; variousness of, 56–58, 60, 63; voice of, 85, 93

James, Henry, 110, 140
James, William, 14, 161 n. 15
John of the Cross, 36, 43, 44
Jongleur (clowning, play), xxv, 2, 12, 21–22, 25, 31–32, 53, 59, 82, 94, 100, 153, 162 n. 3
Jung, C. G., xxvi, 54–55, 58–59

Kermode, Frank, 160 n. 5, 178 n. 27
Kessler, Edward, 54, 56
Knowing (*episteme*), xxiii, xxiv, 6, 14–15, 18, 43–45, 63, 71, 87, 91, 124–25; as prophecy, divination, 18, 78–81, 84

La Guardia, David, 161 n. 16, 173 n. 15
Landscape, xxiv, xxvi, 123, 130–31, 141; as emblem, 121, 128, 133, 135, 140; as graveyard, 141, 177 n. 22; as mindscape, 61–62, 110–11, 116, 120–21; as seductive, 120, 122; as wilderness, 122; *see also* Place, Topos
Language (discourse), 28, 32, 38, 65, 75, 92–93, 95, 110, 145;

antithetical primal words, 48; boundary crossing in, 17, 21, 29, 44, 88, 92, 95, 109, 151; erotic, 9, 12, 20, 33, 69, 141; microstructures of, 88–90; as marriage, 12, 105; as tree, 132; as Seigneur, 105; in the vernacular, 2, 91, 95, 96, 98, 101–2; *see also* Word-play and letterplay
Law, 26, 29, 31, 92, 108, 149, 151
Leggett, B. J., 173 n. 5, 174 n. 18
Leiter, Louis, 27
Lentriccia, Frank, 161 n. 16
Lewis, D. Wyndham, 144
Light, xxvi, 5, 33, 44, 56, 66, 69–70, 76, 83, 85, 90, 134, 135, 154; *see also* Evening Star
Liminality (threshold), xxv, 41, 48, 63, 69, 118–19, 134, 148, 150, 152, 153; *see also* Ambivalence, Temple and labyrinth
Litz, A. Walton, 55, 159 n. 2
Lombardi, Thomas F., 121
Longfellow, Henry Wadsworth, 97, 145
Lucretius, 68, 96
Lutwack, Leonard, 109

MacLeod, Glen G., 163 n. 18
Magnus, Laury, 118, 168 n. 5, 171 n. 14
Mandelbaum, Allen, 137
Map, 150–51, 152, 178 n. 26
Marlowe, Christopher, 84
Marvell, Andrew, 121
Mazzaro, Jerome, 95, 103, 160 n. 14
Melville, Herman, 64–65, 80, 81, 83, 84
Memory, 51, 68, 96, 115, 122, 136, 137; institutes of, 115, 174 n. 17; as mother, 57
Metaphor, 13, 109, 110, 120, 123, 125–26, 128, 131, 133–34, 135, 148, 149, 152, 153, 176 n. 5, 178 n. 26
Miller, J. Hillis, 41, 165 n. 2
Milton, John, 2, 26, 75, 83, 84, 110
Moore, Marianne, 85
More, Paul Elmer, 99
Morris, Adalaide Kirby, 160 n. 6

Nativity (home), xxvi, 18, 73, 90, 120, 121, 122–25, 126, 127, 136, 138, 139
Negation (nothingness), xxiv, xxv, 4, 28, 30, 35–37, 44–45, 67, 68, 112; absence of, 48–49, 93; as antinomy, 39; Stevens critics on, 164–65 n. 2; as positive, xxvi, 37, 40–42, 46, 48–49, 53, 117, 146; *see also* Asceticism, *Via negativa*
Nietzsche, Friedrich, xxv, 41
Norton, Charles Eliot, 13, 95, 96, 99, 170–71 n. 9
Numerical structures, 17, 36, 88, 94, 146; *see also* Geometric images
Nygren, Anders, 160 n. 12

Ode to Psyche (Keats), 150
Origen, xxiv, 8–9, 12
Orr, Mary Ackworth, 169 n. 8
Ovid, xxv, 9

Paradox, xxv, 32, 37, 39–40, 47, 58, 77, 104, 130, 140, 152; "Cretan Liar," 165 n. 6; *see also* Enigma
Parody, xxiv, 12, 23–25, 27, 29–31, 33, 34, 128, 142; of self, 51, 153
Pastoral, 78–79; *see also* Garden
Pearce, Roy Harvey, 165 n. 2
Peterson, Margaret, 5, 160 n. 7
Place, xxvi, 18, 61–62, 109–15, 124; as mythic, 114, 149; theory of, 128–29; as topos, 116, 135, 145, 146; *see also* God, Landscape, Space
Plato, xxiv, 3–4, 57, 72, 95; *Diotima*, xxvi, 58, 167 n. 7; on Evening Star, 169 n. 8; *see also* Eros
Plotinus, xxvi, 42, 45, 167 n. 7
Pope, Alexander, 23, 141
Pound, Ezra, 97, 101, 170 n. 2
Prophecy (divination), xxv, xxvi, 17, 44, 62–63, 65, 78, 79–83, 84, 145; Tiresias, 48
Prospectus to the Recluse (Wordsworth), 128

Quine, W. V., 39

Ransom, John Crowe, 123
Repetition, 7, 30, 34, 45, 51, 68, 70, 74, 76, 90–91, 143, 153, 168 n. 5
Reynolds, Barbara, 12, 95
Richards, I. A., 110–11, 168 n. 2, 173 n. 5
Richardson, Joan, 96, 162 n. 4
Ricoeur, Paul, 134
Riddel, Joseph, 15, 17, 174 n. 4
Rodin, Auguste, 144, 145
Roethke, Theodore, 56
Romanticism (romance), xxiv, 1, 4–6, 19, 32, 34, 118, 142; as the irrational, 1; Stevens's relation to romantic poets, 2, 34; Stevens's theory of, 4–5, 11, 160 n. 5

Santayana, George, 69, 70, 96–97, 168 n. 6
Sappho, 73, 93
Schwartz, Delmore, 126
Scripture, xxiv, 15, 23, 31, 34, 58, 60, 68, 73, 85, 90, 148–49
Seduction, xxiv, 1, 11, 122; parables of, 3, 14, 16–19; and violence, 10–11
Seeger, Alan, 128
Serio, John N., 123
Shakespeare, William, 50, 52, 82, 85, 110
Shami, Jeanne, 177–78 n. 26
Shaw, J. E., 96, 104–5
Shelley, P. B., 2, 5, 13, 32, 33, 57, 63, 110
Sidney, Sir Philip, 55
Silvestris, Bernard, xxvi, 167 n. 7
Sinclair, John, 137
Skepticism (irony), 8, 23, 26–27, 30, 68, 72, 100, 113
Solitude (isolation), 11, 19, 36, 41, 45, 67–68, 70, 75, 121–22, 130, 138; *see also* Boundaries
Solomon (Canticles), xxvi, 3, 8, 12, 19, 33, 60–61
Space (spatiality), 17, 37, 61–62, 87, 107, 111–17, 130; sacred, 114–15, 147, 149; spatial emblems, 121, 128–29; 133, 140, 145, 150; *see also* Directional emblems, Place, Temple and labyrinth, Topos

Speculative theology (mysticism), xxiv, 3, 4, 8, 12–13, 14, 33, 36, 44, 58, 87; *see also* Asceticism, Bernard of Clairvaux, Origen, *Via negativa*

Spinoza, Baruch, 112–13, 173 n. 11

Stevens, Elsie Kachel, 22, 55, 94, 99, 105, 122, 177 n. 11

Stevens, Holly, 2, 121, 136, 159 n. 2, 162–63 n. 13

Stevens, Wallace: attachment to soil, 123–24; on belief, 23, 27, 30, 41; on Dante, 99, 100; as dictionary buff, 82, 151; on Freud, 4, 47–48; at Harvard, 13, 96, 99, 137, 161 n. 19; hiking, 121–22, 123, 169 n. 14, 174 n. 2; on influence, 101; on the irrational, 1, 4; as jongleur, 22, 25, 31; as lawyer, 92, 108, 113, 123; on mental voyaging, 150; on metaphor, 109, 134; on place, 107, 116, 121–22; poetic influence on, 70, 96–97, 100, 105, 121, 137, 145, 169 n. 14; on scale of poetry, 92; and the sense of home, 124, 136–37, 138; on solitude, 122

—Works:

Adagia, xxiii, 23, 26, 29, 107, 108, 109, 117, 134

Anatomy of Monotony, 41

Auroras of Autumn, The, 36, 83–84, 122

Bantams in Pine-Woods, 2, 24

Bird with the Coppery, Keen Claws, The, 23, 24, 25–27

Candle a Saint, The, 57

Celle Qui Fût Héaulmiette, 128, 143–47

"Collect of Philosophy, A," 100

Comedian as the Letter C, The, 116, 155

"Connecticut," 123–24, 138, 139

Connoisseur of Chaos, 49, 52, 115, 125

Countryman, The, 149

Credences of Summer, 36, 38, 114, 122, 128, 132–35

Cy Est Pourtraicte, Madame Ste Ursule, et Les Unze Mille Vierges, 3, 6–10, 13, 100–101, 130

Description without Place, 57, 121

Discovery of Thought, A, 101

Dove in the Belly, 2, 23

Dutch Graves in Bucks County, 84

Esthétique du Mal, 8, 34, 36, 59, 114

Extracts from Addresses to the Academy of Fine Ideas, 38

Extraordinary References, 121

Farewell to Florida, 57, 61–63

"Figure of the Youth as Virile Poet, The," 116

Final Soliloquy of the Interior Paramour, xxvi, 3, 55, 63, 66, 69–70, 85–94, 107

Golden Woman in a Silver Mirror, A, 57

Hand as a Being, The, 20, 55

Hermitage at the Centre, The, 128

Holiday in Reality, 128, 129–32

Homunculus et La Belle Etoile, 71–72

Idea of Order at Key West, The, 55, 62–63

"Imagination as Value," 47, 92

Indian River, 123

"Irrational Element in Poetry, The," 1, 4

"John Crowe Ransom: Tennessean," 123

Large Red Man Reading, 84

Like Decorations . . . , 36, 79

Lot of People Bathing in a Stream, A, 120, 127

Madame La Fleurie, 55, 56, 57

Man and Bottle, 96

Man on the Dump, The 50, 128, 139–43

Man Whose Pharynx Was Bad, The, 35

Man with the Blue Guitar, The, 25, 68–69, 124–25

Martial Cadenza, 74–76

Monocle de Mon Oncle, Le, 23, 24, 27–31, 54, 66, 163 n. 18

Motive for Metaphor, The, 126

Mountains Covered with Cats, 47

Negation, 26

New Life, 99

"Noble Rider and the Sound of Words, The," 58, 100

Nomad Exquisite, 123

Notes toward a Supreme Fiction,

Stevens, Wallace (*cont.*)
    xxiii, 2, 4, 13, 14, 24, 31–
    34, 40, 42, 46–47, 53, 57,
    130
    Nuances of a Theme by Williams,
        66, 67–68, 71
    O Florida, Venereal Soil, 61, 123
    Of Mere Being, 97, 176 n. 2
    Old Lutheran Bells at Home, The,
        43
    One of the Inhabitants of the
        West, 74, 77–84, 87
    Ordinary Evening in New Haven,
        An, 18, 19, 42, 50, 109–10,
        121
    Owl in the Sarcophagus, The, 23,
        57
    Owl's Clover, 175–76
    Peter Quince at the Clavier, 11
    Plain Sense of Things, The, 50–52
    Planet on the Table, The, 151
    Plus Belles Pages, Les, xxiv
    Poem That Took the Place of a
        Mountain, The, 128, 135–39
    Prologues to What Is Possible, 42,
        66
    Quiet Normal Life, A, 66
    Reader, The, 35–36, 66–67
    "Relations between Poetry and
        Painting, The," 14
    Re-statement of Romance, 3, 5–6,
        56
    River of Rivers in Connecticut,
        The, xxv, 129, 147–55
    Sail of Ulysses, The, 40, 43–46,
        49, 116, 120–21
    St. Armorer's Church from the
        Outside, 35
    Six Significant Landscapes, 61
    Snow Man, The, 38–39, 111
    Stars at Talapoosa, 70–71
    Study of Images II, 13
    Sunday Morning, 11, 15, 57
    Things of August, 40, 75
    Thirteen Ways of Looking at a
        Blackbird, 17–18
    This Solitude of Cataracts, 149
    To an Old Philosopher in Rome,
        69, 74
    To the One of Fictive Music, 54,
        57
    Two Figures in Dense Violet Light,
        61

"Two or Three Ideas," 5, 41
United Dames of America, 57
Valentine, A, 141–42
Valley Candle, 38, 66, 68, 70, 71,
    121
Well Dressed Man with a Beard,
    The, 42
World as Meditation, The, 3, 14–
    19
Suckenick, Ronald, 68
Swinburne, Algernon, 24, 75, 164
    n. 27

Temple and labyrinth, xxv, 36, 108,
    114, 117–19, 128, 133, 141,
    148, 152, 154; *see also* Arche-
    type, Liminality
Tennyson, Alfred, Lord, 19
Thomas, Dylan, 1, 63
Thomas, Lewis, 53
Thomas Aquinas, Saint, 12
Time, 18, 27, 50, 80, 151; medita-
    tion on, 75–76, 142
Tolliver, Harold E., 78
Topos, 18, 38, 47, 50, 63, 81, 108,
    115–16; *see also* Bridge, Color
    symbolism, Cosmic Tree, Di-
    rectional emblems, Evening
    Star, Garden, Metaphor
To the Evening Star (Blake), 73–74

Unheimlich (uncanny), 108, 126,
    136, 138, 176 n. 6

Valediction Forbidding Mourning, A
    (Donne), 18
Vendler, Helen, xxiii, 6, 28, 30, 41,
    50, 75, 126, 150, 152, 169 n.
    12
Via negativa, xxv, 36, 37, 38, 40,
    42, 44, 49, 93; *see also* Asceti-
    cism, Center, Negation, Specu-
    lative theology
Villon, François, xxv, 29–31, 143,
    164 n. 27
Violence (destructive force), xxvi, 2,
    4, 6, 9, 10–11, 43, 49, 74, 82,
    84, 123
Virgil, 82, 102, 137, 141
Vita Nuova (Dante), xxvi, 91, 94–
    96, 100, 103

War, 74–76, 77, 82
Whitman, Walt, 1, 79–80, 83, 88, 91, 108, 133, 145
Williams, William Carlos, 67, 98
Word-play and letter-play, 17, 45, 47, 51, 52, 62–63, 88–90, 91, 94, 118, 131, 142, 143, 155, 161 n. 17, 175 n. 1
Wordsworth, William, 24, 128, 133

Yates, Frances, 115, 174 n. 17
Yeats, William Butler, 1, 41, 68, 143